Elias Canetti

Twayne's World Authors Series

German Literature

David O'Connell, Editor
Georgia State University

TWAS 843

Elias Canetti
Photograph copyright by Isolde Ohlbaum

Elias Canetti

Thomas H. Falk

Twayne Publishers ■ New York

Maxwell Macmillan Canada ■ Toronto

Maxwell Macmillan International ■ New York Oxford Singapore Sydney

Elias Canetti
Thomas H. Falk

Copyright 1993 by Twayne Publishers

All rights reserved. No part of this book may be reproduced or
transmitted in any form or by any means, electronic or
mechanical, including photocopying, recording, or by any
information storage and retrieval system, without permission in
writing from the Publisher.

Twayne Publishers   Maxwell Macmillan Canada, Inc.
Macmillan Publishing Company 1200 Eglinton Avenue East
866 Third Avenue   Suite 200
New York, New York 10022   Don Mills, Ontario M3C 3N1

Library of Congress Cataloging-in-Publication Data

Falk, Thomas H.
   Elias Canetti / Thomas H. Falk.
   p. cm. – (Twayne's world authors series; TWAS 843)
   Includes bibliographical references and index.
   ISBN 0-8057-8276-1
   1. Canetti, Elias, 1905-   – Criticism and interpretation.
I. Title. II. Series.
PT2605.A58Z685 1993
833'.912 – dc20   93-7654
                                      CIP

The paper used in this publication meets the minimum
requirements of American National Standard for Information
Sciences – Permanence of Paper for Printed Library Materials,
ANSI Z39.48-1984.

10 9 8 7 6 5 4 3 2 1

Printed in the United States of America.

Contents

Preface

> It is wonderful to *study*, namely to take up and contemplate names and things one has never yet contemplated; to tell oneself what one notices about them; what one would like to retain about them; to register it in the large, casual hoard of one's experiences; register it in such a way that one may never think about it again. One thereby creates a realm of personal adventures and discoveries, and the things that one re-encounters *within* this realm have a twofold character: each is both a discovery and a piece of oneself.
>
> – Elias Canetti, *The Human Province*

Written in 1956, these words serve as the primary basis for this examination of the work of one of the twentieth-century's distinguished writers and thinkers. It may seem that today we cannot afford the luxury of study, yet our times, and the future, perhaps require more than ever that we create the "realm of personal adventures and discoveries" and experience a piece of ourselves.

Compared with that of other writers, Elias Canetti's oeuvre is quite modest. He has written only one novel, three plays, an autobiography covering just the first 30 years of his life, an anthropological-philosophical study of crowds and power, several volumes of notes and aphorisms, 15 essays collected in a single volume, and a few slim books with some occasional writings. But no one should be misled by the small number: the complete work constitutes a picture of rare achievement and triumph seldom found.

Interest in Canetti's work has increased since he became a Nobel laureate in 1981, but he has not enjoyed the popularity other writers have gained following such distinction. Some critics and apologists have suggested that Canetti is a "difficult" writer. His novel and plays, for example, are within the tradition of the theater of the absurd; they represent an existence out of harmony with its surroundings. In this way they are, indeed, difficult to understand and accept, and Canetti does not apologize for making such demands on his readers and audience. Nevertheless, anyone interested in studying and in contemplation will find Canetti a stimulating and accessible teacher.

Canetti's philosophical and aphoristic writings show him to be a preeminent storyteller as well. He engages his readers in issues of fundamental importance to the contemporary world by recounting stories and myths from throughout time and all parts of the world. Canetti feels strongly about certain issues, and he can be a stern moralizer. He does not offer his readers grand systems for resolving problems, but once he has gained their attention, he never lets go.

There are a few matters in Canetti's writings that are problematic. For example, in his novel the protagonist is a full-fledged misogynist, and readers – especially after they have also read the autobiography – may suspect that Canetti harbors similar views. Other issues, such as his relationship with his mother, may involve psychological problems that are beyond the purpose and scope of this study. In general, this exploration of Canetti's writings allows him to speak for himself on these matters.

Since there are few examinations of Canetti's works now available in English, the present study may serve as both an introduction and an invitation to his writings. The works themselves are available in reliable, accurate, and sensitive English translations.

It is not easy to properly acknowledge the support I have received during the years I have devoted to the study of Elias Canetti's writings. There are, however, a few friends who deserve thankful recognition: first, some colleagues to whom I wish to express my gratitude because they listened to me and encouraged me to continue my work and then, some students who gladly and finally recognized that my enthusiasm for Canetti was quite valid after all.

I also want to recognize in this acknowledgment that I received immeasurable courage to write this book from Tanya and Charlotte. Each contributed in her own special way, perhaps without always knowing how.

But most of all I want to thank Julia. Without her neither this book nor many other projects during the past 25 years would have been completed.

Acknowledgments

I would like to thank the following publishers for permission to use excerpts from:

The Play of the Eyes by Elias Canetti, translated by Ralph Manheim. Translation copyright 1986 by Farrar, Straus & Giroux, Inc. Reprinted by permission of Farrar, Straus and Giroux, Inc.

The Secret Heart of the Clock by Elias Canetti, translated by Joel Agee. Translation copyright 1989 by Farrar, Straus & Giroux, Inc. Reprinted by permission of Farrar, Straus & Giroux, Inc.

The Torch in My Ear by Elias Canetti, translated by Joachim Neugroschel. Translation copyright 1982 by Farrar, Straus and Giroux, Inc. Reprinted by permission of Farrar, Straus & Giroux, Inc.

Auto-da-Fé by Elias Canetti. English translation copyright 1947 by Elias Canetti. Copyright renewed 1974 by Elias Canetti. Reprinted by permission of The Continuum Publishing Company.

Crowds and Power by Elias Canetti. English translation copyright 1962, 1973 by Victor Gollancz Ltd. Reprinted by permission of The Continuum Publishing Company.

The Conscience of Words by Elias Canetti. English translation copyright 1979 by The Continuum Publishing Company. Reprinted by permission of The Continuum Publishing Company.

The Human Province by Elias Canetti. English translation copyright by The Seabury Press, Inc. Reprinted by permission of The Continuum Publishing Company.

The Tongue Set Free: Remembrance of a European Childhood by Elias Canetti. English translation copyright by The Continuum Publishing Company. Reprinted by permission of The Continuum Publishing Company.

Chronology

1905   Elias Canetti born 25 July in Rutschuk (now Ruse), Bulgaria, the first of three children of Jacques and Mathilde (Arditti) Canetti.

1911   Family moves to Manchester, England, where Canetti learns English and begins school.

1912   Father dies unexpectedly at age 30.

1913   Mother and children spend summer in Lausanne, where Canetti learns German in three months before moving to Vienna.

1916   To escape the ravages of World War I, the family moves to neutral Switzerland, where Canetti attends school in Zurich.

1921   Mother moves the family to Frankfurt am Main, where Canetti completes secondary school and has his first encounter with the power of the crowd during a mass demonstration.

1924   Returns to Vienna, where he matriculates at the university as a student of chemistry, receiving a doctorate in 1929. In April he attends his first Karl Kraus lecture, where he also meets Veza Taubner-Calderon, his future wife.

1927   On 15 July Canetti witnesses the behavior of the masses during the demonstration that led to the burning of the Palace of Justice in Vienna.

1928-1929 Spends the summers in Berlin and meets many artists, including Bertolt Brecht, Isaak Babel, and George Grosz while working as writer and translator of Upton Sinclair's novels for Wieland Herzfelde's Malik publishing house.

1929-1930   Returning to Vienna, works on his plan for the "Human Comedy of Madmen," a series of eight novels.

1930-1931   Writes his novel, *Die Blendung*.

1931-1932   Writes his drama *Hochzeit*, which is distributed in manuscript form by the S. Fischer Verlag, Berlin.

1932-1933   Becomes acquainted with Hermann Broch, Hermann Scherchen, Fritz Wotruba, Robert Musil, Alban Berg, Georg Merkel, and Abraham Sonne.

1933-1934   Writes his drama *Komödie der Eitelkeit*.

1934   Marries Veza Tauber-Calderon.

1935   *Die Blendung* is published by Herbert Reichner Verlag, Vienna, Leipzig, Zurich.

1937   Mother dies in Paris.

1938   In March Hitler annexes Austria to Germany; in November Canetti and his wife flee Vienna for Paris.

1939   They settle in London, where Canetti works exclusively on his socioanthropological study of crowds and power.

1942   As a "safety valve" Canetti begins writing the *Aufzeichnungen*.

1946-1947   *Die Blendung* is translated and appears in London as *Auto-da-Fé*, in New York as *The Tower of Babel*.

1949   *Die Blendung* is translated and appears in France as *La Tour de Babel*. The book receives the Grand Prix International du Club Français du Livre.

1952   Writes his drama *Die Befristeten*.

1954   Visits Marrakesh and writes his notes about the trip, which are later published as *Die Stimmen von Marrakesch*.

1955   The monograph *Fritz Wotruba* is published by the Brüder Rosenbaum Verlag, Vienna.

1956   *Die Befristeten* is performed in England as *The Numbered* by the Oxford Playhouse Company in November.

1960 *Masse und Macht* is published in Hamburg by the Claassen Verlag. It appears as *Crowds and Power* in 1962 in London and New York.

1963 Wife, Veza, dies. In fall *Die Blendung* is published in Munich by the Carl Hanser Verlag, from now on his exclusive publisher.

1965 *Hochzeit* and *Komödie der Eitelkeit* are performed in Braunschweig, causing considerable protest from the audience. The first volume of *Aufzeichnungen* is published. Others follow in 1970, 1973, and 1987.

1966 Is awarded the Dichterpreis der Stadt Wien.

1967 Is presented the Deutscher Kritikerpreis. *Die Stimmen von Marrakesch* is published.

1968 Receives the Großer österreichischer Staatspreis.

1969 The Kafka essay, *Der andere Prozess: Kafkas Briefe an Felice*, is published. Canetti is awarded the Literaturpreis der Bayrischen Akademie der schönen Künste.

1971 Marries Hera Buschor. Begins writing his autobiography for his brother Georges, who dies in Paris before it is finished.

1972 Daughter, Johanna, is born. Receives the Georg-Büchner-Preis.

1975 Is awarded an honorary degree from the University of Manchester. *Das Gewissen der Worte*, a collection of essays, is published.

1976 Receives honorary degree from the University of Munich.

1977 The first volume of the autobiography, *Die gerettete Zunge: Geschichte einer Jugend*, is published.

1979 Canetti is cited with the distinction "Pour le Mérite" from the Federal Republic of Germany.

1980 The second volume of the autobiography, *Die Fackel im Ohr: Lebensgeschichte 1921-1931*, is published.

1981   Awarded the Franz Kafka Preis and the Nobel Prize for Literature.

1985   The third and last volume of the autobiography, *Das Augenspiel: Lebensgeschichte 1931-1937*, is published.

1987   The last volume of notes and aphorisms, *Das Geheimberz der Uhr*, is published.

Chapter One

Years of Learning

The Tongue Set Free, The Torch in My Ear, The Play of the Eyes

Among writers, especially as they reach advanced age, it is not uncommon to publish diaries, journals, notes, or materials collected over a lifetime as an adjunct to their major works. Such items are frequently edited by these writers to present a more direct narrative of their lives and work. Emendations can remove personal references that might create embarrassment or a public image the writer would like to avoid. Perhaps without malice, such publications offer writers the possibility of inventing or reinventing themselves.

An autobiography presents writers with the opportunity to be highly selective in telling the story of their life. They select the materials and the right set of circumstances to present themselves. The most famous example of autobiographical writing in German literature is, of course, Goethe's *Dichtung und Wahrheit* (poetry and truth). In this work Goethe tells a great deal about himself, but the reader is never certain whether it is *Dichtung*, that is, ideas that Goethe has fabricated or fictionalized about his life, or *Wahrheit*, the true facts of his life. For many readers the fictionalized version of life is more fascinating than a true accounting, with its dates, facts, and otherwise uninteresting or irrelevant details.

Elias Canetti has written his autobiography, detailing his life from his earliest memory at age two until the death of his mother in 1937. It has been published in three volumes: *The Tongue Set Free*,[1] *The Torch in My Ear*,[2] and *The Play of the Eyes*.[3] Numerous scholars have debated the purpose, intention, and veracity of Canetti's autobiography, yet no clear statement – how much is *Dichtung*, how much *Wahrheit* – has been developed.[4]

Canetti has always been a very private man, granting but a few interviews in which he would only discuss his writings. Thus, it is possible to conclude that the public image he has presented in the volumes of his autobiography will be the only image available for a very long time. In his essay "Dialogue with the Cruel Partner"[5] he discloses the three forms in which he has maintained records of thoughts and events over the years: notes, memo books, and diaries. Selections of the notes have been published as aphorisms. The memo books, as he describes them, are small calendars in which he sets down no more than the names of people or places, or specific ideas that concerned him at a particular time; these memo books served to stimulate more comprehensive thoughts at some later time when they might be considered in a diary entry. The diaries are the record of his most extensive thinking on problems or issues prior to articulating his views in writings or public lectures. Canetti, however, has made his actual diaries a complete secret for others; he wrote them in an altered stenographic code that would require consider-able effort to decipher. Consequently, any effort to establish a com-pletely valid understanding of the first 30 years of Canetti's life – even if one had access to all the notes, memo books, and diaries – would be at best difficult, at worst impossible.

"Geschichte einer Jugend," the story of a youth, is the subtitle of the first volume of the autobiography and might well serve as a guide to reading this part of Canetti's oeuvre, because he is such an ex-traordinary storyteller. His autobiography is a series of vignettes that not only report events of his early life but also recall the experiences that shaped his mind. His story combines his love of faraway places with a love of the past, revealing a clearer understanding of his views of the world a half century later. Throughout the three volumes, there are sketches that relate to specific literary characters or events as well as encounters that influenced his lifelong pursuits of specific philosophical issues.

In one of his rare interviews, Canetti explained the reason for writing this autobiography. He spoke of his close relationship to his youngest brother Georges and the significant influence he had on his writing: "During his last illness I resolved to write the story of our childhood. I wrote it for him and in the hope it would help to heal him. I had told him that the book was written and entitled *The Tongue Set Free*! Unfortunately, I was unable to show him the begin-ning of the book. He had died. The book is dedicated to him and would not exist without him."[6] This statement illustrates Canetti's steadfast and unquestionable conviction that his writings have extraordinary powers. He attacks the world with a vengeance and he believes he can make it better.

An aphorism describes Canetti well: "The philosopher is characterized by the tiny number of his chief ideas, and the stubborn and irksome way he reiterates them."[7] Canetti's autobiography, like all his other writings, examines these chief ideas, using many examples from his life to support their validity. To examine how each person or event is treated and described in the autobiography would be too far-ranging and rather repetitive. Each volume deals with a specific period of time and is also divided into the cities where Canetti lived. *The Tongue Set Free* covers the period from his birth in 1905 until 1921, when he lived in Ruschuk, Manchester, Vienna, and Zurich. *The Torch in My Ear* begins with his residence in Frankfurt am Main, Germany, from 1921 to 1924, then covers his Vienna years from 1924 until he had completed his novel in 1931; an intervening chapter is devoted to his experiences in Berlin during the summers of 1928 and 1929. *The Play of the Eyes* is dedicated to Canetti's life in Vienna from 1931 until 1937. The wealth of information included in the autobiography is so vast that it is impossible to consider every entry. Consequently, this study will concentrate on only a few events and a select number of people that have profoundly shaped Canetti's life.

The Tongue Set Free

When the septuagenarian Canetti commenced to write the story of his life, he concluded that "anything I subsequently experienced had already happened in Ruschuk" (*TF*, 4), the city in northeast Bulgaria, now called Ruse, where he was born. His earliest memory takes him back to the summer of 1907 when he was only two years old. His parents were vacationing in Carlsbad that year and they had taken a young Bulgarian girl with them to serve as a nanny. Canetti remembers a maid carrying him from his room into the hallway, where they meet a man who approaches them and tells the child to stick out his tongue. The man takes a knife from his pocket, advances the knife toward the child and says, "Now we'll cut off his tongue" (*TF*, 3). The frightened child is unable to withdraw his tongue to escape the advancing knife, but at the last moment the man retracts the blade, returns the knife to his pocket, and tells the child, "Not today, tomorrow" (*TF*, 3). Apparently, each morning began with this terrifying ritual.

Ten years later Canetti learned from his mother the details surrounding that early memory. Presumably the nanny had met the young man in town and would visit his room at night. The purpose of the morning episodes was to make sure the child did not speak about these encounters. The threat was seemingly successful and "the child quite literally held his tongue for ten years" (*TF*, 4). This brief vignette illustrates the power of the command, an issue Canetti examined many years later in great detail in *Crowds and Power*.[8] The young man had ordered the child to be silent and the child was obedient not only at the time, but for 10 years. The command was issued by a source of greater strength, there was "no hope of fighting" it, and it was not "open to doubt" at the time (*CP*, 305). In his study, Canetti points out that "every command consists of momentum and sting. The momentum forces the recipient to act, and to act in accordance with the content of the command" (*CP*, 305). The two-year-old child, however, did not carry out the command to the fullest because he finally – after 10 years – disobeyed the dictate by speaking to his mother about the morning episodes. Consequently, the sting, that element of the command that is retained in the mind of the victim, has been evaded after all, making the force of the command ultimately ineffective.

This earliest memory also introduces the hallmark of Elias Canetti: the writer who cannot be silenced. It would be very wrong to believe that Canetti "held his tongue" and remained completely silent until he was 12 years old. Virtually every episode that follows this first memory is filled with stories about speaking and the power of language. The first part of this volume of the autobiography is devoted to Canetti's many encounters with languages during the six years he lived in Ruschuk.

Reared in a family of well-to-do Sephardic Jews, Canetti learned Bulgarian and Ladino, the old Spanish language that his forebears had brought with them when they were expelled from Spain 400 years earlier at the time of the Inquisition. Since Ruschuk was an important land and water trading center on the lower Danube, Canetti's contacts with foreign languages were extensive: "on any one day you could hear seven or eight languages" (*TF*, 4). Exposure to this great variety of languages undoubtedly provided good early training for the concept of the "acoustic masks" that Canetti later developed, maintaining that each person has a limited number of lexical items, which are produced in an auditory manner unique to that individual.

There are many other stories that Canetti tells of his early life in Ruschuk, stories that had a profound influence on him for the rest of his life. The recalling of these events decades later in the writing of the autobiography provides an interesting insight into the role that memory plays in the creative process. Canetti's principal languages up to age six were Bulgarian and Ladino, the former spoken by the servants in the home while the latter was used by the immediate family and relatives. From the serving maids Canetti learned many stories and fairy tales that were indigenous to Balkan culture and that he first heard and learned in the Bulgarian language. Not long after he left Ruschuk, Canetti forgot Bulgarian completely, yet he continued to remember the fairy tales, not in Bulgarian but in German, a language he did not learn until he was eight years old. Canetti calls this phenomenon a "mysterious translation" that he is reluctant to investigate for fear of destroying his "most precious memories" (*TF*, 10). He continues with the observation that "the events of those years are present to my mind in all their strength and freshness (I've fed on them for over sixty years), but the vast majority are tied to words that I did not know at that time" (*TF*, 10).

A plausible explanation for this phenomenon may well be found in the various theories of the creative process proposed by artists and writers, as well as by the psychological and philosophical thinking prevalent since the early years of this century and not uncommon among the Romanticists 100 years earlier. In each description of the creative process, it is proposed that the original experience undergoes some type of transformation before it finally becomes suitable artistic material. What Canetti calls the "mysterious translation" is not unlike the ideas proposed, for example, by Friedrich Schlegel, who suggests that wit (i.e., knowledge) is attained through divination (i.e., some unexplainable process)[9] or by Novalis, who believed that the complete work of art will always contain some faint shimmer of the chaos from which it came.[10]

Canetti speaks further of his continued use of Bulgarian fairy tales. He observes that "it seems natural to me to write them down now; . . . It is not like the literary translation of a book from one language to another, it is a translation that happened of its own accord in my unconscious" (*TF*, 10). Although normally opposed to psychological theories, it is clear that Canetti recognizes that these early experiences have undergone some inexplicable transformation; his present rendition of the stories is different in language and artistic form from the tales he heard as a child. Throughout the autobiography one can find examples where Canetti concludes stories, some of which might strike him or the reader as possibly unbelievable, with exclamations such as That's the way it was! or That's the way I remember it! This clearly indicates that he attempts to differentiate between the factual and the fictional.

Canetti offers another interesting example of the creative process in a story of a fire in a neighborhood house. He was four years old when this event occurred, and it was the first time he witnessed a burning house. From a slight distance he observed how some people were stealing items from the fiery dwelling, appearing to him as "tiny black figures" running in all directions, identified by onlookers as thieves (*TF*, 25). Fifteen years later, when he was a student in Vienna, he discovered those "tiny black figures" again in Breughel's paintings. Sixty years later, he admits that he no longer could distinguish between the early experience in Ruschuk and what was added to his image by the painter. Unlike other artists whom he appropriated later "by contemplation and reflection," Canetti found Breughel "present within me as though, certain that I would have to come to him, he had been awaiting me for a long time" (*TF*, 25). Here the creative process follows a different route. Rather than simply undergoing a "mysterious transformation," the initial experience is transformed and attached to an existing work of art (or to an existing philosophical concept). Once this first step in the transformation has been completed, however, it is still necessary for this newly established experience to pass through the previously described transformation – the "mysterious translation" – before it is ready material for fiction.

Canetti's family in Ruschuk was large, and life was vigorous and eventful. Grandfather Canetti, as head of the family business, ruled with an iron fist over three generations. There were not only the aunts, uncles, cousins, and brothers to celebrate the Sabbath and holy days together but also a myriad of servants from various ethnic groups, Bulgarian peasant girls who lived with the family, and strangers who would be invited to join the festivities. Many are remembered with stories or anecdotes that reveal the influence they had on Canetti then and later in life. There was, for example, an Armenian who, while chopping wood in the backyard, sang sad songs that young Elias understood only in his heart. Or his cousin Laurica, whom Elias attempted to kill because she would not show him her notebook filled with writing. There was the weekly example of the crowd when a large group of gypsies came begging at the family home. And there were the times when his Uncle Bucco would bestow a blessing on the young child but always followed the benediction with laughter, transforming Elias's pride into humiliation. But the three people who had the greatest and most extensive effect on Elias Canetti were his father, mother, and paternal grandfather.

Grandfather Canetti

Grandfather Elias Canetti, after whom young Canetti was named, was a dynamic and powerful self-made businessman who "was feared in his family, a tyrant who could weep hot tears if he wanted to" (*TF*, 17). He expected every male member of his family to work in his thriving wholesale grocery business in Ruschuk; if they refused, they were denounced with a most terrible curse. Within the Sephardic community, the grandfather enjoyed great popularity as a superb storyteller and a fine singer.

The celebration of Passover in the home of pious Jews provided the young Canetti with his first experiences of high drama and the power of oration, both talents he would later develop to a high degree of excellence. On the seder evening, with the entire family in attendance, the grandfather and grandson – the eldest and the youngest members of the family – would read the story of the Jews' exodus from Egypt as it is told in the Haggadah. The child would ask the Ma-nishtanah (questions about the significance of the various rituals of the celebration), and the grandfather would respond with the story of the exodus. Young Canetti was very aware of the role he played: without his questions there could be no celebration of the ritual on the seder evening. In addition, he felt that his grandfather's changing singsong response was personally directed to him; they were two actors in an important dramatic event.

When Elias was six years old, his parents decided to leave the oppressive dominance of the grandfather's home and business and

join the mother's brothers in their business in Manchester, England.
The grandfather was outraged at their decision and made every effort
to thwart their plans. Whenever he saw the child, he hugged and
kissed him and broke out in tears. He "proclaimed that I was his
dearest grandchild and he could not live without me" (*TF*, 32). When
the mother admitted that she was "the author of the emigration
project . . . he turned his back to her and never spoke to her again"
(*TF*, 33). The most terrible event, however, took place just prior to
their departure, when the grandfather "cursed his son solemnly" in
the presence of a horrified family (*TF*, 33). Canetti recalls that he
"heard them speaking about it: Nothing, they said, was more dreadful than a father cursing his son" (*TF*, 33). What made this childhood
experience especially poignant was that the father died very unexpectedly a year later. Both the young boy and the grandfather attributed the death to the curse. The seven-year-old boy, then and
later, perceived the death as an example of the power of words.
Since the father suffered no obvious physical ailments, Canetti could
only attribute the cause of death to the power of words, a subject he
would study in all its variations and manifestations throughout his
life.

Father and Mother

Canetti's parents, Jacques and Mathilde, met when they were students in Vienna. From that happy period in their lives, they had acquired two great passions: a love of the German language and a fas-
cination with the theater. Both wanted to become actors, a dream
prohibited by their parents' demands that Canetti's father enter the
family business and his mother assume the role of the dutiful house-
wife. But they did continue to speak German, their own private language, in Ruschuk, where Ladino was used by the rest of the family.
Noting the feelings of joy that seemed to accompany his parents'
German conversations, the child made repeated attempts to learn
this magic language, but the parents denied his requests, which led
to resentment, especially toward his mother.

Among the tales Canetti recalls from those early years in
Ruschuk, two especially seem to characterize the differing personalities of his parents. He often asked his mother to tell a story from her
childhood when she had ridden in a sleigh across the frozen
Danube. The party was approached by a pack of wolves and only

survived the attack when two men in another sleigh came along and shot one wolf, driving the remainder of the pack away. The wolves from this story, Canetti writes, "became the first wild beasts to fill my imagination" (*TF*, 9). This story was subsequently enhanced by the Bulgarian fairy tales that Canetti heard. The wolf was transformed from the rapacious animal of the mother's story into a werewolf. The old superstition of a human being turned preternaturally into a wolf, often joined by vampires, became a much more menacing figure in the imagination of the child. Ultimately the transformed creature became real when Canetti's father, as part of the Purim celebration, masqueraded as a werewolf in the child's presence. The father attempted to calm the screaming child, revealing himself and placing the mask in plain sight, but the child would not believe him. "The story of the werewolf had thus come true" (*TF*, 20). The mother's tale is an account of an actual event, without fictionalized embellishment. The father, however, possessed of the talents of the true actor, made fiction real. Other anecdotes from later in life likewise show the mother as a very serious individual, while the father is a creative, even joyful, person.

In 1911 the family moved to Manchester, England, an event of great consequence for the young boy. Indeed, he did say that "anything I subsequently experienced had already happened in Ruschuk" (*TF*, 4). But all those earlier events occurred prior to the time Canetti learned to read. He remembered that earlier life by its sounds, sights, and smells. In England, however, Canetti adds reading and books to his life, and from this time onward virtually all events important for him are in some way associated with books.

Shortly after Canetti started school, his father began to give him books from a special children's series: *The Arabian Nights*, Grimm's fairy tales, *Robinson Crusoe*, *Gulliver's Travels*, *Tales from Shakespeare*, *Don Quixote*, Dante, *William Tell*. His father encouraged him to try to read these books, and they then had a wonderful time each evening talking about the stories in English. "It would be easy to show that almost everything that I consisted of later on was already in these books" (*TF*, 40). During this year, Canetti and his father enjoyed a particularly close relationship, whereas he was rather distant from his mother. One of the last conversations that Canetti remembers having with his father took place one Sunday while strolling along the Mersey river. In response to the question of what the boy wanted to be when he grew up, Canetti said he wished to become a doctor. The father, who had become a businessman much against his own wishes, then promised his son: "You will go to the university and you will be what you want most" (*TF*, 42).

Undoubtedly the event in Elias Canetti's life with the greatest and most far-reaching consequences was the death of his father. All three volumes of the autobiography include many references to that occasion, and the first and third volumes have specific chapters devoted exclusively to Canetti's search for the explanation of his father's death.[11]

In late summer 1912, a year after arriving in Manchester, Canetti's mother fell ill. Since the doctors could discover no discernible sickness, they concluded that the indisposition was caused by the poor English air and advised her to take a cure at a spa on the Continent.[12] Leaving the three children in the care of a governess and maid and under the father's supervision, she went to Bad Reichenhall in Germany. After a few weeks her health seemed to be improving, so it was decided that she should continue the cure for several more weeks in order to return to Manchester in fully restored health. When she requested an extension after six weeks, Canetti's father became impatient and telegraphed her to return to England forthwith, which she did. Canetti's firsthand report says nothing about the day or evening of his mother's return except that his father did not visit the children's room that evening. The next morning, however, he made his customary visit with its loving and joyful games before breakfast. Only a few minutes later, Canetti heard shouting from downstairs, ran to the dining room, and saw his father lying on the floor. At 30 years of age and in seemingly perfect health, Canetti's father had died of a sudden heart attack.

For the next 23 years, from 1912 until 1935, Canetti attempted to learn the cause of his beloved father's death. He received various explanations: his grandfather maintained it was caused by the curse he had invoked upon his son; a family friend, Mr. Florentin, speculated that a newspaper report of the commencement of the Balkan War and the possibility of many casualties even within his family brought about the death of the peace-loving father. Just as the grandfather's curse was to serve as an example of the power of the word throughout Canetti's life, so the concept of war – all wars –

hereafter would "absorb me as the most personal thing that could happen to me" (*TF*, 59).

It was, however, his mother's account of the events leading to his father's death that most provoked and influenced Canetti. Even more crucial was the way she told him the story over that 23-year period. Since a physical examination after the death revealed no cause for the heart attack, Canetti periodically queried his mother. "What I learned from her changed every few years; as I gradually got older, new things were added, and an earlier version proved to have been 'solicitous' of my youth" (*TF*, 57). His obsession to learn the truth – "my father's death was at the center of every world I found myself in" (*TF*, 58) – finally obliged him to accept his mother's last version, which, he claims, he still believes. Canetti does, however, retain some skepticism. He questions the veracity of her final account by adding that it was "the truth as she saw it" (*TF*, 60).

What seemed to have happened at Bad Reichenhall, according to the final version, was that the mother's physician fell in love with her and urged her to leave her husband and become his wife, a request she never entertained, indeed rejected completely. She had wanted to extend her cure because she enjoyed being with people who shared her intellectual interests, an experience she greatly missed in Manchester. In the course of discussion, her doctor had introduced her to the writings of Strindberg, a writer whom she continued to read her entire life.[13] The uniqueness of this literary encounter was that "she felt challenged to give answers and found within herself daring, unexpected drives" (*PE*, 222). Here she met an author who "thought as ill of women as she did" (*PE*, 222). Under no circumstances, however, did she apply this misogyny to herself. She consistently and resolutely identified herself with the prideful male protagonist Coriolanus, from Shakespeare's play.[14] When Canetti's mother returned to England, her husband demanded that she tell him everything that had happened at Bad Reichenhall. "He wanted a confession and she had none to make. He didn't believe her" (*PE*, 223). Suspecting her of infidelity, he could not believe that the physician would even consider marriage to a woman with three children if she had not been unfaithful. He then asked whether they had conducted their literary discussions in German. The mother responded affirmatively, suggesting that it was the only reasonable language to use when speaking to a German doctor. Not satisfied, the father announced that he would not talk to his wife until she told the complete truth. After a silent but sleepless night, Canetti's father went to his children's room for his customary visit, went down to the dining room, had the heart attack, and died.

After more than two decades of merciless questioning and torturous encounters and confrontations, Canetti believed he had found the reason for his father's death. "Her infidelity had consisted in speaking German, the intimate language between her and my father, with a man who was courting her. All the important events of their love life . . . had taken place in German" (PE, 224). Canetti admits in conclusion that he "hadn't the heart to tell her that she was guilty in spite of her innocence, because she had listened to words she should never have allowed, spoken in this language" (PE, 224).

When his father died, Canetti was 7 years old, his mother 27, and the brothers 4 and a year and a half. During the early months, the disconsolate widow relied heavily on the strength and support of her oldest son, perhaps more than should have been expected of a boy his age. He was her constant companion; they took their meals together; he even slept in the same room with her, preventing her from committing suicide on numerous occasions.

During this distressful period, there developed a most unfortunate relationship between Canetti and his mother. Each had a great need for the other, but they also developed an antipathy toward each other when that need was rejected and independence was sought. For example, the boy would exhibit considerable hostility towards anyone, including his mother, if a man showed her even the slightest real or imagined amatory interest. At first it was as if he insisted on protecting her, but in time he may well have felt that she should be punished for the role she played in his father's death. Perhaps in retaliation, his mother later made every effort to instill her misogynous views in her son. As a result, even as a grown man, he would invent imaginary women friends for fear that his mother would verbally attack and abuse real friends.

Fear of his mother's reactions to his women friends seems to have been well-founded. Canetti met his first wife, Veza, when he started studies at the university in Vienna in 1924. They did not marry until 10 years later, and even then he kept his marriage a secret from his mother for another year. When it finally seemed that his mother could accept his marriage, she turned on her son "with a dire prophecy: just as I had deserted her, so I would desert Veza" (*PE*, 228).

While Canetti was enjoying the success of the publication of *Auto-da-Fé*,[15] his mother "saw Veza banished and forgotten in a tiny apartment just like her own in Paris. . . . I hadn't deceived her and she hadn't let herself be deceived; no one could hide his wickedness from her, she had the gift of seeing through people, and she had passed it on to me. I was her son" (*PE*, 228-29). It had taken 23 years to reach this point where mother and son seemed to have achieved a strange truce: the mother realized and foretold the fate of Canetti and Veza's future, and the son had revealed that the father's death was caused by the mother's linguistic infidelity. But Canetti was wrong. His mother, whose patron saint was Coriolanus, had the last word in a letter she sent to him several months after his visit: "she wrote that she never wanted to see me again" (*PE*, 229).

Less than a year after his father's death, Canetti's mother decided to leave England. Although she had several brothers who apparently supported her during the period of mourning, she disliked Manchester because it lacked all manner of intellectual stimulation. For her the citadel of culture was Vienna and the language of the intellect was German. Canetti had shown great interest early in life in learning the magic language of his parents, an enthusiasm that seemed to wane during the year that he and his father were so joyfully occupied in learning English. To prepare her son for entrance into third grade along with the other eight-year-old boys of Vienna, his mother undertook a brutal and merciless plan to teach him German. After just three months he was quite fluent and entered the Viennese school in fall 1913.

Her teaching method exemplifies her resolve to have her way. She had lost the husband with whom she shared German and now her son was to fill this need. The method she employed was so extraordinary that Canetti recalls it in great detail. "How can I depict that instruction believably? I know how it went – how could I forget? – but I still can't believe it myself" (*TF*, 67). Using an English-German grammar as a textbook, she would read a sentence and have her son repeat it several times until he pronounced it properly. At that point she would tell him the meaning in English just once, expecting him to remember it. This procedure was repeated with many more sentences. The next day she tested him, having him repeat the

German sentence and follow it with the English translation. If he missed one or another sentence, she would deride him, scold him, and shout: "My son's an idiot! . . . or Your father knew German too, what would your father say!" (*TF*, 68). Never once did she praise the boy, who lived constantly in fear of derision. Nevertheless, "she regarded the terror I lived in as pedagogical" (*TF*, 69). Finally she gave him the book so that the oral drills could be reinforced by reading, his progress was enhanced to the point where he could converse in German with his mother, and he had acquired "a belated mother tongue" (*TF*, 70). But the most important aspect of learning German for Canetti, the future writer, was that it "tied me indissolubly to that language" (*TF*, 70). Of the many languages Canetti had encountered and the languages he knows, it is the magic language of his childhood, the "belated mother tongue," that he has used exclusively in his writings.

The first volume of the autobiography, *The Tongue Set Free*, is Canetti's story of the first 16 years of his life. After leaving Manchester, the family lived in Vienna from 1913 to 1916, and when the conditions of World War I made life too insecure they moved to Zurich, Switzerland, remaining there until 1921. These were years of learning for Canetti. It seems as though the precocious youth pursued all his school studies with great vigor and dedication. Canetti includes in his autobiography portraits of his teachers in which he celebrates their contributions to his life of the mind. Using the divisions of medieval guilds, the first volume is his apprenticeship years; the next, *The Torch in my Ear*, describes his 10 years as a journeyman; and the final volume portrays the young master.

The Torch in My Ear

The second volume of the autobiography examines a critical period in the author's life, from 1921 to 1931. Friends of Canetti's mother seem to have persuaded her that it would be beneficial to remove her 16-year-old son from his idyllic and utopian Zurich and expose him to the harsh realities of life in post-World War I Germany, with its problems of unemployment, inflation, and political turmoil. Under much protest from Canetti, the family moved to Frankfurt am Main, where he lived until he completed his secondary school studies at the Gymnasium in 1924. In April of that year, he moved to Vienna, the city that would be his home not only during his years as a student at the University of Vienna, where he earned a Ph.D. in chemistry in 1929, but also for another nine years until November 1938, when he and his wife were among the last Jews to flee from Vienna following the annexation of Austria to Hitler's Germany.

If learning in his earlier years had been directed by teachers or ensued from fortuitous encounters and subsequent enthusiastic pursuits, learning during this decade of Canetti's life was the work of a serious young man. During the first several years in Vienna, Canetti's struggle with his mother continued and finally resulted in a separation; he stayed in Vienna and his mother and two brothers moved to Paris. As painful as this break must have been for Canetti, it provided him with a vital freedom to develop his own personality.

Canetti had been in Vienna only a few days when, on 17 April 1924, friends introduced him to two people who would have a profound impact on him for the rest of his life: Veza Taubner-Calderon, his future wife, and Karl Kraus, the great Viennese critic, satirist, and editor of *Die Fackel* (The Torch). Canetti acknowledges his indebtedness to Kraus by giving this volume of his autobiography a title composed of two important contributions from Kraus: *The Torch* is from the journal in which Kraus published many of the thought-provoking essays and fictions that Canetti heard at Kraus's public readings; the *Ear* represents the way Kraus taught Canetti to hear the many sounds that made up all levels of Viennese society. Of course, there were other important voices that Canetti heard during these early years in Vienna, and he recognizes them here with shorter essays and vignettes. Also during this decade of Canetti's life, two major events occurred that were to shape his mind and his work: his experiences with crowds during the workers' demonstrations protesting the murder of Walther Rathenau, a prominent labor leader and politician, and the crowds that participated in the 15 July 1927 burning of the Palace of Justice in Vienna.

From the host of people presented in this volume of the autobiography, one is examined here in detail: Karl Kraus.

Karl Kraus

In his speech accepting the Nobel Prize for Literature, Canetti expressed his indebtedness to four men who had had a profound influence on him. "The first is Karl Kraus, the greatest German satirist.

He taught me to hear the sounds of Vienna with unwavering devotion. More importantly, however, he inoculated me against war – an inoculation which was necessary for many back then."[16]

On the day when Canetti attended his first Karl Kraus lecture, the satirist was at the height of his career. On 17 April 1924 he was giving his three-hundredth lecture to an audience of 1,500 eager listeners assembled at Vienna's Great Concert House Hall.

Karl Kraus (1874-1936) was already beginning to make a name for himself in the last few years of the nineteenth century.[17] As a young man, he was already a regular participant in the discussions at the Café Griensteidl, the meeting place of the distinguished Jung-Wien (Young Vienna) literary group. Here he became acquainted with the leading writers of that time and caused considerable outrage when he attacked Hermann Bahr, Hugo von Hofmannsthal, and Leopold von Andrian, all highly respected writers. Kraus's 1897 pamphlet *Demolirte Literatur* (Demolished Literature) illustrates his powerful style of writing, employing quotations from his subjects' works in order to parody and satirize them. A year later he published his polemic *Eine Krone für Zion* (A Crown for Zion), an assault on the Zionist movement and its leader Theodor Herzl; here Kraus argued that unconditional assimilation with the socialists was the only viable solution for Jews.

Kraus's fame increased in 1898 when he acquired an extended readership as the "chroniqueur" of the Viennese magazine *Die Wage* (The Scales). Within a year his celebrity as correspondent and humorous feuilletonist had grown to such heights that he was offered a similar position on the staff of Vienna's leading newspaper, the *Neue Freie Presse* (New Free Press). He declined the offer, preferring to make that paper the subject of his attacks on journalism for many years to come. Instead, he established his own periodical *Die Fackel*. In the lead editorial of the first issue, the 25-year-old Kraus wrote that the mission of *Die Fackel* was not "what we will do, but what we will undo," and with that he began his critical attacks on corruption, nepotism, and the press.

The first issue of *Die Fackel* sold 30,000 copies within days and continued with about 10,000 subscribers for its first half decade. In the years prior to World War I, subscriptions grew from 29,000 to as high as 38,000, decreasing after the war and through the 1920s to approximately 10,000 subscribers. Thereafter, the numbers declined gradually. When Kraus died in 1936, *Die Fackel* had appeared for 37 years, with 922 issues. What is even more amazing than the longevity and immensity of the periodical is the fact that most of *Die Fackel* was written by Karl Kraus himself. Canetti, a voracious reader, undoubtedly read virtually every issue that appeared during the mid- to late 1920s. Kraus's lectures and readings, however, seem to have made an even greater impact on him: he mentions attending 100 lectures (*TE*, 71).

Much of what Kraus published in *Die Fackel* and elsewhere was material he had prepared for his public readings and lectures. The first such reading took place in Berlin in 1910; his appearances continued in various European cities until Kraus had completed 700 in April 1936, just two months before his death. The topics presented at these public events in the years that Elias Canetti attended may be summarized in three categories: Kraus's attacks on the press, on theater criticism, and on politicians; his readings from his own works; and his "Theater der Dichtung" (Literary Theater), in which he read from the works of other writers.

During the 1920s, Kraus launched a successful attack on Imre Bekessy, a Hungarian journalist who had established himself with his newspaper *Die Stunde* (The Hour) in Vienna shortly after World War I. This Viennese press lord was financed by profiteers and racketeers, received extensive favors from the Austrian government, and conducted a systematic program of blackmail, extortion, and corruption. Kraus unveiled the truth about Bekessy's activities, printed and distributed posters with the battle cry "Hinaus aus Wien mit dem Schuft" (Get that scoundrel out of Vienna), and through satire and polemics made Bekessy's life so unpleasant that he was finally forced to flee the city.

Another longtime Kraus opponent was the well-known Berlin theater critic Alfred Kerr, whose reviews often resembled yellow journalism more than critical analysis. When in 1926 Kerr presented himself as a pacifist and champion of human and civil rights, Kraus started his attacks by presenting and publishing some of the really bad poetry Kerr had published pseudonymously during the war. Legal confrontations between the two were eventually resolved, but Kraus continued the fight by citing the theater critic's work, claiming that the best weapon is always the opponent's own words.

The Bekessy and Kerr affairs taught Canetti the power of the word. Kraus was by no means just a journalist campaigning for some personal cause; he seriously believed that he was educating the public by speaking and writing the truth as he saw it. "In Kraus's hands, polemic and satire became weapons with which to direct men away from everything superficial, corrupt and dehumanizing in human thought and action" and to lead them "back to the 'origin' of all values, and so, in effect, to accomplish a regeneration of culture as a whole."[18] Fifty years after hearing Kraus, Canetti, in his essay "The Writer's Profession," similarly insists that it must be the writer's "pride to resist and fight . . . the envoys of nothingness . . . to find a way out of it and one shall mark the road for everyone. Whether in grief or despair, one shall endure in order to learn how to save others from it" (*CW*, 246). That is Canetti's law for today's writer, and specifically for himself.

The third person whom Kraus attacked, this time unsuccessfully, was Vienna's chief of police, Johannes Schober. He had ordered the police to use rifles to control the crowds that gathered to protest the acquittal of the men who had killed two innocent bystanders in a confrontation between rightist and prosocialist groups. The incident took place on 15 July 1927, the day the crowd set fire to the Palace of Justice. Eighty-nine people, including women and children, were killed and about 300 were wounded. Two months later, Kraus carried out a poster campaign demanding Schober's resignation. The crusade failed. The moderate Pan-German nationalist Schober emerged politically strengthened and two years later headed the Austrian government that eventually destroyed the Austrian Republic and paved the way for Hitler's Annexation.

The date 15 July 1927 was very important for Elias Canetti, at the time a chemistry student.[19] After reading about the verdict in the newspaper, he was so outraged that he raced on his bicycle from his apartment in suburban Ober Sankt Veit to the center of Vienna. There he was engulfed by the crowd, just as he had been some years earlier during the demonstration in Frankfurt. This experience formed the basis of his lifelong study of *Crowds and Power*, as well as a significant portion of *Auto-da-Fé*.

At any reading, a high point would be Kraus's recitation from his monumental tragedy *Die letzten Tage der Menschheit* (The Last Days of Mankind). Written between 1915 and 1917 and first published in several issues of *Die Fackel* in 1918 and 1919, the completed version was published in 1922. This is not an ordinary play; it is the ultimate example of Kraus's "Theater der Dichtung," the "Literary Theater." When Kraus completed this major work, it consisted of a prologue, five acts, and an epilogue, a not unusual structure, but it had over 200 scenes and was 800 pages long. Using direct quotations, montages, and collages, Kraus projects the disorder and chaos of World War I. In one scene, for example, he presents the voice of Pope Benedict XV, the truly pious and charitable pope at the time of the war, praying for the end of the blood being shed among the nations. In the very next scene, Kraus quotes directly from another Benedict, the editor in chief of Vienna's *Neue Freie Presse* Moritz Benedikt, as he dictates an article rejoicing over Austria's sinking of numerous Italian ships and the way the fish of the seas will feast on the bodies of the dead sailors.[20] By juxtaposing these scenes, the former of the vicar of the Holy See, the latter of a jingoistic journalist celebrating the destructive and inhumane powers of the Imperial navy in the Adriatic Sea, Kraus establishes his powerful antiwar message. If not heeded, the result will be the final destruction and damnation of the human race.

The Last Days of Mankind has never been staged in its entirety. Not only does its length make a meaningful production impossible, but Kraus never intended it for anything other than his "Literary Theater." Kraus was a master at imitating the voices and noises of all the characters he created in his play. The publisher Frederick Ungar, who attended most of Kraus's readings, described these evenings, when Kraus would appear on the stage and sit at a small table on the darkened stage, with only a small lamp illuminating him: "The first impression was one of shyness; but when he started to read, his passionate condemnation of the war, of everything that was corrupt in Austria, and the force of his conviction, compelling in its sincerity, had a powerful impact upon his audience. But he himself was also carried away by the emotion of his visionary fervor. His clenched right fist trembled with emotion under the lamp's glaring light. And the mastery of his diction was further enhanced by the mastery of his recitation – he had all technical means at his disposal." Ungar continues his account of the readings with a quotation from a contemporary writer: " 'For an hour and a quarter he wields the rod of his word. Now his voice is hoarse with quiet wrath, now it sounds melodious, as if he were weaving in a stanza from a folk song, now it rises to a roaring thunderstorm, in which one can hardly distinguish word from scream; at another moment it cuts the air like blows from glittering weapons' " (Kraus, x).

Those readings certainly were heady encounters for Elias Canetti, then in his early 20s. And in the 100 lectures and readings he attended, Canetti also heard Kraus read from the works of other writers. In the 1920s, as part of his "Literary Theater," Kraus prepared one-man readings of nine plays by the great nineteenth-century satirist and playwright Johann Nestroy. This gave Kraus the opportunity to perform the roles of the characters by assigning to each a different voice and dialect, as well as singing the numerous songs Nestroy included in each of his plays. The origin of Canetti's concept of the acoustic mask can certainly be traced back to these evenings at Kraus's readings.

During the same years, Kraus also presented a 14-part cycle based on the work of the genius of opéra comique Jacques Offenbach. Kraus found in these operettas a powerful parody and satire of France during the Second Empire. In his essay on Kraus, Walter Benjamin points out that "Kraus, in his recitals, does not speak the words of Offenbach or Nestroy: they speak for him."[21]

For Canetti, however, the most exciting moments must have been when Kraus recited Shakespeare. Canetti had started reading Shakespeare when he was only 10 years old and now, a decade later, he was hearing the masterful Karl Kraus deliver the great orations from *King Lear*, *Timon of Athens*, or any of the other twelve dramas that Kraus included in his Shakespeare cycle. But in his acerbic essay, Benjamin is far less charitable in discussing Kraus's Shakespeare work. He believes that Kraus is no longer presenting the many true and important acoustic masks of the world of Vienna, as he had done in *The Last Days of Mankind*. Rather, Benjamin suggests that Kraus reveals himself through the character of Timon, the grumbling misanthrope (Benjamin, 263).

Shortly after attending the first Kraus lecture, Canetti joined the large crowd of true believers. He was totally perplexed when his future wife Veza did not show the same veneration for his great master. Veza always sat in the first row at the lectures, causing Canetti to ask in outrage: "How did she dare sit in front of Kraus? Every sentence of his was a demand. If you couldn't meet the demand, you had no business being there" (*TE*, 159). And of himself, he writes: "For a year and a half, I had gone to every reading, and I was filled with him as with a Bible. I did not doubt a single word he said. Never, under any circumstances, would I have acted against him. He was my conviction. He was my strength" (*TE*, 159).

Although such comments sound like pure and simple idolization, it must be emphasized that during that early period Canetti learned a great deal from Kraus at those lectures. Kraus's readings from *The Last Days of Mankind* did, after all, teach him to abhor war and to perceive the acoustic masks that make up each individual, as Canetti consistently acknowledged from those first days in 1924 until he received the Nobel Prize a half century later. Furthermore, Kraus's demands that language and critical reasoning be used with the utmost care and adherence to rules have certainly contributed to Canetti's becoming one of the great stylists and thinkers of this century. Finally, it must be remembered that Canetti had spent his formative years in the seclusion of Zurich and, consequently, had to learn about the corruption of journalism, government, and politics as they are practiced in the real world.

In the summer of 1928 Canetti was in Berlin assisting Wieland Herzfelde, publisher of the radical Malik publishing house, to prepare a biography of Upton Sinclair. In those years, Berlin was Europe's most exciting cultural metropolis, filled with all the great art and artists, yet also home to all the excessiveness that is part of any large city. Canetti, at age 23, overwhelmed by this experience, met many important cultural figures – George Grosz, Brecht, Isaac Babel, and Wieland Herzfelde's brother John Heartfield, to name just a few. What astonished Canetti most was the way he was treated by these celebrities: "not with scorn, but with curiosity, and, above all, never with condemnation" (*TE*, 268). This encounter with writers and artists was the first time after four years of Kraus's influence that Canetti was among people who had strong and conflicting views. Speaking about himself and the influence Kraus had had on him, Canetti admits that he "was filled with all his [i.e., Kraus's] contempt and condemnation and acknowledged nothing that was determined by greed, selfishness, or frivolity. All objects to condemn were prescribed by Kraus. You were not even allowed to look at them; he had already taken care of that for you and made the decision. It was a *sterilized* intellectual life that we led in Vienna" (*TE*, 268-69;

Canetti's emphasis). Although it may not have been obvious to Canetti at the time, it becomes clear that the Berlin experience initiated the later falling-out with his idol, Karl Kraus.

The autobiography does not speak about Canetti's conflict with Kraus after that summer visit to Berlin, although the break was of great importance to Canetti's further intellectual development. There are, however, two major essays included in *The Conscience of Words* that address this issue in detail: "Karl Kraus – The School of Resistance" (1965, also known under the title "Why I don't write like Karl Kraus") and "The New Karl Kraus" (1974).

"I attended a hundred lectures by Karl Kraus; for nine years I let every spoken and written word of his take effect on me: for five years without resistance, for four with growing criticism" (*CW*, 219). Writing the essays on Kraus 40 to 50 years after his initial encounter, Canetti undertakes the difficult task of describing and defining the essence of Kraus. Using his former idol's technique of the "acoustic quotation," Canetti begins with Kraus's well-known self-definition from an early issue of *Die Fackel:* "The census has revealed that Vienna has 2,030,834 inhabitants. Namely, 2,030,833 souls and me" (*CW*, 214). This seemingly humorous, offhand remark establishes the egocentric Kraus not only as someone unique among the more than 2 million, undoubtedly misguided, souls but also as the one and only individual in the entire city whose duty it was to convert and save all those others. In the early years Kraus served Canetti as total master; Kraus was judge, jury, and executioner of all laws that he himself had promulgated. Canetti referred to Kraus's law as one that "glowed: it radiated, it scorched and destroyed," and "every verdict was carried out on the spot. Once pronounced, it was irrevocable" (*CW*, 31).

Kraus's obstinate persistence was agreeable to Canetti as long as Kraus's outrage was directed against such moral issues as war or corruption. Here Kraus was indeed often a lone voice – but never the only voice – publicly proclaiming what others often failed to recognize and chastise. His "acoustic quotations" in the late 1920s revealed not only the horrors of war when he read from *The Last Days of Mankind* but also called attention to Bekessy's corrupt newspaper empire, Alfred Kerr's questionable theater criticism, and the blame borne by Vienna's police chief Johannes Schober for the deaths at the 15 July burning of the Palace of Justice. There were, however, other times when Kraus pursued the motto of *Die Fackel*, "what we will undo," with an unjustifiable vehemence. For example, it was not enough for Kraus to have defeated Kerr; he continued his pursuit in *Die Fackel* with four further articles titled "Little Pan is Dead," "Little Pan Is Still Rattling," "Little Pan Already Stinks," and "Little Pan Still Stinks" (*CW*, 215). Canetti finally saw in Kraus's continued attacks not only overkill but an unforgivable mean-spiritedness.

As time went on, Canetti also learned that Kraus never allowed his audience to hold a different opinion on who was or was not a distinguished writer. Canetti was not troubled by the praise that Kraus heaped on favorite writers such as Nestroy, Shakespeare, and Goethe. It was, however, entirely different with writers that Kraus had declared unworthy, because Kraus demanded that his listeners and readers share his views with total and blind obedience. After a while, when the initial euphoria and unquestioning dedication to Kraus was diminishing, Canetti started to reject the dictatorial power of Karl Kraus.

It is not possible to establish an exact date or the precise circumstance when Canetti's liberation from Kraus began. Likewise, it is difficult to know exactly when Canetti was no longer under the strict domination of his mother. It is, however, reasonable to suggest that a great change in Canetti's life occurred in September 1929. After finishing his doctoral degree in chemistry in June of that year, he spent another summer in Berlin, where he had been commissioned to translate several novels of Upton Sinclair. Returning to Vienna with a means of livelihood, Canetti devoted half of each day to his translation tasks and the other half to preliminary work on the series of novels that he projected for his "Human Comedy of Madmen." The journeyman years seem to be over; the life of the master writer begins.

The Play of the Eyes

This third volume of the autobiography is devoted to the years 1931 to 1937. Unlike the other volumes, it does not proceed in chronological order. But its primary purpose is to portray Canetti as a mature writer and thinker during this period. In the fall of 1931, after a year's work, Canetti completed his novel *Auto-da-Fé*, published in 1935. His next task was to write the play *The Wedding*, which though it was accepted by the theater division of the S. Fischer publishing house in 1932 went unpublished until 1964.[22] The third work, completed in early 1934, was the play *Comedy of Vanity*, first published in 1950.[23] Canetti's major preoccupation during these years was the preliminary work on his study of crowds and power.

The most important experiences for Canetti during these politically turbulent years in Vienna were, however, his encounters and friendships with some of Europe's most distinguished artists. There were not only writers such as Hermann Broch and Robert Musil but also the musicians Hermann Scherchen and Alban Berg, as well as the painter Georg Merkel and the sculptor Fritz Wotruba, to mention only a few.

Two influential men from this period will be examined here in detail, illustrating Canetti's interaction with them and their impact on his thinking. In 1933, Canetti met Fritz Wotruba, to whom he devotes not only two chapters in the autobiography but also an essay published in 1955. The other personality Canetti encountered in 1933 is Abraham Sonne, a most elusive individual who assumes the role that Canetti's mother and then Karl Kraus played in the early years of the author's life. Sonne, however, made a most constructive contribution to the life of the young Canetti. In the first two volumes of the autobiography, the tongue and the ear were the senses that played the prominent roles; in this volume it is the eyes. Wotruba's work provided the visual stimulus and Dr. Sonne's brought greater intellectual insight.

Fritz Wotruba

With the publication of his autobiography, it became evident that Canetti had had a great affinity for the fine arts throughout his life. There are ample references to the great masters of the past: Breughel, Rembrandt, Michelangelo, Goya, and Matthias Grünewald. Among the artists who were his contemporaries, Canetti acknowledges the profound influence that George Grosz's *Ecce Homo* series had on him when they met in Berlin in 1928. In the early 1930s Canetti became acquainted with the sculptural accomplishments of Anna Mahler, daughter of the composer Gustav Mahler and the flamboyant Alma Mahler. Through Anna Mahler, Canetti met Fritz Wotruba (1907-1975), Austria's most distinguished twentieth-century sculptor.[24]

In addition to the two chapters assigned to Wotruba in the auto-biography, "A Twin Is Bestowed on Me" and "The 'Black Statue,' " Canetti refers to him countless times in this third volume. The 1955 essay *Fritz Wotruba* became the exhibition catalogue for the tour that made Wotruba's sculpture known throughout the western world.[25] To understand the relationship that the writer and the sculptor established and valued in these earlier years, it is useful to briefly outline the myth of sculptural creation and the nature of the work in which Wotruba was engaged.

All of the basic ingredients of sculptural creation are combined in the ancient Greek myth of Pygmalion and Galatea, described in Ovid's *Metamorphoses*. This early association of sculpture and magic symbolically reveals some basic insights into the essence of sculpture. Pygmalion was a man and a sculptor who fell in love with the beautiful goddess Venus. Since she would not have him, he made an ivory statue of her. When he continued to pray to her, Venus finally took pity on Pygmalion and entered into the statue, giving it life as Galatea. Pygmalion then married Galatea, and they had two sons.

Sculptors have portrayed the moment of the statue's transformation since ancient times and have often succeeded in simultaneously suggesting the inanimate quality of their materials and the living nature of the human figure. Thus, artists can control reality by fashioning an object that portrays the ideal outcome of their desires. Venus's pity, a symbol of magical powers, imbues the sculptor's work with life, making possible a union of creator and created and, consequently, also providing for a continuation of a family line that includes the world's sculptors.

There are several suggestions in Canetti's writings placing Fritz Wotruba and his work in ancient and mythical times. Indeed, Canetti's essay begins: "It is an old and indestructible idea that the sculptor stands at the Inception. Whoever speaks of the creator thinks first of the forming of creatures in space, and no other art has so strongly preserved its primordial character" (*FW*, 8). Observing Wotruba's hands, Canetti is ever conscious of their power and sensitivity, comparing their touch with the touch "of God's finger in *The Creation of Adam* on the ceiling of the Sistine Chapel" (*PE*, 105). Yet at the same time that the hands of the sculptor stand at the inception of life, Canetti also recalls that they have great destructive power.

After they became close friends Wotruba told Canetti about his
father, who had beaten his older brothers. "Fritz's eldest brother
had been sent to jail for murder and armed robbery, he had died
miserably in Stein on the Danube" (*PE*, 105). The fear that he would
likewise perform violent acts – committing the sin of Cain – drove
Wotruba to "his daily battle with stone . . . his work owes its existence to the conflict between his father and his brothers, and to the
fate of his brothers" (*PE*, 106). These are the qualities and the
themes that return sculptors to the beginning of time and to the earliest and most basic conflicts in human life.

In the same way, Canetti was at this time searching for the origin
of power and crowds. Although there is no specific information in
the autobiography on which books he was reading or which sources
he was consulting, there are scores of references to the fact that he
was almost totally preoccupied with this problem during these years.
(When *Crowds and Power* was finally published in 1960, Canetti included a bibliography of some 350 titles relating to myth, religion,
history, anthropology, biography, and psychiatry, but advised that
this was only a very selective list.) If Wotruba hewed stone until he
achieved the sculpture inherent in the material, his "twin" Canetti
was hewing books to secure the origin of crowds and power.

Fritz Wotruba worked in various media, but it was his sculptures
in stone that Canetti most admired. This is the oldest form of sculpture and is used by artists who are comfortable working with a highly
resistant, obdurate material. Ancient sculptors believed that their art
was mainly one of releasing the forms and meanings that were hidden or imprisoned within the stones. Working as carvers in this sub-
tractive process, they would cut away from a stone block until the
forms in their mind's eye were revealed, a process that requires not
only great strength but also indefatigable patience. These are character traits of the artist that Canetti was only now learning to appreciate, because he had really seen the work of too few artists who had
dedicated themselves to hard work in their respective fields. It
should be recalled that at this point Canetti had written his novel in
one year and his two early plays in only a few months. He did not
know that he would have to dedicate the next quarter century to
Crowds and Power. Canetti greatly admired, for example, Robert
Musil, who worked untiringly for decades on his monumental novel
The Man without Qualities. At the same time, he felt only contempt

for a writer such as Franz Werfel, who, although very popular and highly successful, was forever "foaming at the mouth" (*PE*, 167), with nothing of value or substance to say.

Just as the sculptor works with the hardest materials yet cannot show the difficulty in the final work of art, likewise Canetti learned from his "twin" – as well as from other great writers and models like Kafka and Stendhal – that great writing would only come through the hard work of releasing the forms and meanings hidden or imprisoned within words. In 1975, the year Wotruba died, Canetti included in his notes and aphorisms the following entry portraying the great affinity he had with his friend: "It would be wonderful to still find a brother who has said it with the same hardness."[26]

Dr. Sonne

Virtually nothing is known about the man called Dr. Sonne, a man to whom Canetti attributes the greatest importance. Canetti reports: "It seems that when only fifteen he had written, under the name of Abraham ben Yitzhak, some poems which had been compared to Hölderlin . . . only a very few hymnlike poems, perhaps less than a dozen, of such perfection that he had been numbered among the masters of the newly revived [Hebrew] language" (*PE*, 147). And in Martin Buber's correspondence there is a reference to "Abraham Sonne (1883-1950), known as the Hebrew poet Abraham ben Jizchak, lecturer at the Jewish Educational Institute of Vienna. 1919 to 1920 secretary general of the Zionist Executive Committee in London. Since 1938 resident in Jerusalem."[27] From Canetti's autobiography we learn that Dr. Sonne, although a seminal personality in Elias Canetti's life, was a totally unassuming scholar in many fields, a man who lived in almost total seclusion, a person completely disinclined toward ambition leading to fame, and – most important – an individual who spoke only after careful consideration and then with the greatest precision.

In addition to scores of references throughout this volume of the autobiography, Canetti has entitled one entire section "Dr. Sonne" and devotes four chapters to the man: "Silence at the Café Museum," "Sonne," "High Authority," and "The Spanish Civil War."

Canetti and Dr. Sonne first took note of each other in 1933 or 1934 at Vienna's Café Museum, a famous gathering place for painters and sculptors. Although they saw each other almost every day, they were not introduced until a year and a half later. Canetti went to the café each day and noticed the man who always sat alone, reading many newspapers, speaking to no one. What specifically attracted Canetti to this person whose name he did not yet know was that he looked like Karl Kraus. "I kept my distance; without knowing who he was I had great respect for him. I felt his concentration as if he had been Karl Kraus, but a silent Karl Kraus such as I had never encountered" (*PE*, 113). At the time, Canetti was trying to find a way to escape the influence Kraus had on him; this nameless and silent likeness assisted him. "Little by little, my veneration detached itself from Karl Kraus and turned to his likeness" (*PE*, 115). This change in Canetti's life was to have the most felicitous consequences.

Their actual meeting a year and a half later came about as a result of an interesting discussion Canetti had with his good friend, the writer Hermann Broch. Thinking about the numerous people they knew in Vienna, they wondered whether there was such a thing as "a good man" (*PE*, 126). Initially, they were inclined to think that it was impossible for a good man to exist in their turbulent environment; they both "harbored a pristine image of the good person" (*PE*, 127). Yet, little by little, they formulated a definition: the good person must not be naive but "must know what he is doing," must possess "a number of drives and motives to choose among," cannot be unknowledgeable about the world and people while at the same time "not let them deceive him," and must be "vigilant, sensitive and alert" (*PE*, 127). If this person possessed all these qualities and virtues he had to then answer affirmatively the question: "Is he [the good man] nevertheless good?" (*PE*, 127). After reviewing all the people they knew well, Broch thought of one person who satisfied all requirements: "My friend Sonne! He's our good man!!!" (*PE*, 128). Only a short while later, Canetti finally met this good man, Dr. Sonne.

What struck Canetti especially was the totally impersonal manner of Dr. Sonne's discourse. Unlike normal coffeehouse conversations with "floods of I-talk, protestation, confession and self-assertion, . . . self-pity and self-importance," Dr. Sonne "never talked about himself," rarely addressed Canetti directly, and generally spoke only "in the third person to distance himself from his surroundings" (*PE*, 133). Their conversations were far-ranging and profound. Reference can be made here to only a few.

Canetti gives no details of discussions the two men had about Austrian political events and about how events in Germany would affect them momentarily, but he summarizes everything with a single statement: "Catastrophe was in the air" (*PE*, 133). Dr. Sonne offered precise and insightful analyses of the events that shaped Canetti's world in the 1930s: the decline and fall of the First Austrian Republic, the frightful and totalitarian reign of both Chancellor Dollfuss and Chancellor Schuschnigg, the battles of various political parties that often resulted in a form of civil war, the rise of Austrofascism, and the ultimate horror of Austria's annexation to Germany in March 1938. "It was only seeing Dr. Sonne that made this period bearable for me. He was an authority to which I had daily access" (*PE*, 133-34).

Also from Dr. Sonne, Canetti learned "that it is possible to concern oneself with a wide range of subjects without becoming a windbag" (*PE*, 135). This was of considerable importance as Canetti was attempting to articulate his personal – and at times rather unconventional – views not only on crowds and power but on every other issue he would investigate for the remainder of his life.

One interesting example of Dr. Sonne's impersonal and detached personality and the effect this had on Canetti can be found in the way each man dealt with Canetti's writings. When they were first introduced, Canetti had already written (but as yet not published) his novel and two plays, but he felt he had to protect his work from the "supreme authority"; he could not show it to Sonne until it was published and could not be changed. Sonne, on the other hand, had heard about Canetti's work and had even attended one of Canetti's public readings, but he "never said anything, because he knew that as soon as the book was out . . . I would bring it to him" (*PE*, 192).

When *Auto-da-Fé* was finally published in October 1935, Canetti presented a copy to Dr. Sonne with the following German inscription: "Dr. Sonne, mir noch mehr. E. C." ("For Dr. Sonne, to me still more. E. C.") (*PE*, 205). This dedicatory inscription reveals several interesting aspects of Canetti's attitude toward the "High Authority," his title not only for Dr. Sonne himself but also for the autobiography chapter dealing with Dr. Sonne's analysis of Canetti's novel.

Canetti's addressing the man as "Dr. Sonne" indicates that their relationship was still very formal and quite impersonal. The signature "E. C." is Canetti's way of humbling himself in the presence of the man he holds in such high esteem. (Apparently, in all copies that he gave to other people, he wrote out his full name.) To understand the phrase "to me still more," it helps to recall that the German word "Sonne" means "sun," which for Canetti at that time meant the "luminous, searing, winged, source and . . . end of all life" (PE, 206). The unpretentiousness of the inscription, this attitude exhibiting freedom from all pride, learned from the man he held in the highest regard, becomes the hallmark of Elias Canetti.

After Canetti gave Dr. Sonne a copy of Auto-da-Fé, they continued their daily discussions at the Café Museum, but days turned to weeks and Dr. Sonne never mentioned the novel. Canetti was most eager to hear Dr. Sonne's commentary, but "I never once asked him. I had learned to respect every corner of his silence . . . His independence . . . taught me the meaning of an independent mind, and in my dealings with him I was certainly not going to disregard what I had learned from him" (PE, 207). And, indeed, five weeks after he had received the novel, Dr. Sonne asked Canetti whether he would be interested in hearing his comments on Auto-da-Fé.

For two hours, Dr. Sonne "illuminated the book from every angle" (PE, 208), talking to Canetti not as the author but as a reader, creating a distance for critical discourse. Gradually Canetti understood the reasons for Dr. Sonne's remarks: "he knew the book would have a hard life and he was arming me against the attacks that were to be expected" (PE, 209).

Sonne commenced his criticism with observations that Canetti should anticipate and advice on how he should deal with such problems. For example, he noted that the work "would be attacked as a book of an old and sexless man," that Canetti's "portrayal of the Jew Fischerle lent itself to misuse by racist propaganda," and that the characters of Therese and Pfaff would be perceived as wholly unrealistic (PE, 209). Dr. Sonne was convinced, however, that "when the catastrophe had passed" the critics would realize that Canetti's characters were "types that had brought about the catastrophe" (PE, 209). Other insightful observations by Dr. Sonne became for Canetti "a reservoir of secrets" to be treasured for the next five decades (PE, 209). The commentary of that day provided Canetti with immunity to all attacks on his novel.

In the two years prior to their forced departure from Vienna in 1938, Canetti and Dr. Sonne often talked about the Spanish Civil War

(1936-39). It seemed quite clear that the events in Spain were only a prelude to what was to occur in all of Europe. Dr. Sonne feared that Hitler's "fanatical sense of historic mission" would involve the European countries and eventually the entire world in a horrible war (*PE*, 294). Their conversations, however, often expanded beyond current events to include issues and topics related to Spanish history and the arts. Dr. Sonne had a deep knowledge of Spain's history and literature and could easily translate documents from the three languages that made up Spain's past, Spanish, Arabic, and Hebrew. They spoke of the great painter Goya (1746-1828) and the extraordinary courage exhibited in his engravings *The Horrors of War*. With his abhorrence of war, Goya portrayed that "most evil and dangerous of human traditions" as a witness who fervently wished that his depiction of horror might persuade viewers against war (*PE*, 293). Dr. Sonne reminded Canetti that Goya "didn't look the other way" (*PE*, 292) because only through total insight could horror and evil be perceived and prevented.

Also prominent in their discussions was the name of the Spanish satirist, novelist, and wit Quevedo (1580-1645), one of the greatest writers of the Golden Age. In this context, Canetti makes a very important observation about himself: "A writer needs ancestors" (*PE*, 296). This statement, perhaps only fully articulated some years later, illustrates the importance Canetti has placed on the writer being part of a larger and longer literary tradition. The writer garners strength and courage from those who have preceded him and will himself serve the same function for those who follow. It is interesting to note that Canetti, who had then just published his *Auto-da-Fé*, saw himself in the company of Quevedo, Swift, and Aristophanes, all great and courageous satirists of their times, languages, and countries.

Examining the events of the times and the history of Spain with Sonne, Canetti also learned to value the origins of the Sephardic Jews, their cultural traditions, and the way they preserved their civilization for centuries following their banishment from Spain. Dr. Sonne taught Canetti his personal history during these two years and thereby prepared him for the banishment he would soon experience. They were both forced into exile in 1938. Canetti took his European cultural heritage and the German language with him to London. Dr. Sonne went to Jerusalem. "Neither of us wrote any letters" (*PE*, 150).

Chapter Two

War between Head and World

Auto-da-Fé

In 1973, almost a half century after he had written *Auto-da-Fé*, Canetti published the essay "The First Book: *Auto-da-Fé*." In this reminiscence the author tells of some important events and experiences that led to the writing of this extraordinary novel. In his customary way Canetti was influenced by seemingly trivial episodes in his private life as well as by incidents of great historical importance. Furthermore, as his autobiography shows – especially the first and second volumes – the nascence of this work lies in even earlier years of Canetti's life.

Auto-da-Fé was initially to be only one of eight books of the *Comédie Humaine an Irren* (*Human Comedy of Madmen*). Each novel would focus "on a figure on the verge of madness, and each of these figures was different from all others down to his language, down to his most secret thoughts. His experiences were such that no one else could have had the same ones. Nothing could be exchangeable and nothing could mix with anything else. I told myself I was building eight spotlights to illuminate the world from the outside" (*CW*, 210). For almost a year, from fall 1929 to fall 1930, Canetti worked on developing eight characters, each of whom he identified by a word describing the particular form of madness. These are *Wahrheitsmensch* (a man obsessed with truth), *Phantast* (the technological visionary who lived only in cosmic plans), *Religiöse Fanatiker* (religious fanatic), *Sammler* (collector), *Verschwender* (spendthrift), *Tod-Feind* (enemy of death), *Schauspieler* (the actor who could live only in rapid metamorphosis), and *Büchermensch* (book man). Ultimately, Canetti concentrated on the book man, who is the protagonist of *Auto-da-Fé*, the only novel of the eight to be completed. Canetti does not regret the loss of the other characters, since in this way he was forced to focus fully on just one specific form of madness (*CW*, 210; *TE*, 322).

The title of the novel and the name of the major character underwent several changes, even though the basic premise remained unaltered. The first name given to the protagonist was Brand (conflagration), designated by the letter *B*, which also stood for *Büchermensch*. The reason Canetti selected this name was that he had decided at the outset that this character would destroy himself in a fire he set to his library. At a later date he changed the name to Kant, since the name Brand seemed too obviously to predict the outcome and fate of the character. When he finished writing the novel in August 1931, the title was *Kant fängt Feuer* (Kant catches fire) and the name of the protagonist was Kant. Canetti's only concern at the time was that the name could be associated with the distinguished German philosopher Immanuel Kant. After waiting until 1935 to find a publisher for his novel, Canetti, on Hermann Broch's advice, changed the name of the novel and of the character for the last time. The man's name is now Kien (meaning pinewood or kindling), and the title is *Die Blendung* (blinding or dazzlement).[1]

The place in which Canetti lived while writing the novel was important to him. In April 1927, after living in various rooms rented to university students, he moved to one of the outlying districts west of the city of Vienna. From his room there he not only had an idyllic view of the Lainz deer park and the gardens of the archbishop's residence, but he could also see the walls surrounding the extensive grounds of the sanatorium for the mentally ill, Am Steinhof. The landlady reluctantly gave him permission to hang photographic reproductions of Michelangelo's frescoes in the Sistine Chapel and a large phototype of Matthias Grünewald's Isenheim Altar. This was the visual environment in which Canetti lived for six years, writing his novel and his first two plays.

The other significance of this new address is that the landlady served as the model for the character of Therese in the novel. Therese looked like the landlady in the way she walked and held her head. Furthermore, Canetti reveals that the landlady's first long speech about the youth of today and the high cost of potatoes is quoted verbatim as Therese's first major speech in chapter 3 of the novel (*A*, 36-37). He claims that the speech so annoyed him that, although he heard it on various later occasions, he committed it to memory immediately and quoted it from the first time he heard it. Of course, the speech serves as the first example of the protagonist's misunderstanding of the character of Therese.

The historical event that was of major importance for Canetti, as well as all of Austria, took place on 15 July 1927, when a group of workers set fire to the Palace of Justice in Vienna. They were protesting the verdict of innocence of those who had murdered two people in a shooting in the Burgenland region some months earlier. When the crowd of demonstrators blocked the streets, making it impossible for the fire department to extinguish the conflagration, the police commissioner gave the order to shoot. This resulted in the death of some 90 people and in hundreds of injuries.

That morning, Canetti had read about the verdict in the official government newspaper *Die Reichspost* and was outraged by the blatant miscarriage of justice. He quickly went to the scene of the unrest, joining the workers who were marching from all parts of the city to the Palace of Justice. Previously, there had been numerous incidents in which workers had been the victims of injustice, but it was this case that brought about a spontaneous reaction on their part. And it was likewise for Canetti a spontaneous act to participate in the demonstration. Earlier in life he had witnessed crowd behavior, but only as a bystander. This time he "became a part of the crowd, . . . he fully dissolved in it" (*TE*, 245).

In his reminiscent essay and his autobiography, Canetti claims that this event "had the deepest influence on my subsequent life" (*TE*, 244) and "also on the creation of *Auto-da-Fé*" (*CW*, 205). Writing a half century later, he maintains that:

> It was the closest thing to a revolution that I had physically experienced. A hundred pages would not suffice to describe what I saw. Since then, I have known very precisely that I need not read a single word about what happened during the storming of the Bastille. I became a part of the crowd, I dissolved into it fully, I did not feel the least resistance to what it did. I am surprised that I was nevertheless able to grasp all the concrete details occurring before my eyes. (*CW*, 205-6)

Canetti concludes the description of that day by summarizing the impact the events had on his life:

> During that brightly illuminated, dreadful day, I gained the true picture of what, as a crowd, fills our century. I gained it so profoundly that I kept

> going back to contemplate it anew, both compulsively and willingly. I re-
> turned over and over and watched; and even today, I sense how hard it is
> for me to tear myself away, since I have managed to achieve only the tiniest
> portion of my goal: to understand what a crowd is. (*TE*, 252)

Although the experience of that day would form the basis of his major study of *Crowds and Power*, much of what Canetti observed was
developed in the fiction of *Auto-da-Fé*.

Canetti recalls one occurrence on 15 July that could serve as an
example of a member of the *Human Comedy of Madmen*, as well as
a character in the novel. Near the burning Palace of Justice, but
slightly apart from the demonstrating crowd that was under attack by
the police, Canetti saw a solitary man endlessly crying out: "The files
are burning! All the files!" (*CW*, 206; *TE*, 245-46). Considering the
horror and destruction taking place at this momentous occasion,
Canetti reasonably responded with the entreaty, "Better files than
people!" The man, however, was incapable of understanding
Canetti's plea and continued his lament over the burning files. This
comical and absurdly horrifying incongruity may have angered
Canetti at the time, but the strange man and his lament were
recorded in his memory and used in variations in the novel and in
other fictional writings.

In the days and weeks following this extraordinary day in the history of Vienna and Austria, Canetti was fully preoccupied with what
he had seen and experienced. There was one direct link between the
events and his study of literature. His idol, Karl Kraus, took it upon
himself to place posters throughout the city calling for the resignation of the police commissioner who had given the order to shoot at
the crowd. Kraus was the only person of prominence in Vienna to
express outrage at what had taken place. Canetti recalls walking from
one poster to the next admiring the courage Kraus had displayed
through this act; he "felt as if all the justice on earth had entered the
letters of Kraus's name" (*TE*, 246). This serves as further confirma-
tion of the writer's responsibility to society.

During the summers of 1928 and 1929 Canetti had two opportu-
nities to leave Vienna and experience life in the center of European
culture, the city of Berlin. Through an invitation from the publisher
Wieland Herzfelde, Canetti was to go to Berlin to write essays and
prepare translations of several books by the American author Upton
Sinclair for publication by the Malik publishing house. Berlin in the

late 1920s was the place where everything was happening. Estab-
lished and aspiring writers, painters, and musicians came from all of
Germany, as well as Vienna, Rome, Prague, England, and the United
States, to live and work in this radical and liberal cultural center.
Much of the activity was due to the energy, sensitivity, and judgment
of Jews, who made up a significant part of the liberal population. But
Canetti experienced other aspects of Berlin as well. There was the
"Red Berlin" with its political cabaret, the left wing boulevard
papers, and dissenting weeklies; "naughty Berlin" had cocaine ped-
dlers, nude parties, sensational murderers and crime syndicates;
"literary Berlin" with its cafes, subversive lectures, psychoanalysis,
and numerous Oriental cults; as well as the Berlin that served as the
political, financial, commercial, and industrial center of the dynamic
Weimar Republic.[2]

In Berlin Canetti met many of the artists who made up the intellectual life of the metropolis. He mentions three in particular who
had a profound impact on him: the artist George Grosz, the Russian
writer Isaac Babel, and Bertolt Brecht. All three, along with
Herzfelde, were members of the radical left. From Grosz, Canetti
received a copy of the graphic series *Ecce Homo* illustrating religious
hypocrisy, which along with militarism was one of the chief objects
of Grosz's scorn at the time (*CW*, 208). Isaac Babel, already an established writer and dramatist, took a special liking to Canetti and is
remembered for his openness and willingness to talk to him about
anything, unlike many of the other celebrities Canetti met in Berlin.
When Canetti met Brecht in Berlin, he did not know him as a playwright, only as a poet, even though Brecht was already a well-known
dramatist. Brecht's effect on Canetti was the opposite of Babel's, for
Brecht took delight in shocking the younger and naive Canetti with
his radicalism and cynicism.

After his well-regulated and tempered life, Canetti found the
Berlin experience bewildering. He describes his state of mind: "I was
in the most expansive excitement, and at the same time I was terrified. I took in so much that it had to confuse me" (*CW*, 209). But it
seems that "the wilder sexuality" was especially despicable to him.
He compares Berlin with Vienna: "Anything was possible, anything
happened; compared with that, Freud's Vienna, in which so much
was *talked* about, seemed harmless chattery" (*CW*, 209). On his second visit to Berlin in summer 1929, Canetti made a special effort to

avoid the wild life and forced a quieter lifestyle on himself, devoting time to meeting just "regular" people rather than artists and intellectuals. Returning to Vienna after the second summer visit, Canetti retreats to his quiet room to contemplate "the extreme and frenzied people" he had met in Berlin (*CW*, 210).

For a year Canetti worked on the projected *Human Comedy of Madmen*, identifying those figures on the verge of madness. In early fall 1930 the "book man suddenly became so important" to Canetti that he "pushed aside all other drafts and concentrated fully on him" (*CW*, 210). Canetti imposed a rigid schedule of work on himself, writing every morning on the manuscript, and finished the novel in October 1931. As part of the self-imposed discipline, Canetti read Stendhal's *The Red and the Black*, which showed him how it is possible to advance the novel in a very clearly defined and strict manner. This was important, for Canetti had observed that although "the world had crumbled" (*CW*, 210) and the writer was obliged to portray it in this way, "a writer had to invent extreme individuals with the most rigorous consistency, like the individuals the world consisted of, and he had to place these extreme individuals next to one another in their separateness" (*CW*, 210). Just because "nothing was comprehensible anymore" "did not mean that one had to tackle a chaotic book" (*CW*, 210). Stendhal "made me stick to clarity" (*CW*, 211). After Canetti had written only a few chapters he received another book, Kafka's *Metamorphosis*. This was a most fortuitous event. "There, in utmost perfection, . . . there was the rigor that I yearned for. There, something was achieved that I wanted to find for myself. I bowed to this purest of all models" (*CW*, 211). When, on occasion, he felt discouraged with the progress he was making on the novel and was tempted to give up, Canetti would look at and gain encouragement from the phototype of the Isenheim Altar and remember that Grünewald had "undertaken something enormously difficult and stuck to it for four years" (*CW*, 212). In retrospect, Canetti recognized his arrogance, but at the time it was "an indispensable goad" (*CW*, 212).

Auto-da-Fé is divided into three parts: "A Head without a World," "Headless World," and "The World in the Head." The main character of the novel is Peter Kien. Other major characters are Therese Krumbholz, his housekeeper and wife; Fischerle, also known as Siegfried Fischer, a hunchbacked dwarf who exploits Kien;

Benedikt Pfaff, a retired policeman and caretaker of the apartment house; and George Kien, Peter's younger brother, who is a psychiatrist and director of an asylum for the insane in Paris.

The narrative form of *Auto-da-Fé* is complex because it is constantly changing. The novel is not told from one particular perspective but alternates from one to another character in no pre-established permutations. Furthermore, Canetti sometimes uses direct discourse, at other times inner monologue, or sometimes both as a stream-of-consciousness discourse. It is even possible to have one character's inner monologue respond to that of another. The only constants in the novel are the readers, who must continually adjust and readjust their perspective. This makes for very exciting reading, but also for very difficult or even incomplete interpretation. Consequently, this treatment provides an introduction of the protagonist and the major secondary characters, discussion of the significant conflicts and issues presented in each of the three parts of the novel, and selected examples of Canetti's narrative techniques.

Prologue

Canetti adheres with unfailing pertinacity to the oldest and most basic prescription for the well constructed plot as articulated by Aristotle in his *Poetics*: "A whole is that which has beginning, middle, and end. A beginning is that which is not itself necessarily after anything else, and which has naturally something else after it; an end is that which is naturally after something itself, either as its necessary or usual consequent, and with nothing else after it; and a middle, that which is by nature after one thing and has also another after it."[3] Given the polytypical nature of Canetti's novel, Aristotle's statement of the well-constructed plot may be the only definition that can be applied.

The first several pages of the novel not only introduce the main character but also preface virtually all major themes and issues to be treated. Without explanation or mention of names, the first chapter, entitled "The Morning Walk," begins with a dialogue between Peter Kien and Franz Metzger. The protagonist and the nine-year-old boy exchange a few innocuous comments when Kien suddenly poses a question that, at first glance, seems infelicitous, since the reader only learns the location of the conversation on the next page. Kien wants to know whether the boy would rather have a piece of candy or a book. When the boy replies that his preference would be a book, Kien responds with joy and suggests that that is his reason for standing in this place, which will later be identified as being outside of a bookstore. Furthermore, in only five pages the author has Kien recall that he was not at all unlike young Franz when he was nine years old. Canetti uses this method of foreshadowing or anticipation with great skill throughout the novel.

The next line of the discourse has Kien asking Franz why he had not told him earlier that he was standing in front of the bookstore because of his liking for books. Without any explanation, different punctuation, change in tense or mood, Canetti introduces a type of monologue that his characters will employ with great frequency throughout the novel. This record of their mental activity plays the same role as the interior monologue of the traditional stream of consciousness novel, but it has none of the characteristics of that type of novel, such as the "prespeech" levels of consciousness that commonly lack punctuation, logical transitions, conventional syntax, or evidence of intervention by the author.[4]

As the conversation continues, Kien asks the lad what his father's name is. The reply that it is Franz Metzger must be examined carefully, because all names – whether of a person or a place – are important in Canetti's fiction. The word *Metzger* is the German equivalent of "butcher," but with none of the negative connotations of the English word. It does, however, imply that reference is being made to a common shopkeeper who works with raw strength rather than intellectual power; his son hopes for the latter in his future. The character of the father will be replaced later in the novel by Benedikt Pfaff, a brute of a man who can beat other people bloody with his bare hands. Given that the boy and Kien meet during the morning walk (*Der Spaziergang* in German), it could be suggested that the author is combining the words *Metzger* and *Spaziergang* to make of it a *Metzgergang,* or a useless, futile errand on Kien's part.

The topic changes so that Kien's professional activities can be introduced. In reply to whether he would like to travel some day to a foreign land, the boy mentions India with its tigers and China with the great wall. China and the great wall represent Kien's work as a world-renowned sinologist who lives and works in his own personal library, a library that has been walled up to such an extent that it is impenetrable. India and the tiger introduce Kien's great adversary, his maid and wife Therese, who gains control over Buddha and is always seen slinking and prowling about the apartment, ready to pounce on Kien.

Since Kien and the boy are standing in front of a bookstore, they speak first about a Chinese book that Kien has taken out of his briefcase and shown to the boy. They marvel at the book and the thousands of characters that make up the language, an exoticism the nine year old aspires to acquire just as Kien has in his own lifetime of work. The books displayed in the shop window, however, arouse Kien's great antipathy for their commonness and lack of value. It is Kien's passion for the rare book from the Orient and his loathing for the common book and for those who treat books in an ignoble manner that make up the core of the conflict between him and Therese.

One of the delightful aspects of the novel is that Canetti, through the sinologist Kien, introduces the reader to ancient Chinese history, literature, philosophy, and culture. Although the character of Kien can be described as a pedant of the worst kind, Canetti's teaching of sinology is pleasurable at all times. On the second page of the novel, Kien points to two Chinese characters and tells the boy that they stand for the great Chinese philosopher Meng Tse, also known as Mencius (371-288 B.C.). A few lines later, just as the boy is leaving to go to school, Kien tests him to see whether he remembers what he had learned about Mencius. It is almost as if the author is telling the readers that they, too, must pay close attention.

The remaining part of the introductory section (less than a third of a page) is a presentation of the protagonist. It is important to note that this is the only good reference to the character and his environment. The narrative is not yet filtered through the psychologically unbalanced eyes of Kien and the other major characters but is presented through the impartial eyes of the nine year old.

Upon questioning, it turns out that Franz Metzger and Peter Kien live in the same apartment house at 24 Ehrlich Strasse (honesty street), but Kien cannot recall ever seeing him there. The reason the boy has not been noticed is that Kien "always looks the other way when anyone passes [him] on the stairs" (A, 10). Throughout the entire novel, Kien consistently refuses to perceive his surroundings honestly; this is the essence of his personality. He is identified as a professor without a school, but the boy's mother even questions the validity of this.

Indeed, although Kien sees himself as the world's foremost sinologist and there is not infrequent mention of his working in his study, there is never any evidence that he is actually engaged in scholarly work. Quite to the contrary, the only association Kien has to sinological studies is from a psychologically unbalanced relationship: he speaks with the ancient Oriental sages. The boy thinks Kien is a scholar solely because there exists an enormous library, although this has been seen only by his family's maid. And if this maid is the equivalent to Kien's housekeeper Therese, she has to be understood as an unreliable source of information on the scholarly quality of the library, which in turn becomes a questionable basis of support for Kien's claim to be a great scholar.

Understandably but naively, the youth hopes some day to have a library containing all books in all languages, including Chinese, of course. At this point, the pedant living upstairs on "honesty street" could advise the boy that such an undertaking would be impossible, but he does not. In parting, Kien invites young Metzger to visit his library to see, not necessarily the books, but some pictures of the Far East. Franz is very excited about this opportunity and tells Kien that he will come the same day after school. Of course, Kien immediately rejects the boy, telling him that he has work to do and that he should not come for at least another week. Before Franz goes off to school, Kien instructs him that when he does come he should tell Therese that Kien has given him permission to inspect the library. But when Franz later tries to enter Kien's apartment, he is physically and verbally rejected by Therese, an act that Kien values so highly that he decides to marry the housekeeper and thereby make Therese the guardian of his books. That is also the moment when his downfall begins.

Peter Kien and Therese Krumbholz

Professor Peter Kien, age 40, is supposedly the greatest living authority on sinology. For years he has lived in the top floor apartment of 24 Ehrlich Strasse. More precisely, he is a misanthrope who has withdrawn to his 25,000-volume library. Believing that truth is synonymous with knowledge, Kien has shut himself off from human beings to be closer to truth. For over a decade no one has seen Kien. He has even declined a chair of oriental philology at a major university so that students will not distract him from his pursuit of knowledge. At international congresses of sinologists he is always scheduled to give a major presentation, but at the last moment declines to appear in person and has some younger colleague read his paper for him. When colleagues ask for his photograph because they cannot remember what he looks like, he has none to send and is unwilling to have one taken. Kien himself does not know what he looks like; he has no mirrors in his home. He sees his reflection only in the window of a book shop.

Kien has committed the content of all his books to memory. He uses the books only to check the accuracy of his statements, but he is never wrong. It is said that Kien thinks in quotations, that his library is in his head, that his memory is so precise that he even turns pages of the books in his head. Writing is the only form of communication he tolerates; talking is disorderly and dangerous. Anything not directly related to his scholarly work is carefully entered in a notebook especially kept for those things Kien wants to forget.

Kien has only one desire in life: "the possession of a well-stocked library, in perfect order and enclosed on all sides, in which no single superfluous article of furniture, no single superfluous person could lure him from his serious thoughts" (A, 23). In his apartment, Kien's library takes up four rooms; the only other rooms are a kitchen and a maid's room. The windows have been walled up and skylights have been installed to provide each room with space for book shelves from floor to ceiling on all four walls. One of these rooms is also used as a study, furnished with a desk, two armchairs, a movable pair of steps for fetching books from the higher shelves, and a divan on which Kien sleeps. There is no furniture in the other rooms. All of the rooms are carpeted to provide a noise-free environment.

The maid brings the meals, which he takes at his desk so that he can continue work without interruption. He never pays any attention to the food. "He reserved consciousness for real thoughts; they depend upon it; without consciousness, thoughts are unthinkable. Chewing and digesting happen of themselves" (A, 28). This was the life that Peter Kien had established and followed for many years, a life devoted totally to his books and his scholarship.

Eight years earlier, Kien had to fire his housemaid because a book was missing from his library. At the time, he placed an advertisement in the newspaper: "A man of learning who owns an exceptionally large library wants a responsibly-minded housekeeper. Only applicants of the highest character need apply. Unsuitable persons will be shown the door. Money no object" (*A*, 26).

Therese Krumbholz answers the advertisement and becomes the new housekeeper.[5] A woman "on the right side of fifty" (*A*, 26), Therese had no doubt that she was of the highest character. She is attracted to the position because it offers a job "with a single gentleman" (*A*, 26) and, of even greater interest, money is no object. When she asks about the salary, Kien merely replies: "Whatever you like" (*A*, 27). As Kien's housekeeper, Therese is in charge of keeping strangers from entering the apartment; she "take[s] over the custody of the books" (*A*, 26). Each day she is to thoroughly dust one of the four rooms, starting all over again on the fifth day.

Therese serves as the counterfigure to Peter Kien. While he is virtually without a physical appearance, Therese has a distinct and never-changing physical make-up and deportment that constitute her visual mask. She always wears a floor-length, blue starched skirt; her feet are invisible, and rather than walking she appears to be gliding and waggling from place to place. She generally holds her head crookedly, often with one ear touching her shoulder, revealing the other as large, flabby, and prominent. It is, however, in her speech, her acoustic mask, that she shows herself the opposite of Kien. For virtually no reason at all, she blurts out the following speech:

> Some people have a cheek. Excuse me, such ragtag and bobtail. The father was a common working man. Where they get the money from, I'd like to know. But there you are. Everything for the children, these days. Nobody is strict any more. Cheeky they are; you wouldn't credit it. . . . Excuse me, in my time it was very different. . . . Nothing like that these days. You don't catch people wanting to work now. Don't know their places any more, that's what it is. . . . Who ever heard of such a thing in my time? Let 'em do a job of work, that'd be more like it. I always say, where does the money come from? Prices going up all the time. Potatoes cost double already. It's not surprising, children have a cheek. Parents don't check them at all. In my days, it was a couple of good smacks, left and right, and the child had to do as it was told. There's nothing good left in the world. When they're little they don't learn, when they grow up they don't do a hand's turn. (*A*, 36-37)

Parts and variations of this speech are repeated on many occasions. If there is any purpose in what Therese is saying, it is her effort to offer conversation through mere talk and, indirectly, to establish herself as belonging to a finer class of society than the lower class from which she comes. Therese is not intelligent enough to offer an analysis of the declining values of families and schools or the old virtues of hard work and discipline, to say nothing of the worsening state of the economy. She is, however, crafty enough to hope and to think that her speech might make an impression on the listener.

Kien's sense of language, on the other hand, suffers from over-refinement, and that is his acoustic mask. Therese does not realize that her trite, stereotypical expressions are nothing but meaningless clichés, but Kien, likewise, does not recognize her speech for what it really is. Normally he does not listen to anyone speak, certainly not common people or the usual riffraff. In his philological studies he hears only what the great oriental sages and philosophers are saying, occasionally even engaging them in discourse. In conversations with Confucius, he practices his spoken Chinese. So, in listening to Therese, Kien hears only selectively. He hears certain words and interprets them from his own perspective, rather than trying to understand them in the context in which they are spoken.

Kien believes that, although Therese is uneducated, she values and desires learning. In leaps and bounds of the mind, he concludes that through her continuous physical contact with the books in his library, Therese has said that learning, specifically book learning, is the essence of life. At most, Therese reads the advertisements in the newspaper; there is no evidence that she has ever read a book. Yet Kien tries to find a book for her – an almost impossible task for the sinologist who owns a world-famous library.

Kien finally selects for Therese Willibald Alexis's historical novel of sixteenth-century life in Brandenburg, *The Trousers of Herr von Bredow*. The selection is just an old, tattered schoolbook with grease spots on the binding and sticky pages. Therese immediately prepares a book cover; Kien concludes she has an extraordinary sense of the proper handling of books. He is confirmed in this when he visits the kitchen and finds Therese wearing white gloves and the book "on a small embroidered velvet cushion" (A, 45). Therese is not reading the book; she is trying to get out the grease spots. But Kien is greatly moved by Therese's treatment of this book he was happy to be rid of. All these years he had used books uncaringly in his selfish pursuit of knowledge, but now this simple and untutored housekeeper was teaching him their intrinsic value. Kien decides he has judged Therese unfairly and resolves to be guided by Confucius's dictum: "To err without making amends is to err indeed. If you have erred, be not ashamed to make the fault good" (*A*, 47).

"It shall be made good, cried Kien. I will give her back her eight lost years! I will marry her! She is the heaven-sent instrument for preserving my library. . . . Had I constructed a human being according to my own designs, the result could not have been more apt for the purpose. She has all the elements necessary. . . . Her heart belongs to the books" (*A*, 47-48). Kien runs to the kitchen and says to Therese "Give me your hand!" (*A*, 48). Understanding him literally, Therese stretches out her hand. Kien clarifies his intention, and Therese accepts with one of her clichés: "I make so bold!" (*A*, 48).

For eight years, Therese had hoped that her "place with a single gentleman" (*A*, 26) might lead to sexual gratification. And during all these years of dusting, she had thoroughly examined every nook and cranny of his library, fully believing that Kien had great sums of money or other valuables hidden among the books. Finally, with the impending marriage, Therese expected fulfillment of both desires. Neither Therese nor Kien realized that they were pursuing totally different agendas.

"A Head without a World"

Kien and Therese have occupied the same apartment for eight years before their marriage, but they have each lived in their own world. Although existing communally, their lives have been separate – and harmonious. The struggle begins only when they marry.

Married life, as described in the first part of the novel, consists of one massive collision after another. Even though there is no precise specification, the time to elapse in this part is not more than a few months; the outward events are also few. Kien attempts to return to his scholarly work immediately after the wedding; Therese seeks material and sexual satisfaction. The great clash in their lives comes about because Kien lives the life of the head without a world and Therese lives the life of the world without a head. To some extent their lives are very similar, although motivated from totally different perspectives. Both are so permanently established in their own extreme world – a world of madness – that they are completely incapable of establishing even a faint resemblance of a harmonious relationship.

As Peter Kien maneuvers between the real world and the world in his head, he seems to be only marginally aware of his actions in the former. Since he generally fails to articulate to Therese the reasons for his actions, and Therese usually does not understand what he is all about even when he tells her, real world actions establish nothing more than a common confusion. The reader soon becomes aware of the sense of design that makes up the world portrayed in this novel, where characters live in their own realms of insanity without, of course, realizing it.

That Kien is mentally unsound is very clear. His misapperception of his world first became evident when he chose Therese as a wife and the permanent caretaker of his library. It is only logical, in this psychotic world, that Kien continues to misunderstand Therese's actions. The reader is quite cognizant of the illogic of Kien's thought processes when he continues to assign virtues to Therese that he wants her to have, despite the fact that they are the opposite of what she really is. Even on their wedding day, returning from the ceremony by streetcar, Kien persists in his misapperception.

An old man and two young children vie for the only remaining seat. Therese speaks out: "Children last" (A, 51), and the old man takes the seat, as Therese intended. But Kien understands something very different. The two words set off an extensive and intricate thought process leading to Kien's conclusion that Therese's statement could mean nothing other than that his books come first and the thought of having children last.

Kien and Therese presumably speak the same language, but neither can (or is willing to) understand the other. On the streetcar and elsewhere, each offers a different interpretation of what they hear. This mutual unintelligibility prompted the early English translation of the novel with the title *The Tower of Babel;* the first translation into French was *La Tour de Babel*.

Kien's dementia tends to lead him to seek initial solutions to real world problems in the world of scholarship. A recluse and misogynist who at age 40 takes a wife, Kien has an immediate problem. In an almost stock ridicule of the scholar, Kien will read a book on the proper way to consummate the marriage.

As soon as the newlyweds arrive home, Therese excuses herself to prepare physically for the final celebration of the marriage ceremony. Kien enters his study and realizes that this finale must take place on the only sleeping space available, his divan. In fear he hastily covers the sofa with many books, indiscriminately taken from the shelves. He is certain that his books will protect him from Therese, but when she enters the room in her white petticoat, his fear increases. He was only prepared for the starched blue skirt. Therese advanced and "with one all-embracing stroke of her left arm, swept the books onto the floor," removed her petticoat, laid it on the books, and "made herself comfortable on the divan, crooked her little finger, grinned and said, 'There!' " (A, 59). Kien, now defeated by her physical advance, runs to lock himself in the bathroom where he psychologically regresses to his childhood and weeps. The marriage that was to provide Therese with sexual satisfaction is never consummated.

Throughout Kien's stream of consciousness there are references that from time to time return the reader momentarily to the plot of the story. With great regularity, references to the wedding and its (lack of) consummation recur while future elements of the story are anticipated surreptitiously. Therese in her starched blue skirt, her physical defense against Kien, is a reality that confronts Kien in his strange world. To survive, he will have to devise some scheme that will destroy Therese. References to the skirt apprise the reader of the basic conflict of the story. It gives a "world" to this part of the novel that otherwise offers a "head without a world."

In the first months of the marriage, Therese gains control over their physical environment while Kien attempts to preserve his world of books. She purchases furniture for three of the rooms, but the books remain on their shelves. More than this intrusion into his library space, however, Kien is most disturbed by Therese's constant interruptions. She speaks while he is working and even during meals. A written pact seems to satisfy both of them. Therese acknowledges that the books belong to Kien and are not to be moved; she signs a statement that "in return for the cession of the three rooms, I hereby undertake to remain silent during meals" (A, 61). Kien's world of silence is reestablished, but Therese is actually the greater winner in this confrontation. She now knows how high a price Kien will pay not just for her silence but for retaining what he calls his "personal cosmos" (A, 57), his library. Having won this first round in the acquisition of space and material goods, Therese sets off on her search for the ultimate prize: Kien's bank book.

Of course, Kien has lost the privacy of his library space. His reaction to the loss is to pretend that it never happened. To protect himself from the sight of what Therese has done with his beloved library, he does not open his eyes during waking hours unless seated at his desk. His eyes are used only for reading and writing. Since he can remember the exact location each book occupies on his shelves, he can fetch books with his eyes closed. Rather than realizing that Therese has reduced his "head without a world" to an existence that cannot even perceive his physical environment, Kien makes a virtue of his blindness. With a superficial reading of the mid-eighteenth century assertion by Bishop Berkeley, *esse est percipi* (to be is to be perceived), Kien concludes that the corollary must be: "what I do not perceive, does not exist," and the chapter concludes: "Whence, with cogent logic, it was proved that Kien was in no wise deceiving himself" (A, 71).

Therese, likewise, experiences blindness, but in her own nonreflective, nonphilosophical, inarticulate way. In purchasing some bedroom furniture, she fell prey to the sales talk of the clerk. "What was it the young man in the furniture shop said: 'Yes, around thirty, that's when the best people get married, whether ladies or gentlemen'" (A, 73). At 56, Therese is nevertheless certain that the salesman guessed her age and marital status correctly and certainly without any ulterior motive. If Therese were able to articulate a philosophical maxim, she might conclude: I am how I wish to be perceived. Like Kien, she would consider her reasoning to be based on authoritative logic and she would cite the salesman as proof that she was in no wise deceiving herself. Unable to enunciate her views with quotations from famous philosophers, her self-deception is nevertheless as pronounced and effective as Kien's.

Both are blind; neither shows any evidence of correctly interpreting either their own world or the world around them. The German title of the novel, *Die Blendung*, 'the blinding' or 'being blind,' describes what is happening.

The only episode in the novel in which a major character actually experiences contact with the real world is Therese's purchase of the bedroom furniture. At the shop of "Gross & Mutter" (Big & Mother), the salesman is the antithesis of the Confucian *chün-tzu* – the superior man, the man who conducts himself nobly and in whom inborn humanity is harmoniously blended with cultivated decorum. The *Analects of Confucius* (chapter 4, section 16) states: "The superior man understands what is right; the inferior man understands what is profitable."

The salesman at Gross & Mutter is Herr Grob, the German equivalent of crude, uncouth, rude, uncivil. In the English translation, he is called Mr. Brute and is always referred to as "the superior young man." Brute's entire sales pitch consists of nothing more than a series of sexual innuendos; for example, reference to a double bed leads to a description of a wife seducing her husband. Flattering Therese by suggesting she is barely more than 30 years old, Brute goes on to say that the essence of feminine pulchritude can be found in her big hips, which he almost touches. Therese becomes the total victim of Brute's language game. Various later chapters return to this episode, with Brute portrayed as pursuing Therese for material gain while she maniacally hopes for sexual satisfaction.

Although Brute is a minor figure in the novel, he serves as the only person representing the real world and, consequently, illustrates the brutal deceptiveness that exists even in a sane society. Other themes and narrative techniques are illustrated by an episode in which Kien reacts to Therese's placement of furniture in his library.

One day during Therese's absence, helped by the building caretaker, Kien throws all the furniture out in the corridor, hoping to reestablish the order he had enjoyed prior to his marriage. He closes the library doors behind him and, anthropomorphically, starts to talk with his books: "For some time, more precisely since the invasion of an alien power into our life, I have been labouring with the idea of placing our relationship on a firm foundation. Your survival is guaranteed by treaty; but we are, I take it, sage enough not to deceive ourselves as to the danger by which, in defiance of a legal treaty, you are threatened" (*A*, 90). Kien then recalls an event in Chinese history when books were burned.

It is typical for the character of Kien to search for an event in history that will justify his own actions. Without a historical parallel or reference, nothing can be understood in contemporaneous time; the further back he can go, the more validity his present actions and perceptions have for him. Given his blindness to his real-world environment, Kien's historification removes him even further from reality. Through the narrative technique of interior monologue, Kien's stream of consciousness occurs in a highly structured and arranged pattern, although it does not follow the tradition of the stream-of-consciousness manner of recitation as such.

Kien's mind turns to Shi Hoang Ti, the first emperor of China, who in 213 B.C. was persuaded by his first minister, Lisi, to order the destruction of the classics, particularly the books of the Confucian school, so that the power and influence of the literati would be eradicated.[6] Even the oral literary tradition was to be eliminated, and all opponents to this decree were threatened by a penalty of death. The Confucian canon would have been irretrievably lost if devoted scholars had not risked their lives by concealing the sacred texts. Only works on agriculture, medicine, and divination were to be spared the conflagration.

In his address to his books, Kien refers to this historical event as "the ancient and glorious story of your suffering" (A, 90). But of the books that were spared in Shi Hoang Ti's decree, he shows his contempt: "a vulgar mob of practical handbooks" (A, 91). This is not the only time when the issue of the mob or masses is considered in this novel. Kien, in his own demented mind, is the singular example of the virtues of high art and culture; all else in the novel is assigned with great condescension to the mass of the unlearned and the artless.[7] The topic comes up again as Kien continues to talk to his books. He quotes the Confucian apostle Mencius: "They act, but know not what they do; they have their customs, but do not know how they came by them; they wander their whole life long, but still they can not find their way; even so are the people of the masses" (A, 92). Although the masses do not understand such matters, for Mencius, as for Confucius, they nevertheless pursue a path of compassion.[8] But Kien, in his egomania, interprets the text to mean that one "must beware of these people of the masses. They are dangerous because they have no education" (A, 92).

Given Kien's ultimate fate, it is understandable that the theme of book burning and its attendant self-immolation occurs throughout the novel.[9] Even before marriage threatened his books, Kien has a nightmare in which he attempts to save burning books that are flowing from the breasts of jaguars. (The dream is generated by Kien's examination of Mexican pictorial writings that illustrate and describe ancient sacrificial priests.) But it is the episode about the Chinese books that is the clearest and, for Kien, the most personal treatment of the book burning theme.

Whenever Kien recalls the ancient event, he actually experiences in his nostrils the stinging smell of the conflagration of the books, and he rejoices in the eventual punishment of the instigator Lisi. What Kien does not do is to respond to the event as the scholar and philologist he claims to be. He shows no interest in validating the correctness of the texts that were recreated by the Chinese literati in the century after the original books were burned. And his joy in the death of Lisi ignores the fact that it was Lisi who standardized the written characters throughout the Chinese empire, thereby providing a written language that was intelligible to people of many different dialects throughout that nation. A final irony lies in the fact that had it not been for the accomplishments of Emperor Shi Hoang Ti and his adviser Lisi, the tradition of preparing and honoring the "Historical Record" might not have been established at that early date, thus making knowledge of the book-burning event impossible. All such details, of course, make Kien's monomania much more obvious.

Kien may well be the owner of a distinguished library, but he repeatedly shows little understanding of the content of his books. He is not a sinologist but a bibliomaniac, and his character seems to present a textbook example of schizophrenia – the functional psychosis characterized by unrealistic behavior dominated by a private fantasy. Kien's behavior shows all the basic symptoms of the schizophrenic personality. He has faulty thought processes, engages in bizarre actions, tends to live in an inner world, and is incapable of maintaining normal interpersonal relationships.

He certainly is incapable of knowing or controlling Therese, and his reasons are bizarre: "As far as he was familiar with the history of all cultures and barbarisms, there was not one into which Therese would have fitted" (A, 115). As she searches for his money, her actions are themselves bizarre.

Cataloguing Kien's books on slips made from the blank margins of newspapers, she concludes that she has earned the books, that she is acquiring the library for herself. As she finishes each set of ten strips, she sews them together and deposits "her hard-earned possession" (A, 116) in the pocket of her heavily starched blue skirt.

The cataloguing process also tells the story of her nymphomania. She encounters the name of Buddha in the title of numerous books, and each time she records the title, she pronounces it. The verbal activity initiates a sensuousness of mind and body, leading Therese to conclude that the word Buddha "was the name for the superior young man, not Brute" (A, 117). In her mispronunciation, she initially pronounces Buddha as Puta, then softens this to Puda. Mr. Brute becomes Mr. Puda. The new name is significant. The word *puta* is Spanish and Ladino for whore or prostitute, and *puda* (or the verbal form *pudern*) is the Austrian slang word for fornication. The salesman Mr. Brute has become the prostitute who will satisfy her sexual desires, and Therese has the necessary wealth for his services.

There is irony in Therese's conclusion, for it is the antithesis of the Buddhist doctrine of the realization of basic truths. In Buddhist teaching, the source of all evil lies in the craving for material possessions and sensual pleasures; the disciplined mind promotes spiritual development through perceiving reality without error or deception by irrelevant external elements. Therese has violated the core of Buddhist preaching by crassly craving material possessions and sensual pleasures simultaneously. Her lack of disciplined thinking will result in a totally false perception of reality later in the narrative.

Of the many examples of confusion and humor in the novel, none is more important than an episode dealing with the last will and testament, extending over several chapters in the first part of the book. The avaricious Therese, unable to locate Kien's bank book and not satisfied with her "acquisition" of his library, wants to know the exact worth of Kien's estate; she dreams of a glorious future as the wife of Mr. Brute, with whom she will own a furniture store. Kien, ill at the time, comes to believe that Therese wants to draw up her will in order to provide security and safety for him in the event of her death. It is decided that each will make a will, but only Kien does so.

"The will, as he had written it down, she first suspected to contain a slip of the pen, then a silly joke, and last of all a trap. The capital he still had in the bank might cover his housekeeping expenses for another two years" (*A*, 125). Kien's will and Therese's quick assessment of it at this moment are realistic and absolutely correct. If both were clear-sighted, they would accept the fact that Kien has almost depleted the inheritance that has been his sole source of support for many years. But neither Therese nor Kien can live in a world of sustained clarity.

Therese convinces herself that Kien has indeed made a mistake, that zeros are missing from his figure. Surreptitiously, she takes the will from his desk only to find the number 12,650. She takes a strip of newspaper and copies the numbers with such precision that they flawlessly resemble the original, and then she adds a dozen zeros. "Then she took Kien's pen, bent over the will and changed the figure 12,650 into 1,265,000" (*A*, 132). Lack of space on the document prevents her from adding more zeros and making herself even wealthier.

Uncharacteristically, Therese recognizes that she has committed a crime, and she resolves to go to church. There, reality quickly departs, and Therese identifies "the superior man" Mr. Brute with Christ, Kien with Judas, and herself with a white dove, symbol of innocence and chastity. She returns home and begins an inner monologue about the 1,265,000, which has now become her new reality. Kien's response to this monologue is, of course, complete misunderstanding. Just as he misinterpreted her earlier monologue about children and potatoes as an indication of her love of books, now he believes that Therese has inherited $1 million from some superior person and that she went to church to give thanks for her good fortune. Therese's love for him means that she will give him this dowry, and he will be able to double the size of his library.

In a long harangue about the dowry, each refers to a different imaginary document until Kien demands that Therese give him her will. When she goes to the desk and takes out his will instead, Kien notes that Therese must have changed the numbers, but he is unwilling to accept the reality of the situation. Nevertheless, he agrees to rewrite the will even though neither he nor Therese want their imaginary world destroyed. "A few minutes later they had understood each other for the first time" (*A*, 142). This moment of true understanding is also the point when they begin to destroy each other. They are driven from their mad dreams into a real world of madness.

Comparing the three-fold division of this book with works from the tradition of Austrian theater of the baroque period, it is evident that the action in heaven has been concluded in part 1, life on earth is about to commence in part 2, and hell will be represented in part 3. Although both Kien and Therese will lapse into their individual dreams, manias, and psychological abnormalities in the second part, as they did in the first, this life on earth for Kien as well as for Therese is the struggle for the library. Neither can realize their dreams as long as the other continues to exist and, consequently, both set out in their own way to destroy the other.

Fischerle

It was at the unsavory, low bar-café *Zum idealen Himmel* (The Stars of Heaven) that Kien first met the dwarf Fischerle, his companion through part 2 of the novel, "Headless World." Of the small creature who addressed him in a distinct Viennese dialect Kien observed that the noise came from a mouth that could not be seen. There was "no forehead, no ears, no neck, no buttocks – the man consisted of a hump, a majestic nose and two black, calm, sad eyes" (*A*, 175). For the past two decades Fischerle has been the champion chess player at this bar; supported by his prostitute wife, he is able to devote his time to challenging anyone willing to engage him in a chess match.

Fischerle's great ambition is to obtain enough money to compete against the international chess champion and to become the recognized world master. One night, while serving as Kien's famulus, Fischerle dreams of stealing Kien's bank notes, which he imagines to be in the millions. With this money he imagines traveling to America where he challenges and defeats the world chess champion, Capablanca.[10] Each of a thousand reporters from the world press gives him $1,000 so that the new champion, now known as Mr. Siegfried Fischer, will reveal his identity. With his $10 million, Fischerle sends his wife a million, establishes a foundation with another, marries a millionairess, lives in a gigantic palace, and rides about in a custom-made car. He continues with chess and is always victorious, even when he plays 30 opponents simultaneously. Awakening from his dream, Fischerle realizes that he must concoct another, real scheme to swindle Kien out of his money.

The character of Fischerle serves as a fine example of the concept of the extreme as it is articulated further in *Crowds and Power*. In size Fischerle is so very small and almost nonhuman that he is generally known only as the hump. But in his environment he yields an inordinate power over the physically and mentally much larger Peter Kien, as well as over all the thugs and bullies at the bar. Even though he has no forehead (which implies that he has no brain), he is the champion of an intricate intellectual game. His $10 million and the details of his life of excess are further examples of power, even though they are experienced only in a dream. Later, just prior to his death, Fischerle discloses a new and changed personality when he reviews his dream: "True, you can take liberties in a dream, but dreams reveal a man's true character" (*A*, 349).

"Headless World"

To gain complete control over Kien's actual wealth, Therese has resolved to refuse him access to his library and has thrown him out of their apartment. With only his coat, hat, briefcase, and bank book, Kien spends each day going from one bookstore to the next. For the sake of efficiency, he follows a large city map on which he has marked all of the bookstores to be found in each district. Entering each store, he insists on speaking to the proprietor and announces: "I urgently require, for a work of scholarship, the following books" (*A*, 167).

Thus far, the action of the narrative seems to follow a reasonable course of events. That changes, however, when Kien begins to read off a long list of authors and titles from a "non-existent paper" (*A*, 167) at such a rate that no one can follow him. It is said that Kien, "despite reading" (*A*, 167), is observing the reactions of his listeners with considerable amusement. For each bookstore, he draws up a new list of two to three dozen titles, placing the imaginary pieces of paper in his briefcase as soon as he leaves the shop. The books he acquires are duplicates of those in the library from which Therese has expelled him. Within a few weeks, Kien has an emergency library of a few thousand volumes that will allow him to continue his scholarly activities. The joke, however, is that Kien has not purchased a single book. All of these new books are stored in his memory and thus he carries "the entire new library in his head" while his "briefcase remained empty" (A, 169).

The absurdity of Peter Kien's life continues at the end of each day as he checks into a nearby hotel. Although he appears to be an indigent without luggage, he succeeds in obtaining "a large, quiet room for the night" away from "women, children or common people" (A, 169) by showing the substantial amount of money he has withdrawn from the bank. The porters overlook Kien's eccentricities when they receive a tip equal to half the price of the room. Although he normally avoided mechanical devices, Kien did use the elevator now because he was tired and "the library in his head weighed heavy" (A, 169). After dinner he unloaded the books from his head in the order in which he acquired them, placing them first on a sofa and in the wardrobe, later on the floor, which had been carefully covered with clean sheets of brown paper. As the days pass with the acquisition of ever more books, it becomes necessary for Kien to have a ladder brought to his room because the books he removes from his head are so numerous that the stacks reach the ceiling. This activity continues for three weeks.

This introductory scene to the second part of the novel is in many ways similar to the beginning pages, although the reader of the earlier part is less aware of Kien's strange state of mind. He speaks of reading books for his scholarly work, but again there is no real evidence that Kien is engaged in philological research. In the first part there is reference to fellow scholars who long ago thought highly of his work but with whom Kien has had no contact in more recent times. Likewise, in the second part there is no one who will certify him as the "prodigy of learning" (A, 168) Kien claims to be. At the outset of the novel, Kien describes himself as "the owner of the most important library in the whole of this great city" (A, 11). As he checks into the hotel in the second part, Kien states his profession as "owner of a library" (A, 169), and the porter who received the generous tip even refers to Kien as "the gentleman – proprietor of the Royal Library" (A, 170). This aspect of the character of Peter Kien, repeated in these two parts of the novel, resembles the first fool in Sebastian Brant's *Ship of Fools*, the collector of books who has acquired a great library and is proud that he never reads and learns from his cherished books. Kien, too, is a foolish collector of books.

After three weeks of exhausting work, Kien happens upon the miserable, disreputable bar and café The Stars of Heaven, where he meets Fischerle. This is the first time the misanthrope is exposed to the real world, and if Fischerle had not intervened on his behalf, Kien would have easily perished in this den of thieves. As a sign of gratitude, Kien hires the dwarf to assist him in the nightly unloading of the ever-increasing head-library. Finally, having visited every bookshop in the city, they turn to the only remaining source of books, the municipal pawnshop, the Theresianum.

This pawnshop, which plays a significant role in the novel, is the only real, albeit indirect, association that the novel has to the city of Vienna. By decree, Emperor Joseph I established an imperial pawn brokerage, a *banco della pietà*, in 1707, called the Versatz- und Fragamt (Pledge and Loan Office), where in time of need anyone could borrow at a small fee. Toward the end of the eighteenth century this enterprise was expanded and took over the recently secularized Dorotheerkloster (the Monastery of the Canons of St. Dorothea). Located on the Dorotheergasse, the pawn brokerage came to be called the Dorotheum, a name by which the institution is still known today. Although the establishment is called the Theresianum in the novel, the description of the buildings, their function, and the surroundings greatly resembles the Dorotheum. Readers who know the city of Vienna may be inclined to recognize this place and institution, but it must be stressed that it was never the intention of the author to write a novel whose locale was Vienna.[11]

Much to Kien's dismay, the pawned books are stored not in a place of honor adjacent to the main entry of the Theresianum but on the top-most floor in an annex. Although he never inspects the area to learn what kind of books are stored there (perhaps just the popular books he holds in contempt), Kien is greatly concerned about the possibility that a fire could destroy them. This parallels his concerns narrated in the first part of the novel about book burnings and a fire in his library, also located on the top floor away from easy access. From now until the end of the novel, Kien is personally more and more involved in every mention of fire, the burning of books, or the ultimate, cataclysmic destruction of the world.

In his typically illogical and circuitous way, Kien decides that he has been chosen as savior of the books. Providence brought him to Fischerle, who was waiting for the Messiah all these years in The

Stars of Heaven. "At last came that One" and "that One was Kien" (A, 214). In oratory reminiscent of Don Quixote, Kien admonishes Fischerle, his Sancho Panza, to join him in delivering innocent books from the everlasting fires of Hell. "Think, man, a library on fire on the sixth floor! Imagine it only! Tens of thousands of volumes – millions of pages – milliards of printed letters – each one of these in flames – each one of these imploring, crying, shrieking for help" (A, 217).

Two phrases – "Action, not lamentations! Deeds, not tears!" (A, 217) – make up the battle cry that sends this odd duo off on their holy mission. Just like the Ingenious Gentleman Don Quixote of La Mancha, whose mind had become befuddled by reading quantities of chivalric tales, Kien finds verification for his actions in oriental tales of Buddhist practices. And Fischerle, like the moronic peasant Sancho Panza, realizes that he must perform his role so that he can purloin the money remaining in his master's purse. Unlike the characters in Cervantes's novel, however, there is no reversal of roles at the end of this novel. Kien does not return to sanity, and Fischerle does not plead with him to continue to help humanity.

Kien's delirium grows further as he takes up his post at the Theresianum. "The compassionate office which he had recently taken upon himself had mellowed his soul and called forth noble metaphors" (A, 239). In his mind Kien assumes the person of Christ. But Christ's great weakness, according to Kien, was the wasteful feeding and healing of humankind described in numerous biblical parables: "how many books . . . might have been saved by those miracles" (A, 239). Indeed, Kien is fully convinced that former scholars had misunderstood the original biblical documents. "The unexpected appearance of *Logos* in the Gospel of St. John gave abundant grounds for doubt" (A, 239), leading the philologist to a preliminary conclusion that the gospel referred not to men at all, but to the word – to books. Kien knows that someday he will reexamine the scriptures and become the world's authority on scriptural exegesis, just as he has been the world's authority on sinological texts. In his delusion of grandeur there is no end to Kien's capabilities.

To save the books at the Theresianum, Kien stands on the stairway leading to the book section. As patrons arrive to pawn their books, Kien gives them money, admonishing them to keep the books and never again to use them for the acquisition of material wealth.

Fischerle devises a scheme to enrich himself. He makes up parcels of books and hires four people to request exorbitant sums from Kien for the packages. If Kien hesitates, the hustlers remind him of Therese and tell him that she is dead. Kien is ready to believe this, for he has convinced himself that he caused Therese's death by locking her inside the apartment where she starved. With her death, Kien finally gains power and control over Therese, who had become the symbol of fear and terror. Surviving her reinforces Kien's superiority as a man of letters over the untutored woman: "Death is the end of each one of us, but comes first to the illiterate!" (A, 259). Therese, of course, is still very much alive.

Therese has been doubly unsuccessful since Kien's departure. She has been unable to locate the bank book, and she has been rejected by Mr. Brute. To fulfill her dreams of money and sexual satisfaction, she evaluates the library books as worth millions and transfers her affections to the caretaker of Kien's apartment building, Pfaff. Together, they set off every few days to pawn Kien's books at the Theresianum. When Therese recognizes Kien and detects his fat wallet, she realizes that she has finally discovered the bank book. With Pfaff's aid, she takes Kien's money, a scuffle occurs, and Fischerle comes to save the money. Therese yells that she has been insulted, that Kien is a thief, that they are all burglars. Patrons of the Theresianum attempt to separate the foursome, but to no avail. Confusion creates pandemonium. Reports of the events are so overcharged that the impression is created that a terrible riot is taking place inside the building.

A woman, seeing Fischerle lying on the ground, runs into the street to announce a murder. Someone else believes that Kien must have been shot. Outsiders debate whether there was a shot or just the backfire of a nearby car. More information suggests that the murderer is a redheaded man, allowing another to politicize the event as one created by the Reds. Speculation about whether the dwarf is married to the woman leads some to propose that such an inappropriate union is a result of too few available men now after the war. And young people's behavior today is causing riots. Some maintain that a baroness is selling a pearl necklace for 10,000 or 20,000 schillings and either her husband or a footman is the corpse; this is acceptable since the unemployed are starving. The long sequence of rumors and misinterpretations ends with the crowd crying out: "String 'em up I say! Mean it too! The whole lot of them. And the Theresianum too. Burn it! Make a nice blaze" (A, 291). The lack of content and logic in all these exclamations reminds the reader of Therese's diatribes.

The scene, of course, replicates Canetti's experiences on the day the Palace of Justice in Vienna was burned. Even the man who then had cried out "The files are burning" appears here as the Theresianum elevator operator who can only repeat again and again that he has been on the job for 26 years. Certainly rumors ran through the crowd in the same way, exaggerating and falsifying to such an extreme that eventually there was no remaining element of truth. In the narrative, once the police arrive, the four principals are identified as the cause of the disturbance. But still the crowd is incapable of recognizing the truth of the event; people continue to rely on their biases in assigning blame and guilt. Even with the dispersal of the mob, there is no unified opinion on the object of the crime. There is a clear suggestion here that the participants in a historical event may never be able to realize its significance and truth.

Benedikt Pfaff

The caretaker of the apartment house at 24 Ehrlich Strasse, Benedikt Pfaff, proudly introduces himself as a Police Constable, Retired, known by his former colleagues as "der rote Kater" (translated as Ginger the Cat). His name offers a good description of his character. *Pfaff* is the pejorative word used to describe a cleric, priest, or parson and thus should be understood as a negative to his first name. *Benedikt*, of course, refers to the Roman Catholic religious order established in the sixth century by St. Benedict of Nursia. In the same way as the Rule of St. Benedict provides for each monk to profess a solemn vow of obedience to the abbot of the monastery, so Benedict Pfaff rules over his family and the apartment house.

The chapter entitled "The Kind Father" describes Pfaff's realm. The family of five included his wife, his daughter, and "three times over himself; himself as policeman, himself as husband, himself as father" (A, 367). As caretaker of the family and the apartment house, he commanded that his wife and daughter turn over all the money they received for their services of washing the stairs and opening the street door at night. In addition, they had to cook enormous meals for this tripersonal ruler and serve them at the moment he came home. Once, when his wife was five minutes late because she was otherwise so overworked, Pfaff became impatient and beat her to the point where he killed her, although it is more correct to state that she really died of overwork.

The day after his wife's funeral, Pfaff demanded that his daughter, Anne, become his servant, allowing him to perform his duty as father, lawgiver, teacher, and guide of his monastic community. While he was still working, before his retirement, "he locked her into the back room, so that she could devote herself more exclusively to the cooking" (*A*, 368). When he came home he made even greater demands on his daughter than he had on his wife, commanding her to pledge absolute obedience to him or reap the full wrath of his physical power. Anne survived for only a few years in this environment and died of consumption.

Once Pfaff was retired, he invented a scheme for exercising power over all who lived in the house. In the wall of his dwellings, adjoining the main hallway leading to the front door of the apartment house, he drilled a hole about a foot and a half from the floor. Looking through this peephole he could see everyone who entered or left the house, albeit he had to identify them by their trousers or skirts. In the event that he observed someone of whom he disapproved, he would leap up, run out to the hallway, and lay them flat with a few blows of his powerful fists. This not only rid the house of those whom Pfaff found undesirable, but it also provided the residents with a security system for which they had to pay dearly.

The misanthropic Kien paid Pfaff a small "honorarium" of 100 schillings per month to guard him from intruders who might disturb him. Pfaff is referred to as a "*landsknecht*, loyal, reliable fellow, as strong as a bear, who never let beggars, hawkers and other scum over the threshold" (*A*, 263).[12]

George Kien

George Kien, formerly a gynecologist and bon vivant, is now a famous psychiatrist, theoretician in psychoanalytical studies, and director of his own Psychiatric Institute in Paris. He is Peter Kien's brother.

Although fleeting reference is made to George Kien in earlier parts of the novel, it is only in the part 3 that this character is developed. Of all the characters, both major and minor, George is the first who seems to have normal human attributes. His presence also suggests to the reader that George – in the tradition of the deus ex machina – will bring about some form of salvation for his brother Peter. Even for the reader who is not an expert psychoanalyst, it is perfectly clear that all the characters exhibit one or another form of aberrant behavior. The introduction of George Kien's predecessor at the Paris Institute makes it possible to establish an easy and quick summary of their psychological problems. The essence of their insanity, according to this analyst, is that "madness is the disease which attacks those very people who think only of themselves. Mental disease is the punishment of egoism" (A, 396).

The psychiatrist George Kien, however, appears to offer a much more humane analysis and treatment for those under his care, and the reader is temporarily inclined to believe that he could even cure the protagonist. As director of his asylum he has developed a new theory for treating his psychopathic patients. Intrigued by the mad world in which they live, George had the idea of transferring himself into their world and playing the role of an appropriate character in order to find access to his patients. Should a patient suffer from alternating personalities, George could create a character that would be friends with both parties at the same time. This procedure is the reverse of what Freudian psychoanalysts refer to as transference.

Once Kien had become the confidant of the various personalities within the patient, he would be highly supportive of each so that he could discover their most inward motivations before he drew any conclusions on the patient's disorder. The cure that George Kien offered was to bring the two or more personalities together again and rejoin them at their former points of contact, repeating this procedure until they would remain together permanently in the patient.

This fanciful theory for the cure of mental disorders is, to say the least, highly questionable, but it does illustrate Canetti's great skepticism and doubt in the ability of psychoanalysis to cure the disorders of the mind. In the final analysis the great psychiatrist and actor George Kien did nothing for his patients, because in essence he became someone who thought only of himself, as his predecessor had defined the insane. "He lived simultaneously in numberless different worlds. Among the mentally diseased he grew into one of the most comprehensive intellects of his time" (*A*, 398). His ultimate fantasy is to increase the number of patients, and thus his own personality, from the 800 in his present institute to 2,000 to 10,000 patients: "pilgrimages from every land will fill my cup of happiness. A commonwealth of all the world is to be expected in almost thirty years. I shall be People's Commissar for Lunatics. Travel over all the inhabited earth. Inspections and reviews of an army of a million deranged minds" (*A*, 413-14).

"The World in the Head"

The third part of this multidimensional novel brings all the carefully plotted elements to a successful conclusion, as is demanded by the Aristotelian definition of the well constructed plot. The author will resolve the fate of the major characters and their lot in life in keeping with the way in which they were created. In addition, he will likewise dispose of the minor characters and events, so that there will be nothing left unresolved at the conclusion of the narrative.

The character of Fischerle was already killed in the second part, where he served as Peter Kien's guide through the "Headless World." In this part of the novel, Benedikt Pfaff becomes Kien's caretaker and exploiter. He had rescued him after the riot at the police station, where Kien delivered a lengthy harangue claiming that he himself had murdered Therese. Now Pfaff lets Kien live in his caretaker apartment downstairs, while Pfaff settles in with Therese upstairs. Kien is put to work immediately tending to Pfaff's peephole. Pfaff had made this small hole in the hall's wall at the height of a person's knee so that he could observe all people entering or leaving the apartment house. Kien quickly turns the task of observing people from this perspective into a scientific study. He takes careful note of the trousers passing by, but – being a true misogynist – ignores all annoying skirts. He is especially pleased that he has not seen the blue starched skirt worn by Therese: "that special and unmistakable blue, shrill, insulting and vulgar, was worn by no one" (*A*, 381). Using the logic proposed by the philosopher Bishop Berkeley again, Kien concludes that since he has not perceived the blue skirt, then Therese must no longer exist. And he is satisfied to live with this hallucination. As time goes on Kien undertakes a "systematic study of

the classification of men by trousers" (A, 386), which would be published as a " 'Characterology of Trouser' . . . with an 'Appendix on
Shoes' " (A, 387). Kien ignored all women because for him – now
that Therese no longer exists – women are all "illiterates, unendurable and stupid, a perpetual disturbance. How rich would the
world be without them . . ." (A, 387).

With the usual touch of irony displayed in the novel, as soon as
Peter is rescued by his brother, George, from his enslavement in the
small cubicle, he will conclude his study of the microcosm without
women and commence his inquiry of women in the macrocosm. One
would hope that such an investigation, guided by the psychiatrist,
would lead the ailing Peter Kien back to normalcy – that he would
realize that his erroneous perception of women is based solely on
his unfortunate experience with Therese. That, of course, is too
much to hope for.

Through extensive discourse George and Peter attempt to define
themselves and the role they must play to resolve the predicament
that Peter is in. It becomes clear to George that his method of treating the mentally ill will not succeed with his brother. Peter's mind,
totally dedicated to either the taxonomical aspects of his philological
studies or to his own particular perception of the world, is completely shut to any human compassion. George concludes that the
brothers are opposites, suggesting that he has a memory for feelings
while Peter has a memory for facts. "Both together, a memory for
feelings and a memory for facts – for that is what yours is – would
make possible the universal man. . . . If you and I could be moulded
together into a single being, the result would be a spiritually complete man" (A, 436). The fallacy of this conclusion is that it only describes the two personalities in a most extreme and unrealistic way.
Both are, in their own ways, complete egoists.

To satisfy himself George realizes that he must analyze Peter's
problem, offer a solution, and return to his patients in Paris as
quickly as possible. A very superficial examination leads to a plan of
action that will profit only George: "He was to deal with and get rid
of the woman, to reduce the caretaker to his proper station, to talk
the man of character out of his belief in a crime, and to lead him
back in triumph to his cleansed and liberated library" (A, 438). And
that he does without delay. Therese is dispatched to the other side
of the city, where she is set up in her own dairy shop after promising

to never see Peter again and giving George all the pawn tickets for Peter's books. Pfaff, likewise, is removed from his caretaker post at 24 Ehrlich Strasse by George, who claims to be the head of the Paris police to persuade Pfaff to leave his peephole. Pfaff is ordered to redeem all the pawned books before he is established in an animal business close to Therese's dairy shop. The two are ready to move in and live together again, but each is bound to report to Paris immediately if the other strays even close to Peter Kien's dwelling. The library is returned to its former condition, Peter moves back, and George returns to his patients in Paris.

The return to his earlier way of life is easy for Peter Kien because he never really left his life of the mind. Indeed, he was physically removed from his library and his sinological studies for some time and made to roam the city with its disreputable bars and unsavory characters, but Peter was never fully cognizant of his physical environment. He lived for his books and his books provided him with a justification for life. He turns to his books to find freedom from blame for causing Therese's death. In a long litany, he offers evidence that women are the fountainhead of all evil in the world. From Buddha's writings he quotes reasons why women should be held in an inferior position: they are prone to anger, jealousy, envy, and stupidity. Kien concludes that Confucius held women in such low esteem that he could not even comment on them.

When George faults his brother for seeking evidence only in India and China, Peter retorts with a long list of women in Europe. He begins with reference to the great German epic of the Nibelungen and outlines the cowardly role that Kriemhild plays to gain the treasure of the Nibelungen. Through provocation and intrigue, and with no danger to herself, Kriemhild took Hagen and Gunther prisoner and cut their heads off. Kien reminds his brother that it was Kriemhild who sewed a cross on her husband Siegfried's coat so that Hagen would know exactly the one spot on his body where Siegfried was vulnerable and consequently could kill him. Kien lauds the unknown poet of the epic who ends this great medieval poem with the slaying of Kriemhild.

Examples from other literary, mythological, and historical sources are cited by Kien. He begins with Helen of Troy, who brought about 10 years of war in which the finest and most noble men of Greece were killed. The list continues with discussions of the

roles played by Aphrodite, Calypso, Penelope, Hera, Hebe, Cleopa-
tra, and others. With each example, Kien points out the evil and destructive part women have played in the writings of Europe.

Reference to Michelangelo's masterpiece, the painted ceiling of
the Sistine Chapel, offers an example of Kien's myopic reading of the
visual arts. The description of the portion of the fresco he is considering is quite correct and the argument he proposes is not unrea-
sonable. What makes Kien's observations difficult to dismiss is that
he is reading a generally unfamiliar scene. While normal scholars
have concentrated on the great mastery of the panel depicting the
creation of Adam, Kien studies the adjacent scene portraying the
creation of Eve. Kien notes correctly that this scene is located between the larger scenes of the creation of Adam and temptation and
expulsion, but also points out that the creation of Eve is at the exact
center of the fresco portraying the creation and fall of man as told in
the book of Genesis.

Typically for Kien, he points out that Eve was created when God
removed a rib from the sleeping Adam. Not yet fully created, with
one foot on the earth and the other still in Adam's side, Eve is already offering prayers to God, which Kien calls flatteries. "Flatteries
addressed to God are called prayers" (A, 444). He observes that all
of Eve's subsequent actions up to the expulsion from paradise are
cloaked in canny, calculated prayers of deception that God accepts
because "he accepts her homage" (A, 444). And all this while Adam
sleeps. The next ceiling fresco already depicts the fall of man. "When
Adam wakes God leaves them, cruelly together; she will kneel to him,
her hands folded as they were before God, the same flatteries on her
lips, loyalty in her eyes, the lust of power in her heart, and so that he
shall never escape her again she will tempt him to depravity" (A,
444). This is a unique description of the temptation and expulsion
scene, and while correctly portraying the account given in Genesis, it
is not quoted in its entire context of either the biblical passage or
Michelangelo's frescoes.

The result of all this scholarly labor brings Kien not a whit closer
to normalcy; indeed, it only gives him a more solid footing in this
world of madness. It is clearly futile to suggest that his understanding
and interpretation of the great works of world literature, art, and
philosophy may be faulty. Kien, the book man, has set out to prove a
point and has found ample evidence to substantiate his view. Since

he really took no note of his physical environment, it must be concluded that all of the events narrated in the novel have had no effect on him. If anything, they have made him more convinced of his beliefs. At one point toward the end of the book, Kien observes very correctly that a "hallucination continues for as long as it is not contested" (*A*, 381). That is certainly true for the protagonist Kien, but it is equally true for the other characters.

The one theme that is developed from dream and fantasy at the beginning of the novel to total reality at the conclusion is that of the fire. Kien dreamed about it, he married Therese because she promised to save the books in case of fire, he cites examples of great libraries being destroyed by fires, and he imagines the books on the top floor of the Theresianum in flames. The final chapter of the novel, which depicts Kien's life after he is again established alone in his library, is entitled "Der rote Hahn" ("The Red Cock"). Given that he lives on the top floor of the apartment house, the expression that seems appropriate for consideration is *den roten Hahn aufs Dach setzen*, meaning to set a house on fire. That is precisely what Kien does. Thinking the Theresianum is on fire, he moves the library ladder to the center of the room and looks out of the skylight; he "heard the despairing cries; they were the books screaming . . . the Theresianum is burning" (*A*, 461).

"Geblendet schloss er die Augen" (Blinded he closed his eyes) (*A*, 461). He reviews his entire life in this blinded state. Then he strikes up an entire box of matches to look for and rub out the blood stains on the carpet brought about by Therese's imagined death. He hears a knock on the door, but rather than opening it, he stops up his ears, as if he could also shut out sound. He rejects the idea of calling his brother for help, believing that George will only come to steal his library. "He is trying to rob him; everyone is out for a will, everyone counts on the death of his nearest . . . [Kien] will avenge himself on all his enemies! He has murdered his wife . . . and George will get no books" (*A*, 463). He barricades the doors with huge piles of books, returns to the ladder in the middle of the library, "climbs up to the sixth step, looks down on the fire and waits" (*A*, 464). As he is consumed by the conflagration "he laughed out loud, louder than he had ever laughed in all his life" (*A*, 464). And so ends the only completed book of the *Human Comedy of Madmen*.

Chapter Three

Masks and Transformations

The Wedding, Comedy of Vanity, Life-Terms

"Above all else, I consider myself to be a dramatist and everything associated with dramatic work represents the nucleus of my personality."[1] This is a surprising statement if one considers only that Canetti has published just three plays. If, however, one also considers how Canetti has included parts of his novel and numerous character sketches in his public readings, for example, his statement becomes far less astonishing. In conversations, occasional interviews, and in some written statements, Canetti has mentioned – without giving titles – having written other plays, but no further information about such works is available. An examination of the three plays that were published will facilitate an understanding of his dramatic work.

The earliest adventure of a dramatic nature that Canetti describes in his autobiography was his active participation in the reading of the Haggadah at the time of Passover. As the youngest male in the family, he joined his grandfather in performing the question-and-answer ritual explaining the significance of the holiday. Canetti's first creative experience with dramatic work occurred at age six when the family moved to Manchester, England. There, in his room, he spoke to the wallpaper, making up elaborate stories and assigning specific parts to the "many dark circles in the pattern of the wallpaper" that seem "like people to me" (*TF*, 38). When he was all alone he could become quite animated and "tried to persuade the wallpaper people to do bold deeds, and when they refused, I let them feel my scorn" (*TF*, 39). When the governess caught him in this unusual game, she tried to make him give up the "unhealthy" activity, but he would not. He merely changed the process and articulated his stories silently.

A host of other dramatic encounters in his youth could be described as preparatory work. Certainly the extensive reading of classical dramas that he shared with his mother contributed greatly to

Canetti's early proclivity for dramatic literature. And shortly after World War I, when he was living in a boardinghouse in Zurich, the 14-year-old Canetti wrote his first play, "Junius Brutus," a historical tragedy in five acts of 2,298 lines of blank verse. The play, written in three months (but never published), was dedicated and solemnly presented to his mother on Christmas Day 1919. Young Elias soon realized "how miserable this work was, and that it didn't entitle me to the slightest hopes" (*TF*, 198). He clearly learned from this event, however, "the distrust that I later felt against everything I wrote down in haughtiness and self-assurance" (*TF*, 198).

A dozen years passed before Canetti wrote plays again. During this apprenticeship period, Canetti matured, he read a great deal, and he participated in events that influenced his dramatic work profoundly. Many of these encounters are described in considerable detail in the second volume of his autobiography *The Torch in My Ear*, while he reflects on other aspects of his dramatic work in the third volume, *The Play of the Eyes*, and in his notes and aphorisms, *The Human Province* and *The Secret Heart of the Clock*. While it is not possible to examine each observation that Canetti has made on dramatic literature in general and on his plays in particular, it is informative to highlight a few experiences.

Of the many playwrights Canetti read and undoubtedly also saw in performance in Vienna, three seem to have had an indelible impact on him: the greatest writer of Greek comedy, Aristophanes; the nineteenth-century Austrian master of wit and language, Johann Nestroy; and the leading satirist of the day, Karl Kraus. From each Canetti learned a great deal, and each contributed to his concept and theory of the drama.

The writings of Aristophanes (c. 448-380 B.C.) assumed an important role in Canetti's life during the last few months of his residency in Frankfurt in 1924. Indeed, he even describes this time as his "Aristophanic apprenticeship" (*TE*, 53), when he read Aristophanes' works and simultaneously observed that a very similar condition existed in his own world. The basic condition Canetti noted was "the raging plunge of money" caused by the inflation in Germany (*TE*, 53). In those days, Canetti observed the reality of – for example – a loaf of bread costing several billion marks while the price of commodities doubled and tripled in the course of just one day. This total destruction of the structure of society was comprehensible to Canetti only through the works of Aristophanes. He points out that "the cruelty of Aristophanes' vision offered the sole possibility of holding together a world that was shivering into a thousand particles" (*TE*, 53).

From Aristophanes Canetti also learned about the structure of the comedy. An Aristophanic comedy is by no means a light and amusing drama with a typically happy ending, but rather a very serious play using the comedic for the exposition of an important and consequential topic. The typical plan for this comedy presents a protagonist who seriously undertakes some preposterous project, and the play becomes an elaboration of his success or failure. Although Aristophanes' plays do not follow a consistent pattern, structurally each play falls into two parts: one in which the preposterous project or "basic idea" is presented and debated, and the other part in which that idea is put into practice.

Canetti's own *Comedy of Vanity* follows Aristophanes' pattern: a prologue with announcement of the "basic idea" or ingenious plan conceived by a specific actor; the *prados* and *agon*, the former being a presentation by a chorus, while the latter offers a debate between the proponents and opponents of the plan; the *parabis*, which is an interlude in which the characters address the audience quite directly; numerous episodes illustrating the preposterous project; and the exodus that celebrates the successful resolution of the "basic idea." Despite the general absurdity of the situation, the characters are real as types, their verisimilitude coming from their perfectly natural behavior in rather unnatural circumstances. Canetti believes that such a drama will be successful if it can "demand the utmost from the spectator, shake him, take him, and drain him" (*TE*, 54).

Johann Nestroy (1801-1862) owed much of his esteem during Canetti's early years to one of Karl Kraus's finest literary-critical essays, "Nestroy and Posterity," a tribute read before an audience of 1500 in May 1912. Prior to that time, Nestroy was thought of merely as the author of over 80 comedies, most of them in Viennese dialect. Kraus, however, focused on Nestroy's satirical genius and the exemplary fashion in which he mirrored his times, the era of mid-nineteenth-century Biedermeier Vienna. Just as Kraus saw Nestroy as the satirist at the end of a period of decline, Kraus saw himself as the prophet of Austrian decline at the turn of the century. And likewise, Canetti stands at the conclusion of his era. What Kraus wrote about

Nestroy could be said of all three writers: "The satirical artist stands at the end of a development which has forgone art. He is its product and its despairing opposite. He organizes the flight of the spirit from humanity, he concentrates on going back. After him comes the deluge."[2]

From Nestroy, Canetti also learned how the playwright can make effective use of dialects in creating characters. Even though Nestroy's individual characters speak in various Viennese dialects, they can – with the exception of only a very few words – be easily understood even today by every speaker of German. The dialects allow the playwright to create characters representing different and distinct classes, be they economic, social, political, or educational classes. This phenomenon is particularly evident in the two plays Canetti wrote in Vienna, *The Wedding* and *Comedy of Vanity*.

A third characteristic of Canetti's plays that might be attributed to Nestroy is the successful way in which various parts of the stage are used simultaneously. In contrast to the traditional convention of presenting scenes in sequence, Nestroy, in a medieval tradition, divides his stage into two or more areas for action, making it possible to simultaneously offer a particular point of view from different perspectives. Using this technique Canetti can display the views of two or more dozen characters and the audience can follow without the slightest confusion.

Karl Kraus (1874-1936) had an immeasurable effect on Canetti's dramatic work. Aside from everything else he learned at the many Kraus lectures and readings he attended, Kraus's great skill as an orator had an important influence on Canetti. Recalling his first lecture shortly after he arrived in Vienna in 1924, Canetti writes: "When he sat down and began to read, I was overwhelmed by his voice, which had something unnaturally vibrating about it, like a decelerated crowing. But this impression quickly vanished, for his voice instantly changed and kept changing incessantly, and one was very soon amazed at the variety that he was capable of" (*TE*, 70).

Kraus had founded what he called his "Theater of Poetry" (*Theater der Dichtung*), at which he gave spellbound audiences readings of the dramatic and poetic classics, above all Shakespeare, Nestroy, and Offenbach. But the most-famous performances were the readings from his visionary-satirical play *The Last Days of Mankind*, a vast assemblage of scenes documenting the years of the

Austrian apocalypse, 1914-1919. Canetti remembers those readings as times when Kraus "populated Vienna for me" (*TE*, 159).

As the foremost satirical gadfly of his day, Kraus was well known for the masterful way in which he could accuse his enemies and find them guilty. He merely looked closely at their writings, extracted any error however small, and then used their own writing against them. Canetti learned from this experience at Kraus's lectures that "each individual has a linguistic shape distinguishing him from all others" (*CW*, 34), an idea that he would later articulate as the "acoustic mask."

One important characteristic that Canetti shares with these three predecessors is that of taking personal responsibility for the most critical and dangerous roles. According to tradition, Aristophanes played the role of Cleon in his comedy *The Knights* because in those days no actor would have ventured to impersonate a politician. It is known that Johann Nestroy not only wrote over 80 plays but also played important roles in most of them; many provoked the ire of the censors, leading to his arrest and incarceration. In his public readings from *The Last Days of Mankind*, Kraus had reserved the role of the Grumbler for himself. Canetti writes in his autobiography that in Vienna in the 1930s he gave public readings of parts or all of *The Wedding* and *Comedy of Vanity* because no theater was prepared to stage the plays. In later years he even prepared recordings of his plays where he read every role.

From time to time Canetti has indicated that he was writing a book on his theory of the drama. Although this book has not been published, three key concepts emerge as the basis of his theory from various interviews he has given, from his notes and aphorisms, and from his essays and theoretical writings. These concepts are the acoustic mask (*akustische Maske*), the basic idea (*Grundeinfall*), and the transformation (*Verwandlung*). Although they appear in the dramatic and theoretical works of many writers, Canetti's understanding of these concepts is quite unique.

For approaching and interpreting Canetti's dramatic work, a complete understanding of the composition of the "acoustic mask" is essential. In an interview published in a supplement to the Viennese paper *Der Sontag*, 18 April 1937, Canetti articulated some of the aspects of his theory of the drama and outlined specifically how each character of his plays acquires an acoustic mask. Erich Fried includes a verbatim transcript of the interview in the introduction to the volume *Welt im Kopf* (World in the Head), a small collection of excerpts from Canetti's works.[3]

"The drama lives in its own peculiar way in language. One could almost say . . . the drama lives in language and, consequently, I consider the acoustic mask to be the most important element of the dramatic structure" (12). Recognizing that it is difficult to define this concept, Canetti offers an example.

> Go to a popular pub, sit at any table, and strike up an acquaintance with . . . a total stranger. To begin with you will be unable to cheer him up with several kind sentences. However, as soon as he really starts talking – and he will like to talk; that's why he goes to this pub – you must persist in keeping quiet and listen to him intently for a few minutes. . . .
>
> There you will now find that your new acquaintance has a very individual way of speaking. It is not enough to determine that he speaks German or he speaks a dialect, most or all people in this pub do that. No, his way of speaking is unique and should not be mistaken as being that of someone else. It has its own pitch and speed, it has its own rhythm. He changes his sentences infrequently. Certain words and expressions occur again and again. Indeed, his language is made up of only 500 words.[4] He makes do quite well – they are his 500 words. Another person, also "word-poor," speaks a different 500 words. You can, if you listened to him well, recognize him the next time by his language, without even seeing him. He has, in his speaking, become such a figure, clearly delimited on all sides, different from all people, like his physiognomy, which of course is also unique. This linguistic structure of a person, this "remaining-the-same" of his speaking, this language which has been created by him, which he has completely to himself, which will only pass away with him, this I call the acoustic mask." (12-13)

Of course, Canetti does not intend to serve merely as an "ambling phonograph" collecting samples of speech but to use the acoustic mask with all its linguistic possibilities and limitations in his creation of each unique character in his plays. These characters also have a visual configuration when one observes their deportment and manner of walking. Once the linguistic and physical masks have been established, each character represents a particular point of view the author has assigned to them, and, consequently, they take on what might be described as a philosophical mask. In summary, the mask defines all aspects of a particular character.

Unfortunately, the elements of the acoustic mask that are based primarily on the use of specific dialects are essentially lost in the translations of the plays. In *The Wedding* and *Comedy of Vanity*, Canetti's characters speak the dialects that are found in all the various districts of old Vienna and that are peculiar to their social and economic status in that society. Such an environment does not have a good equivalent in the English-speaking world and it is impossible to adapt this aspect of the acoustic mask to another socioeconomic setting; therefore, successful translations have had to eliminate that part of the acoustic mask. One can, however, note the names assigned to places and characters as representing at least a portion of the acoustic mask. For example, one of the main characters in *The Wedding* is Oberbaurat Segenreich. His title translates as senior engineer or construction official, and his name means that he is "richly blessed." Another is Dr. Bock, the 80-year-old family physician, whose name should be translated as Dr. Stud because that is the role he plays. One can also observe that the play takes place in a house on Gütigkeitstraße, kindness street – just another bit of Canetti's irony.

The second key concept evident in each drama is the "basic idea." Canetti insists that "every drama proceed from a completely new basic idea" (15). The play must be so novel in its plot that it presents viewers with a world they have never seen or experienced. It is insufficient for the play to represent characters that exhibit individual interpersonal relationships with other characters. The basic idea must also include a great variety of unique features so that the dramatic environment will illustrate a singular but complete event that is entirely new to the audience.

The notion of the "transformation" refers to Canetti's belief that the theater is not a place for entertainment, but rather should serve as an educational institution. The playwright and the theater are to confront the audience with a reality that results in a catharsis in the Aristotelian sense. Canetti does not seek to describe and interpret the world; he wants to present his "uncomfortable" dramas, grotesque and absurd satires, to bring about a change – a transformation – through confrontation. The reception of his plays shows that audiences are not infrequently reluctant to accept the harsh moral responsibilities that Canetti demands of them so forcefully and unrelentingly in his dramatic works.

An examination of Canetti's three plays illustrates how he executed these key concepts. The published plays are *The Wedding*
(*Hochzeit*), written in Vienna in the winter of 1931-32; *Comedy of
Vanity* (*Komödie der Eitelkeit*), also written in Vienna, in 1933-34;
and *Life-Terms* (*Die Befristeten*),[5] written many years later in London
in 1952-53. The plays had their premieres in reverse order from their
writing. *Die Befristeten* premiered in English translation as *The
Numbered* on 5 November 1956 at the Playhouse Theatre, Oxford,
England; its German premiere occurred at the Theater in der Josefstadt, Studiobühne, in Vienna on 17 November 1967. The other two
plays premiered in 1965 at the Staatstheater in Braunschweig, Germany, *Comedy of Vanity* on 6 February and *The Wedding* on 3
November.

The Wedding

The Wedding has as its "basic idea" the exposition of three protagonists: greed, lasciviousness, and death. The play presents the cruel
and merciless conditions of a society that seems no longer to have a
moral code to live by and is now participating in a repetitive ritual
leading to Armageddon. *The Wedding* is divided into two parts: a
prelude in five scenes and the main act, which presents the actual
wedding celebration.

The prelude serves as a brief introduction to the disparate characters residing in an apartment house on Gütigkeitstraße, all possessed by the singular goal of owning the house in which they live. At
first we meet the landlady, Mrs. Gile, a shrewd old woman whose
granddaughter visits every day to ask to inherit the house while
hoping the old lady will soon die. Each time the grandmother's parrot hears the word *house* he repeats it three times and thereby caws
the major theme of this scene and the entire play. Subsequent scenes
of the prelude illustrate how other residents are trying to cheat the
old woman out of her house: a pompous school teacher, a young
couple, and a very crafty couple who want to purchase the house
cheaply. The fifth scene takes place in the janitor's basement apartment. His wife is lying on her deathbed while he is reading the biblical story of Samson from the book of Judges; blinded Samson pulls
down the house on the Philistines. This foreshadows the events of
the main play.

The wedding celebrated in the main act centers on a depraved, petite-bourgeois family. The father of the bride is Mr. Blest, an engineer, who insists in his vanity that everyone acknowledge that he has built not only this solid house on the Gütigkeitstraße but also this fine family. The other members of the family and wedding party have in common greed to possess property and other people, as well as a demonic obsession with sexual excesses. The nymphomaniacal mother of the bride thinks only of copulating with the groom; the bride lusts for three friends of the family before settling down to the boredom of married life; and – representing the crudest form of sexuality – the 80-year-old family doctor, erotomaniac and pedophile Dr. Stud, brags that he has "had" all the women in the family and at the party. The bride, Christa, summarizes life in this house: upstairs the guileful landlady, downstairs a corpse, and here at this bacchanalian feast she is getting married.

Into this macabre world, Hark, an idealist, introduces a play within the play. He asks what each person would do if his or her beloved were threatened by imminent danger. In this game of illusion each person, of course, thinks only of satisfying their own greed and lust. A sudden earthquake then changes the game into reality. Now that everyone could really save the person they love, they do nothing but try to save themselves. The play closes with cruel, hateful screams that cut into silence. The parrot has the last word: "House! House! House!" (W, 63).

The premiere performance of *The Wedding* in 1965 at the Staatstheater in Braunschweig led to a sensational scandal followed by extensive coverage in the local and national press. The publicity resulted in the closing of the play after only seven performances and undoubtedly discouraged further stagings in the years that followed. Directed by Alexander Wagner, with stage and costumes designed by Manfred Schröter, the initial production seems to have been a faithful rendition of Canetti's text. But spectators were offended by some words, by the way some characters were portrayed, and even by the theme, content, and/or message of the play. The day before the premiere, a Braunschweig newspaper even printed an anonymous charge suggesting that the play was pornographic and contained sexually stimulating and offensive materials. Before the next performance a host of writers and critics, from Günter Grass to Theodor

Adorno, interceded on behalf of Canetti and the performance and vouched for the artistic quality and integrity of the play.

The Wedding is considered Canetti's most stageable play. It was successfully performed under the direction of Karl Paryla in 1970 in Cologne and was enthusiastically received when Canetti himself read it later that year at the Schauspielhaus in Kiel. In October 1985 the city of Vienna celebrated Canetti's eightieth birthday. As "their" Nobel Prize laureate, they made him an honorary citizen of Vienna and Hans Hollmann directed *The Wedding* at the Akademietheater with a distinguished cast. The newspaper *Frankfurter Rundschau* called the performance "Hollmann's crowning accomplishment in staging Canetti's plays."[6]

Comedy of Vanity

The "basic idea" of the second play from the Vienna period, *Comedy of Vanity*, is that humankind would gradually waste away if deprived of its vanity. Vanity, a characteristic quality developed to a greater or lesser extent in each person, is the basic attribute that distinguishes the individual and provides a life-sustaining force.

A government decree to eliminate vanity is imposed on the population:

Official declaration – The Government has decided:

Point One: The possession and use of mirrors is prohibited. All extant mirrors must be destroyed. All manufacture of mirrors must be stopped. If after a period of thirty days a person is found still to possess or use a mirror, he or she will be punished with ten to twelve years imprisonment. The manufacture of mirrors carries the death penalty.

Point Two: The taking of pictures of humans and related beings is strictly prohibited. All extant photographs of human or related beings will be destroyed. . . .

Point Three: The creation of portraits or self-portraits in oil, watercolor, charcoal, pencil or any other medium is strictly prohibited. . . . All extant portraits or self-portraits must be turned in at the nearest government agency. . . . (*CV*, 30)

Point Four: All movie theaters will be closed down. All reels, originals as well as copies, will be destroyed . . . (*CV*, 21)

The consequence of not abiding by each item of the decree is, as in point one, punishment by long imprisonment or even death. A period of 30 days has been set to give people time to comply with the decree.

The play illustrates how a series of unique individuals react to the decree, first in the implementation of the law and then in living with this new restriction. There are at least two dozen distinct characters representing many acoustic masks and individual personalities. In part one of the play we see a carnival-like atmosphere in which all are gathered to destroy their pictures and mirrors, each heeding the call in their own way.

A few examples illustrate the manner in which Canetti creates his dramatic personalities. The teacher Fritz Shakee appears as a traditional enforcer of conduct, but he has a severe stuttering problem whenever he is not acting in an authoritative role. It is Shakee who reads the official decree, during which it is observed that he "has grown in size . . . and reads with a high, loud voice without stammering once" (CV, 29).

S. Bleiss, a photographer prior to the government declaration, has been in the business of perpetuating vanity right along. His favorite gimmick was to take pictures of poor newlyweds standing in front of his car. The couple would not only have a picture but also acquire the capital investment of a car and have the picture as proof of their new wealth.

François Fant is a coxcomb. He has stolen all his mother's mirrors to take to the carnival, where he smashes them with a ball while watching the reflection of his own image in the mirrors. Mme. Emily Fant initially appears to be simply François's doting mother, but quickly reveals that she needs the mirrors in her business so that her girls can check themselves in order to be attractive for their gentlemen customers.

Henry Breeze strolls across the stage, pontificating to his companion Leda Fresh that a self-image of good health provides the individual with a meaningful life. Encouraged by Leda, his magniloquence leads him to boast that his brilliance in talking on a higher level of consciousness makes him "appear more virile" (CV, 31).

In the second half of the play each of the characters has come to terms with the decree 10 years later. Fritz Shakee is now the powerful chairman of the "Group of Four," an enforcement committee of crime fighters. It has come to his attention that young girls have found a way of circumventing the government decree by looking into one another's eyes to see themselves. Fritz Shakee advocates passage of a new law under which the eyes of those young girls will be torn out if they continue their illegal practice. It turns out that Shakee is actually married to one of these girls. In time he grows ill and despondent because he has contracted the "mirror sickness," a disease that can be cured only by looking into a mirror. When his wife illegally procures a mirror for him, Shakee is cured but his original stammering returns. Subsequently, when he tries to bury this illegal mirror, he is consumed by the "voices of stuttering choruses" (*CV*, 87).

S. Bleiss is still perpetuating vanity. "Help yourself to some happiness" (*CV*, 45) is his slogan as he goes from door to door selling time in front of a mirror at five shillings for two minutes. Although occasionally caught in this illegal venture, Bleiss survives since his crime is always also someone else's crime – the perfect black-marketeer. Unlike many other characters, Bleiss has never had a conscience to make him feel guilty. No harm comes to him during this period of prohibition.

The clever businesswoman Mme. Fant continues to indulge her son, but now she has established a "Spiegelbordell," a mirror brothel. Here almost all the characters of the play pay high prices to sit in front of mirrors and admire themselves. Henry Breeze stands before a full-length mirror in a "Luxury Cabin" making pompous and trivial pronouncements. After each proclamation he pushes a button and hears applause, but each time the applause grows weaker until there is none. Dementedly, he shouts basic truths on the condition of the world in a thundering voice as he threatens destruction of the establishment.

In the final scene most of the characters are in Mme. Fant's "Spiegelsaal," her "Hall of Mirrors." Each is confronted by and recoils from a "Thundering Voice" that summarizes their individual personality and the falseness of the mask that each has created. The carnival atmosphere that had robbed them of their individuality at the beginning of the play is transformed into an invocation and affirmation of an individual "Ich!" ("I"). All raise high a mirror or picture of themselves, but never merge into a chorus or group. The "I" of individual vanity prevails.

The premiere performance of *Comedy of Vanity* also took place at the Staatstheater in Braunschweig and was directed by Helmut Matiasek, with set and costumes designed by Manfred Schröter. The press had hailed Matiasek for "discovering" Canetti for the German theater, but their reviews of opening night were generally so negative that the run closed after only eight performances. By and large the reviewers thought highly of the play and placed the blame on the director, who had set the play historically in the period of Hitler's Germany. Matiasek created film segments and photomontages that transformed Canetti's play into a commentary on Nazism. The "mirror sickness" became the Hitler sickness, rather than a general statement on totalitarian systems. "The devices used in the staging changed the play" stated Günther Rühle[7]; that eliminated the catharsis Canetti had intended.

In Austria, *Comedy of Vanity* premiered at the Graz Schauspielhaus in October 1972 as part of the "Steirische Herbst" program (the Styrian Fall Arts Festival). The reviews of this performance were quite favorable, although they did mention that the director, Hermann Kutscher, had not fully realized the concept of the acoustic masks.

The most successful rendition of Canetti's play was the performance in Basel, Switzerland, in February 1978 under the direction of Hans Hollmann. Peter Iden's review quotes Canetti: "After all, 40 years after the *Komödie* was written it has now been performed correctly for the first time in Basel."[8] What made the Hollmann production so successful was his full comprehension of Canetti's concept of the acoustic mask and the uniqueness of the basic idea. In the 1985 *Festschrift* for Canetti, Hollmann describes how he came to understand Canetti, via work with plays by Horvath, Karl Kraus, Aristophanes and Nestroy, and honors him by revealing that he uses Canetti's concept of the acoustic mask in all of his productions.[9]

Life-Terms

For the play written in London, *Life-Terms*, the "basic idea" is a portrayal of a utopian society in which people are no longer tormented by the uncertainty of when they will die. In the prologue two men are talking about the olden days (the present time) when people did not know the *"Augenblick"* (the moment) when they were to die.

Their names were merely names then, rather than the numbers now used to indicate the age when death will occur. Life used to be constantly threatened by the arbitrariness of the hour of death.

Now, at birth everyone is given a locket containing their dates of birth and death and a number that serves as their name and indicates how many years they will live. Although everyone can know his or her own number, it is a crime – labeled murder – to reveal to others the information in the locket. Death has become the ultimate taboo, and to question the accuracy of the established age of one's death is the greatest crime. The Locketeer is the only person who can open the locket at the time of death to confirm the accuracy of the birth and death dates recorded there.

The play has 3 major and 20 minor characters, as well as a "Chorus of the Unequal." The minor characters have names such as the Mother 32, the Boy 70, two Young Men 28 and 88, the Professor 46, and the Boy 10. Their personality and behavior are determined entirely by the number. The Mother 32, for example, is unable to persuade her son, the Boy 70, to be cautious while playing because the son knows that nothing can hurt him – his name is 70. The Boy 10 is allowed to act like a spoiled brat because everyone knows he has only a short life. In a scene with a grandmother and granddaughter, the fairy-tale concept of living happily ever after is negated when the grandmother must remind the girl that she will not live happily ever after, but only until her "moment" (*LT*, 120). Those with high numbers, whether men with 88 or women with 93 and 96, display a superiority and arrogance over those with low numbers; they have been ordained as higher and more valuable citizens in their society.

The major characters are Fifty, Friend, and the Locketeer. Fifty is reluctant to accept the dictatorship of the Locketeer. For many years he has suspected that the lockets were really empty and that the Locketeer was a swindler. He reveals the deception to the Friend and subsequently to the others, the masses, who follow him joyfully, bringing the downfall of the Locketeer's deceptive system. For just one moment the masses rejoice, believing that now they would live forever. With the death of the first person, however, this dream vanishes. The newly established hope for immortality, a new form of freedom, turns out to be only a freedom to die at a time not determined by the Locketeer. Now the time of death is once again unforeseeable; the uncertainty of death is even more unendurable than the certainty of a pre-established moment of death had been before. Fifty may have brought about a freedom, but the burden of this responsibility is more than he is able and willing to endure.

There are few available reviews of the premiere performance of *Die Befristeten* by the Meadow Players of the Oxford Playhouse Company on 5 November 1956, but these are very positive. The play was translated by Carol Stewart under the title of *The Numbered* and directed by Mionos Volanakis, with sets by Wilfred and Samuel Avery. The London *Times* correspondent compares Canetti's play with previous productions of works by Giraudoux and Cocteau and states: "Into this distinguished repertoire Mr. Elias Canetti's play erupts with a strangely mathematical absorption."[10] *Oxford Magazine* reports that "the writing is forceful and plain, as is the production. . . . In scene upon scene they build up the delicate web of tension, achieving with truth and economy effects which grip the mind."[11]

The German language premiere in Vienna under the direction of Friedrich Kallina was not well received. Canetti had just been honored with the 1967 Great Austrian State Prize for Literature, and from the reviews one gets the impression that the Vienna theater establishment felt obligated to give a German language performance. The correspondent from *Die Welt* thought that the production at the small Studiobühne of the Theater in der Josefstadt was "on average good" but that "the whole thing is an amiable play for the mind but not for the stage."[12]

When Hans Hollmann staged a production of *Life-Terms* at the Württembergisches Staatstheater in Stuttgart in February 1983, the press was still inclined to think it was a play for the mind. The performance was very well received, however, because of Hollmann's extraordinary ability to take this parable and make it a dramatic event. There was praise for the performers' "magnificent accomplishments as actors."[13] Although the concept of the acoustic mask is generally not applied to this play by other critics and directors, Hans Hollmann believes that it is essential and applicable for a successful production of *Life-Terms*.

Conclusion

There is no record of major productions of Canetti's plays in the United States. The translator of the plays, Professor Gitta Honegger, did a reading of excerpts from the plays at a meeting of the PEN American Center in New York in the mid-1980s and reports a reading of *Life-Terms* at about that time.[14]

In spite of the difficulties that a production of Canetti's plays may present, there is no reason for not staging these works. From the comments and reviews of performances in the German-speaking theaters, one has the impression that the major objection by audiences to Canetti's works is an antipathy to the philosophical and moral issues the author raises. No one seems to want to hear what this contemporary satirist has to say, just as his predecessors from Aristophanes to Kraus were repeatedly rejected by their audiences.

The concepts of the "acoustic mask" and the "basic idea" in the plays can be examined and articulated with relative ease. But the third concept, the "transformation," can only be tested when the spectator or reader fully confronts the work. Canetti has certainly addressed major issues facing humanity in the modern world: greed, power, lasciviousness, freedom, death, the depersonalization of the individual, and the creation of an inhumane mass society. Susan Sontag has quoted Canetti as saying that he set out to "grab this century by the throat,"[15] and he has done so with power and grace. Some critics have used epithets such as the "difficult" or "uncomfortable" writer in describing Canetti. Not infrequently the controversy surrounding performances of the plays is explained as a public unwilling to see itself in such a brutally honest way – their mask is revealed and they don't like what they see. They are troubled and horrified by their "transformation."

Chapter Four

The Central Theme
Crowds and Power

Yesterday, the manuscript of *Crowds and Power* went off to Hamburg.
  In 1925, thirty-four years ago, I had my first thought about a book on
the crowd. But the real seed for it came even earlier: a workers' demonstration in Frankfurt for the death of Rathenau; I was seventeen.
  – Elias Canetti, *The Human Province*

This is one of the last entries for the year 1959 in *The Human
Province*, Canetti's book of notes and aphorisms. It is interesting,
however, that although Canetti here acknowledges the workers'
demonstration in 1922 as the initial impetus for his study on crowds
and power, the first two experiences he recalls in the first volume of
his autobiography, *The Tongue Set Free*, deal specifically with issues
of crowds and power, and these occurred long before 1922.

The first autobiographical entry, "My Earliest Memory," recalls
an event when Canetti was only two years old. His nanny's boyfriend
threatened to cut off the infant's tongue should he reveal the lovers'
nightly rendezvous. The power of the threat was so great that the
child indeed "held his tongue for ten years" (*TF*, 4). The next entry
not only describes Canetti's family but includes references to the different human and animal groups that make up the population of
Ruschuk during the first half dozen years of his life. In the three volumes of the autobiography, admittedly written 15 to 20 years after
Canetti concluded the first part of his study on crowds and power
(he has occasionally spoken of a subsequent volume), it is interesting
to note the plethora of personal examples of crowds and power that
he experienced. Indeed, it could be said that all his writings in one
way or another treat the topic Canetti examines in this major work.

Canetti's encounter with the Frankfurt crowd in 1922 was undoubtedly so important because he had lived a relatively sheltered

life until that time. Just a year earlier he had left a tranquil, joyful life in Zurich, where he had been spared the horrors of World War I and the dreadful years immediately following. The precocious 17 year old was far advanced in his intellectual development, but he lacked all real life experience. Frankfurt in the early 1920s was a center of political agitation and demonstrations, and the young Canetti came into contact with people from all walks of life. On one particular day he had his first physical experience with a crowd.

A large group of workers was protesting the assassination by right-wing and anti-Semitic fanatics of the distinguished political leader Walther Rathenau. Canetti, watching the demonstration, mesmerized by the shouting marchers, finally joined the crowd even though he had no affinity with the demonstrators. What puzzled him later, of course, was how the physical attraction of the crowd could overcome the intellectual and moral convictions of the bystander. Several years after the Frankfurt incident, when he was already a student at the University of Vienna, Canetti resolved to find an answer to the mystery of what happens to the human being in the crowd and what brings about this "total alteration of consciousness" in the individual (*TE*, 80).

For Canetti, the other influential experience with crowd behavior was his participation in the events surrounding the 15 July 1927 burning of the Palace of Justice in Vienna. More than 50 years later he admits in his autobiography that "the agitation of that day is still in my bones. It was the closest thing to a revolution that I have physically experienced . . . I became a part of the crowd, I fully dissolved in it, I did not feel the slightest resistance to what the crowd was doing. I am amazed that despite my frame of mind, I was able to grasp all the concrete individual scenes taking place before my eyes" (*TE*, 245). Some of the experiences of that day became significant sources for his novel *Die Blendung*, as well as for the two early plays, but Canetti maintains that "the substance of July 15 fully entered *Crowds and Power*" (*TE*, 247).

Canetti began his serious study of crowds in 1925. During his first year at the university he met Fredl Waldinger, a young friend who served as his intellectual sparring partner. Along with other young people, they heeded Karl Kraus's admonition to always articulate every thought with only the most precise linguistic forms; they were becoming more careful and thorough in their discourse. Fredl's interest in Buddhism and Indian philosophy had a twofold impact on Canetti. On the one hand, it persuaded him not to seek the answers to the crowd through continued and intensified physical participation in the crowd. On the other hand, and perhaps more important, it convinced Canetti that it was absolutely essential to greatly expand his exploration of the crowd process.

Another important intellectual experience in 1925 was Canetti's encounter with Freud's book *Mass Psychology and Ego Analysis*.[1] At the time, Freud's name and works were common parlance among the young intellectuals of Vienna. Canetti was particularly critical of Freud's views of the crowd. Freud's conclusions were limited to observations made by other scholars, and his views were based largely on the impact the crowd had on his individual patients. Canetti, in contrast, although still lacking a theoretical basis for his views, had physically experienced the "crowd instinct" (*TE*, 149) and was analyzing it intellectually. In the autobiography, Canetti makes special reference to his profound encounter with Freud's ideas: "I regard this period, from August 1 to August 10, 1925, as the true beginning of my independent intellectual life. My rejection of Freud came at the start of my work on the book, which I didn't deliver to the public until thirty-five years later, in 1960" (*TE*, 149). Following this major confrontation, Canetti devoted essentially the next quarter century to the study of crowds and power; although he wrote his novel and two plays during the same period, one can view these works almost as a tangent to the major study.

Throughout the European intellectual community, the study of crowd behavior and mass psychology had been evident since the turn of the century.[2] The distinguished French sociologists Gustav LeBon (1841-1931) and Gabriel de Tarde (1843-1904) had published pioneering work in the field of crowd behavior and psychology. Their colleague Émile Durkheim (1858-1917), the chief French sociologist after Comte, contributed to this new field with his epoch-making articulation of *The Rules of Sociological Method* (1895). In Germany Max Weber (1864-1920) developed a methodology for the social sciences in which he argued that, unlike the natural sciences, the social sciences cannot be limited to formulating laws of behavior but also must determine the meanings that people attribute to their acts.

Although Alfred Marshall (1842-1924) of Cambridge and Eugen Böhm-Bawerk (1851-1914), the leader of the Viennese school of economics, were principally concerned with the functioning of the market system, they believed that it was dangerous to derive from the purely European experience judgments regarding the quality of social or cultural phenomena. Consequently, they looked to anthropologists to learn how "primitive" societies satisfied basic needs while preserving harmony within their communities.

Of particular interest to scholars, however, were the radical experiments resulting from the 1917 revolution in Russia and the equally extraordinary venture following World War I in the establishment of a new political system in Germany, the Weimar Republic, and in Austria, the First Austrian Republic.[3] In addition to a host of individuals who followed the events taking place in these countries, one group of scholars should be cited for their innovative work. The Institute of Social Research, also known as the Frankfurt School, was established in 1923 by a group of unaffiliated Marxist intellectuals. Although politically inclined, they produced significant studies on the integration of Hegelian Marxism and psychoanalytic theory, on authority, and, later, a penetrating analysis of Nazism.[4] The most important question in the 1930s for true intellectuals, of course, was to understand the frightful rise to power of Hitler and his Nazi party, first in Germany and later in Austria.

There is almost no information on what Canetti was reading and studying during the early years he devoted to learning about crowds and power. On one occasion in 1933, in introducing Canetti at a reading, Hermann Broch made reference to Canetti's study of crowds. Shortly thereafter, as noted in *Welt im Kopf*, Broch advised his young friend to give up that project: "You'll spend your life on that and it will come to naught. Everything about it is too uncertain. Don't fritter away your time. You would be better off writing dramas" (20). Quite the contrary, Canetti did not give up; he intensified his study. What he may have abandoned was the hope of finding a system or methodology for investigation that he could have accepted and worked with. In 1959 he wrote: "However I look at it, my entire adult life was filled with this book; but since settling in England, that is, for the past twenty years, I have worked on scarcely anything else, albeit with tragic interruptions" (*HP*, 184).

When *Crowds and Power* was finally published in 1960 it became immediately obvious to many that 25 years of research and 10
years of writing had produced a major anthropological and social
psychological study. Appended to the book was a bibliography of
some 350 sources from such fields of study as mythology, religion,
history, anthropology, biography, and psychiatry. Even so, scholars
were quick to find major works on crowds and power not included,
and some faulted Canetti for the omissions. In addition to the absence of consideration of Freud, critics have particularly noted the
absence of contributions by Marx and Ortega y Gasset, for example.
Canetti has since explained some of these omissions, discussing
Freud in his autobiography and others in essays and rare interviews.
On occasion he has also spoken of a subsequent volume of *Crowds
and Power* in which he might expand his study. Perhaps he will also
publish further volumes of his autobiography and explain his reasons
for excluding other views of this topic.

Canetti's style of writing has also been the subject of criticism.
He does not adhere to the traditional method of scholarly presentation and argumentation. He begins his exploration without the traditional introductory statements on assumptions, hypotheses, and
methodology. Instead he leads the reader immediately into a series
of definitions of crowds and gradually offers examples of these
crowds and their behavior. Rather than a textbook or a research
monograph, Canetti's study should be described as a conversation
on crowds and power, a conversation filled with a host of examples
illustrating his views and drawn from sources throughout the ages
and around the world.[5] Canetti does not just state facts; he wants to
know why they are so. He offers the reader his ideas with consummate clarity and poetic grace.

Canetti considers many manifestations of crowds and power,
and it is impossible to examine all of them here. For his concept of
the crowd, we will discuss the chapter "The Increase Pack" (*CP*,
107-12) followed by "On the Dynamics of War. The First Death. The
Triumph" (*CP*, 138-40), a chapter showing how such packs are
formed, how they increase, and how they change. "Seizing and Incorporation" (*CP*, 203-11) provides Canetti's concept of power, illustrated here from two other chapters, "The Survivor" (*CP*, 227-28)
and "The Orchestral Conductor" (*CP*, 394-96). The former presents
Canetti's most determined exercise of power, the power of life over

death; the latter describes how a single person can embody numerous aspects of power. Finally, we will examine the last major section of the book, "Rulers and Paranoiacs" (*CP*, 411-62), because it represents Canetti's attempt to present in a summary fashion the concepts of power, crowd, and survival as he has observed them in different cultural environments. Here he employs these manifestations as remonstrations for Western readers.

"The Increase Pack"

Open crowds want to grow in size; closed crowds restrict membership to those belonging to the group. Others are identified as baiting, flight, prohibition, reversal, or feast crowds. Double crowds are made up of women and men, the living and the dead, or the two opponents in time of war. At the core of each crowd there is a "crowd crystal" (*CP*, 73), usually a few members who represent the specific function and purpose of the group and whose aim it is to bring about the intention of the crowd. There are many crowd symbols: fire, sea, rain, rivers, forests, among others. An older form of the crowd is identified as a pack, generally smaller and more restricted. Forms of packs are the hunting pack, which could be made up of animals as well as humans; the war pack, which generally pursues only a single enemy; the lamenting pack, and the increase pack, whose primary function is to grow.

The increase pack is a highly complex pack that applies primarily to human beings. The need to be stronger and greater in number has always been an essential human desire. Human beings cannot propagate as rapidly and numerously as they wish, however, and have resolved that problem through a process of transformation. Evidence of the great human wish and need to be more is disclosed in many myths, rites, and ceremonies. Two examples are given to illustrate how different groups increased their number by means of transformation.

The first example focuses on the rituals of Australian aborigines. Legends tell of their ancestors, who supposedly were half human and half animal; in this case people were associated with kangaroos, and their totemic figures represented this duality concurrently in one specific figure. This came about after years and generations of people surrounded by and associating with kangaroos, eventually looking and feeling like the animal, and gradually becoming the kangaroo totem. In their festivals commemorating their ancestors, the process of transformation called for several men to represent the kangaroo while others would represent the spectators. On other occasions some men might be asked to perform a dance of the kangaroo, their totemic ancestors. With the passage of time these rituals became highly intricate transformations, demonstrating the sacred rites of ancestor worship of the kangaroo totem.

The Australian aborigines adopted this tradition of transformation not only to venerate their ancestral relationship of human and animal as represented by their totem but also to increase the number of their group. The number of kangaroos was always greater than that of the people associated with them, and the aborigines always wished for an increase of kangaroos since that, in turn, brought about their own increase. Not all totems in Australia were based on a relationship with animals. Some totems were plants or insects that were especially prized delicacies, while others, such as mosquitoes, flies, lice, or scorpions, most likely served only as a means of providing great numbers with which the people could associate.

The other example of the increase pack and transformation is based on an investigation of the Okipa buffalo dance performed by the Mandan Indians of North America. A relatively small and sedentary tribe of the plains that typically lived in villages, the Mandans not infrequently found themselves without ready access to the roaming herds of buffalo that provided essential food. Rather than pursuing the bison throughout the plains in times of possible starvation, they created a ritual dance that was to make the "buffalo come" (*CP*, 111) to them. The dance was always successful since it could only be stopped when the buffalo arrived, regardless of how many days or weeks it might take for the animals to appear. The dance commenced when a dozen or more Mandans donned their masks made of a buffalo head, its horns, and skin reaching to its tail. At the same time that the dancer was transformed into the prey, however, he also carried the bow and arrow of the hunter in disguise. Whenever a dancer became fatigued, he had to assume the role of a buffalo who was then symbolically killed and skinned; only then was he replaced by another dancer. This ritual continued until a herd of buffalo actually appeared and joined the Mandans. According to Canetti's source, buffalo are of such a nature that they can actually be lured by the disguised people to join the dancers with their chants and rhythmic movements. Unlike the Australian example, this buffalo dance serves to illustrate how the numbers of the others – the buffalo – can be increased by means of disguise or transformation of the smaller number of people performing their dance.

In a conversation with Joachim Schickel,[6] Elias Canetti noted that the concept of the increase pack can be seen in contemporary times as well. He points to the extraordinary increase in the world's population, to the way in which human beings have bred more and more animals for domestic use and for hunting, and to the enormous escalation in the production of numerous grains. Indeed, he even observes this phenomenon in the almost irrational way in which human beings are inclined to support a continual increase in modern production. Canetti is of the opinion that this human inclination for increase has reached such a dangerous level that it must be restricted before it yields catastrophic consequences.

"On the Dynamics of War. The First Death. The Triumph."

> The inner, or pack, dynamics of war are basically as follows: From the lamenting pack around a dead man there forms a war pack bent on avenging him; and from the war pack, if it is victorious, a triumphant pack of increase. (*CP*, 138)

The first stage in a war comes about when everyone feels threatened because there has occurred a first real or imaginary death. It is not essential that this first death be of an important person or that the death has been caused for a particular purpose. Of importance is the fact that the enemy has killed a member of the group to which one belongs. Initiated by this death, a lamenting pack is formed that simultaneously serves as the "crowd crystal" that quickly establishes the war pack. This is accomplished because everyone who laments the death of one of their members feels threatened with death by those who are now established as the enemy.

Even though a war starts as a result of the death of perhaps just one person, it normally results in the death of enormous numbers. In victory, the lament for the many dead is usually far more moderate than was the lament for the first dead. Victory is celebrated when many of the enemy have been killed or otherwise annihilated. This celebration, however, also reduces the inclination to lament one's own dead who have gone "into the land of the dead" (*CP*, 138) to extinguish the fear that initiated the war.

With the declaration of victory there exists the danger that the war pack will disintegrate and individuals will resort to seeking spoils of the postwar period. This is a problem, especially when soldiers do not feel personally threatened by death; they may feel that they are indeed entitled to take whatever they can plunder. For the military leader, there is a double demand: the soldiers must be permitted to engage in looting, but at the same time an army that is ready to fight must be retained. The solution is a victory feast. On that occasion it is essential to acknowledge the decrease of the enemy while one's own forces have increased. Furthermore, the victory celebration, with parades exhibiting readiness for war again, includes soldiers and civilians alike so that the victory can be properly observed. As victors they now demonstrate not only increase in numbers but also in wealth, some of which will be shared by the people. In some societies prisoners of war are exhibited or even released to show how the number of the enemy decreased. In other societies, however, where the people insist on direct participation in the decrease of the enemy, there will be public executions as part of the victory festival.

Two very interesting examples of the victory feast are given at the conclusion of this chapter. The first tells of mass executions during the "Annual Custom" festival in Dahomey, now Benin, a colony in the former French West Africa (*CP*, 139). During the festival, which normally lasted for several days, the king presided over the public beheading of hundreds of prisoners. In addition to having heaps of heads that the public could witness, the streets were lined with enemies hanging from gallows. On the final day of the festival the king presented the people with gifts of shell-money, for which they had to scramble, and with beheaded prisoners, for whom they likewise fought. The "communion of triumph" (*CP*, 139) allowed everyone to have a piece of the enemy dead.

Reports by eighteenth-century European slave traders who witnessed this festival reveal how the outsiders misinterpreted the significance of the mass executions. Whether from virtue or from business practice, they tried to persuade the king to sell the prisoners as slaves rather than kill them. The king, however, declined because he knew that to retain power over his people he had to allow them to experience the decrease of their enemy and, in turn, their own increase. They had to be shown that it was he, the king, who was so powerful that he ruled over life and death.

The other example of the victory feast refers to the "Triumph" (*CP*, 140), the ceremonial entrance into ancient Rome of a victorious commander with his army, spoils, and captives, authorized by the Roman Senate in honor of an important military or naval achievement. This tradition of the actual display of power and conquest continued until the Romans had achieved such great heights of power that conquest was no longer essential to the Empire. But a victory celebration remained a necessary part of the exercise of power. And so, rather than fighting on a battlefield, the fight was moved to the arena, that oval space in the Roman amphitheater established for combats and other performances. Here the Romans could experience combat vicariously while still celebrating the victory personally as the crowd itself proclaimed the victor. Thus, both power and the pack are preserved.

"Seizing and Incorporation"

The oldest manifestation of power and survival that human beings exhibit (and, as beasts of prey, share with animals) is that of seizing and incorporating – of overpowering and devouring one another. It is not at all difficult to extrapolate more complex and contemporary exemplifications of this very primitive, instinctual act of survival.

The first act of this power play includes all the various activities that precede the actual catching or touching of the quarry. While stalking and lying in wait, the hunter advances with the determined intent of killing the hunted. In the case of a man pursuing an animal that may be stronger or fleeter, it may be necessary to use superior intelligence, skill, or experience to outwit the intended target. Man's keenest device to trick the foe is his power of transformation, where he leads the victim to believe that his intentions are friendly and harmless. During this initial period the hunter not only contemplates the prey as a substance to be devoured, but also considers all the pleasurable stages of incorporating the victim. The time devoted to this aspect of the hunt can be determined by the active and passive gratification the pursuer seeks.

Following the chase, the prey experiences the touch, the oldest and most feared ordeal for the hunted. The senses of sight, hearing, or smell cause far less horror, since there is generally still a space between the hunter and the quarry. Once the victim is touched, it must decide if escape is possible, a conclusion based on either the presence of a real superiority of power or only a perception of greater power. A modern example of this terror can be experienced in an arrest, where the mere "hand of authority" (*CP*, 204) can be so intimidating that the thought of escape is rarely considered.

The next act in the fight for power takes place when the prehensile hand seizes, grasps, or lays hold of the victim. This activity not only comprises the physical application of force but includes numerous symbolic acts as well. Physically it is the hand that surrounds all or part of the prey with an appropriate degree of force and firmness. If it is only a matter of taking sustenance, the grasping hand passes the food to the mouth from where it is consumed and incorporated.

The hand, however, especially when closed, symbolizes many forms of power. Many languages have metaphors where the closed or grasping hand is the ultimate insignia of power: "He was delivered into his hands" or "It is in God's hands" (*CP*, 204). If the seizing hand applies more pressure than necessary, even to the point where the prey is crushed, the hunter actually shows such contempt for the victim, implying that he can do anything to his prey without it being able to reciprocate. Crushing a tiny insect, such as a gnat or a flea, allows a human being to kill a creature without even feeling that a destructive or sinful act has been committed. If the concept of crushing an insect is transferred to another human being, it represents another example of contempt, expressed in such statements as "I could crush you with one hand," "You are an insect," "I can do what I like with you" (*CP*, 205). And just as there is no punishment for killing a bug, there is no retribution for holding another in contempt.

In spite of all its physical power, the human hand, because of its softness, is not able to perform the complete destruction the hunter can imagine. Grinding or pulverizing the enemy to death can be accomplished only by placing it between two hard objects such as the teeth or some rocks. Since the concept of killing prey inside the mouth is abhorrent to humans, the deed is carried out only in a figurative way.

Animals that do not have prehensile ability seem to have developed effective alternate ways of exercising power and creating fear among their enemies. The paws of an animal, with nails and claws, can often wreck greater havoc than the seizing hand. Human beings have always admired the way in which the lions and tigers have seized their prey. With great haughtiness they announce their intentions to kill with a mighty roar that instills great fear in the potential victim long before the stalk commences. The entire process – from stalking to seizing – is conducted according to the agenda established by this solitary king of the jungle, and the quarry can do nothing but submit to its will. It is not at all surprising that those who covet great power, such as tyrants, have endeavored to emulate tigers and lions as they spread great terror among their subjects.

An examination of the act of seizing must include its opposite, the manner by which it is possible to prevent being seized. On this point only the way in which rulers obviate seizure is considered. Those who wish to exercise great power over their subjects have surrounded themselves with well-defined empty spaces to prevent the masses from approaching and seizing. Great palaces were erected in which subjects were held at bay by sentries at a host of gates and rooms that had to be passed before access to the ruler was possible. From this highly guarded position – which in some civilizations is equated with the sun or the sky – the royal personage can easily command the seizure of any subject while remaining protected from seizure himself.

The first step in the actual process of incorporation is the passage of the prey from hand to mouth. Creatures without prehensile ability, of course, begin incorporation with their teeth or beaks. As the hardest substance in the body, the teeth are not only superior weapons for attack and defense, but they are ideally suited for the prehension and mastication of virtually every type of food. Their alignment, from incisors to canines and bicuspids and finally to molars, makes them an appropriate eating device; but when they are visible they can become a frightening medium for power and order.

Wearing one or more teeth from the animals he had slain served a man not only as a memento of the hunt but also displayed his power and could invoke terror in others. Teeth, whether animal or human, with their smooth surfaces, undoubtedly served as a prototype for the first tools. It is suggested that the smooth, hard texture of the tooth led to the polishing of stones and, eventually, to the making of bronze and iron swords that were such effective weapons because of their smooth cutting edges. For modern times, the reference is made to smoothly functioning machines, the preference for "clarity of line and utility" (*CP*, 208) over the decorative in homes and furnishings, and the choice in modern architecture for the straight and orderly. In contemporary language statements such as "everything is going smoothly or functions smoothly" (*CP*, 208) suggest that a procedure or operation is totally within one's power.

It is proposed that the straight and orderly alignment of the teeth may have been a model on which military formations were based. This notion is substantiated by a reference to the Greek legend of the Phoenician founder of Thebes, Cadmus, who planted the teeth of a dragon he had slain. From the teeth, many warriors suddenly sprang up.

Another function of the teeth is to prevent the escape of that which has been captured and imprisoned in the mouth. While many animals only kill their prey after it has entered the mouth, it is essential to use the teeth to further the act of incorporation. It is submitted that the closed teeth may have served as the earliest example of the prison. Reference at this point is made to the story of the Hebrew prophet Jonah, who for his impiety was thrown overboard from his ship to allay a tempest. He was subsequently swallowed by a large fish and imprisoned in its belly for three days. Only after Jonah "cried out of the belly of hell" and promised to do as he was commanded was he delivered from imprisonment. It is further suggested that primitive man may have known other stories of creatures whose mouths were so large that they could imprison him. The horrible image of being cast into the gaping maw of hell has been a symbol of total punishment and eternal incarceration for many centuries.

The next phase of incorporation is most horrifying, because as the prey passes through the throat it disappears completely from light and sight; all thoughts of survival have been spent. Literary allusions are few and often terrorizing, like the journeys to the center of the earth or to the bottom of the sea. If people ever return from such voyages, they are usually marked and disfigured permanently. The normal passage through the body, however, is a long period of incorporation during which all life and substance is extracted from the prey; only refuse and stench remain. This final stage of seizing and incorporating provides a basic idea of the nature of power.

All elements of seizing and incorporating are necessary and basic functions for sustaining one's own life. At the same time, however, they also outline the process of attaining and retaining power, which suggests that the origin of the exercise of power is to be found in the simple, basic process of eating. "Anyone who wants to rule men first tries to humiliate them, to trick them out of their rights and their capacity for resistance, until they are as powerless before him as animals. He uses them like animals and . . . his ultimate aim is to incorporate them into himself and to suck the substance out of them. . . . When they are no more use at all, he disposes of them as he does of his excrement, simply seeing to it that they do not poison the air of his house" (*CP*, 210).

"The Survivor"

"The moment of survival is the moment of power" (*CP*, 227). Throughout this study, the issue of death, or more precisely the avoidance of death, is examined extensively. In virtually every example, it is shown that the horror that the presence and sight of death might generate is transposed into satisfaction with the realization that it is the other who is dead. In a fight or even in a war it is the survivor over the opponent who celebrates the triumphant return with much greater pleasure and enthusiasm, while devoting less time to mourning or lamenting the death of others, including his comrades. The survivor "feels unique" and powerful (*CP*, 227).

Although the concept of survival expresses elements of the wish for immortality, it should not be assumed that the individual only wants to live forever. Immortality means that one wishes to live longer than everyone else and to know it. In fact, it seems that the desire for immortality includes as a most important factor the great yearning that one's name is remembered long after death. In another chapter devoted exclusively to the subject of immortality (*CP*, 277-78), great homage is paid to the French writer Stendhal, who, though not famous during his lifetime, has surpassed his rivals since then and has gained true literary immortality.

There are various types of survival, each based on the relationship of the dead to the survivor and the manner in which the death

has been accomplished. The basest variety of survival results from
one man killing another, as he might kill an animal for food. Indeed,
the animal or man will lie at his feet while he is still standing; the
animal ready to be slaughtered for consumption and the corpse of
the man as evidence that makes the feelings of superiority and triumph possible. The victim is at the total mercy of the survivor who
can take his weapons or even a part of his body as a trophy commemorating and recording the victory. This will further provide the
survivor with strength and encouragement to repeat this form of
killing.

Survival in war, where there are many deaths, has already been
discussed in the section "On the Dynamics of War." Here, however,
it is not just a matter of slaying as many of the enemy as possible but
also of emerging as victorious from the battle. Even though the casualties include both comrades and enemies, the survivor can feel
"fortunate and favored" (*CP*, 228) because he is still alive. If he has
fought bravely and in the midst of battle where many have fallen, the
survivor may also feel superior to others and emerge as a hero. This
will ultimately engender in him a feeling of power, strength, and life
and the belief that he "is the favored of the gods" (*CP*, 228).

This section on survival includes a host of legends and myths describing many types of survivors and forms of surviving, all of which
have as their core the attainment of power of the survivor at the
moment of death of the other.

"The Orchestral Conductor"

Although Canetti offers many examples from ancient times, the modern period may be easier to comprehend. Most people who attend
orchestral concerts have undoubtedly never thought of such an occasion as a paradigm of crowds and power, but Canetti's explication
of "The Orchestra Conductor" presents such an event as an example
of his thesis. He suggests that most people think only of the music
being performed, rather than of the gathering of an orchestra, an
audience, and the conductor. The conductor, of course, is the most
powerful person, even though he may think of himself as merely a
servant whose function is to interpret a musical score as accurately
and faithfully as possible. Since he generally does not participate in
making music by playing one of the instruments of the orchestra, the

conductor is obliged to rely on others to carry out his ideas and wishes. But any thought of subservience is invalid.

Prior to the conductor's appearance in the orchestra hall, there exists a virtual pandemonium. Members of the orchestra enter the stage singly or in undefined groups. They might tune their instruments or rehearse once more a difficult passage of music they will perform later. Some may even engage in activities that have nothing to do with the performance, such as chatting with their fellow musicians. This activity can continue for an unspecified period of time and at any place on the stage. It is only arrested by the announcement and appearance of the conductor.

The audience is, likewise, an unorganized group of individual people. Although they have come to the auditorium for a common purpose, they too enter singly or in small groups and become organized only when they are shown to their assigned seats. The audience generally pays no attention to the cacophony emanating from the stage, preferring to engage in activities they initiate themselves, such as talking to neighboring concert-goers or reading the program. The moment the orchestra conductor appears, however, all members of the audience become one group – they are to be silent, seated in a particular place, and all looking in the same direction, toward the conductor.

Upon entry, the conductor is in complete command of everyone in the orchestra hall. Of all those assembled, he is the only one standing, most often on a rostrum where he can be seen clearly by both the orchestra and the audience. No one can question his authority, neither the musicians whom he faces nor the listeners behind him. From the moment he raises his baton he holds the power of life and death over the assemblage.

For the musicians, that small stick, the baton, or even just the conductor's hand, exercises ultimate control. With very small movements he not only sets the pace that everyone must follow but also commands which instrument may perform and which must be silent. Since he is in possession of the score, he knows exactly what each individual musician must do and, by virtue of this superior knowledge, has the power to assure that everyone attends to precisely the role they are to play. The conductor's dominance over the orchestra is greatly enhanced through the public display of his unquestioned authority.

The audience is under even greater control by the conductor. Without facing them, he subjects them to total obedience, requiring silence from the moment he decides to begin until he ends the performance and lays down his baton. Although the audience may experience great moments of joy and excitement at various times during the musical presentation, they must wait until the conductor allows them to express those feelings through applause. At the appointed time, he not only receives but also expects public adulation, not necessarily for the musical presentation itself but mostly for his accomplishments in leadership. For a given period of time, a host of individuals has capitulated to his complete and unquestioned power.

"Rulers and Paranoiacs"

This final section examines within a greater context the manifestations of power and crowds that Canetti has developed throughout his book. The individual parts of this chapter investigate "African Kings," "A Sultan of Delhi: Muhammad Tughlak," and "The Case of Schreber." The purpose of this part of the study is to illustrate modes of behavior that, although removed in time and place from the contemporary European and North American reader, are in many respects rather similar to those that readers can indeed observe in their own society.

For example, Canetti found a description of the ceremony that took place when an old king died and his successor was selected in the West African country of Gabon, a former territory in French Equatorial Africa. The process was reported in DuChaillu's book *Explorations and Adventures in Equatorial Africa*, published in London in 1861. Although the account is in no direct way related to today's events, it takes little imagination to see in those procedures something very similar to the electoral process practiced in various Western democratic countries. The reader almost has the impression that, after talking about current election problems, Canetti is saying: Let me tell you a story that treats an issue just like the one you are trying to understand! He then reports on the way it was done in another place in earlier times and lets the reader draw the necessary conclusions from his account.

The people in a tribe over which the old king had ruled for a long time had become weary and fearful of their leader. They were unlike other tribes that had the custom of limiting the reign of their kings to a specific period of time and then killing him. So when their king fell ill, they all expressed their sorrow publicly, but in private they all looked forward to his death. When he finally did die, the tribe followed a ritual of six days of mourning. A few responsible and honored men not only buried the old king in a secret place but also set about to secretly select a new king. On the seventh and last day of mourning the men announced the name of the new king to the tribe and to the man whom they have selected. This person was chosen not necessarily because of his leadership ability or because he belonged to a prominent or powerful family, but rather because he was popular with the people and could receive the greatest number of votes.

The period between the announcement of the chosen candidate and the coronation includes activities not unlike those that can be witnessed during the electoral process. It begins immediately after the name has been made public. The entire tribe viciously pounces on the as-yet-uncrowned king; they spit on him and beat and kick him; they curse him and his family relentlessly. While all this abuse is heaped upon the unfortunate candidate, one man will halt the activities and loudly announce: "You are not our King yet; for a little while we will do what we please with you. By-and-by we shall have to do your will" (*CP*, 412). After the future king has taken all the abuse without showing fear and contempt for the tribe, he is taken to the house of the deceased king where the elders and the tribe declare: "Now we choose you for our king; we engage to listen to you and obey you" (*CP*, 412). He is then dressed in the vestments of his office, a silk hat and a red robe.

The coronation is followed by a feast during which the new king receives visitors from all parts of his realm and participates in "six days of indescribable gorging of food and bad rum – of beastly drunkenness and uproarious festivity" (*CP*, 412). When this part of the ceremony is over, the new king can finally begin his reign.

Canetti observes how various crowds have functioned during the course of these events (*CP*, 413). It begins with a "lamenting pack" that mourns the passing of the old king for the six days prescribed by custom. This is followed by a "baiting crowd" and a "reversal crowd" who are actually venting their anger at their long-feared, hated old king, although they appear to be attacking the new ruler.

The new king, of course, recognizes that the antagonistic behavior he is experiencing is "transferred hostility," but he is also made aware that he may be treated similarly if he behaves as did his predecessor. Canetti notes that the new king begins his reign during a revolutionary period, but he calls it a "posthumous revolution" because it is not directed against the new king. The gluttony accompanying the coronation represents not only the activity of a "feast crowd" but also "guarantees future increase" during the reign of the new king. The reader – with a bit of realistic cynicism – can see the parallel between the process in Gabon and that in Western democracies.

There are other reports on customs practiced by different African tribes and their kings illustrating activities that are similar to established habits in the contemporary Western world. What is important to understand here is that Canetti is assisting readers to become observers, ready to comprehend the significance in their own lives of that which they have witnessed.

The other two parts of this section deal with paranoid rulers: Muhammad Tughlak, the fourteenth-century sultan of Delhi, and Daniel Paul Schreber, the *Senatspräsident* at the Court of Appeals in Dresden, who believed he was the ruler of the universe.[7] Both cases are treated in considerable detail and can be examined here only in summary.

Muhammad Tughlak "is of all men the fondest of making gifts and of shedding blood" (*CP*, 424). He ruled over most of India and was said to be the most cultured sovereign of his time. His court was the grandest and most splendid in the world, with daily exhibitions of royal ceremony and festal display. But he was even more famous for his cruelty. On any given day he would punish people with torture or execution for even the slightest transgression. When some people in Delhi spoke ill of him, he ordered everyone in the city to move to Daulatabad. Learning that all but two people – a blind man and a cripple – had obeyed his order, he was still dissatisfied; he ordered the cripple to be flung from a mangonel and the blind man dragged to Daulatabad. Only when the city was entirely empty was he able to say: "Now my mind is tranquil and my wrath appeased" (*CP*, 428).

It was Muhammad Tughlak's wish to rule the entire world. He secretly devised several schemes to accomplish this, believing fully in the wisdom and the righteousness of his plans. Once he sent 100,000 horsemen to conquer China; when all but 10 perished trying to cross the Himalayas, he considered the survivors traitors and had them executed upon their return to Delhi. He used his vast treasury to establish huge armies, and when he ran out of money, he taxed his subjects to the point of beggary. To escape his wrath, the peasants fled the country, but this led in turn to famine and revolt and to ever greater terrorism. "Muhammad felt no remorse for his cruelty; he was firmly convinced that all his measures were justified" (*CP*, 431). When he learned from a high Islamic authority that insubordination against a king could be punished by death, he engaged in the most extensive shedding of blood because he was convinced that everyone had become his opponent and enemy.

Canetti labels Muhammad Tughlak "the purest case of a paranoiac ruler" (*CP*, 433). He was abnormally preoccupied with creating great crowds – his armies, his treasure, his court in Delhi, and a great crowd of corpses. He became the only survivor; his victims were the greatest crowd. His commands were the most powerful since they always resulted in the death sentence. Muhammad Tughlak, like most of the examples in this book, comes from a non-Western culture. Canetti chooses such cases because he believes that the tyranny and despotism they exemplify will be understood by Western readers more clearly than cases drawn from their own societies.

One major Western example comes in "The Case of Schreber," an analysis of Daniel Paul Schreber's *Memoirs of My Nervous Illness*, published in 1903.[8] This celebrated book, referred to in most textbooks of psychiatry as the premier case study of paranoia, was first examined by Freud in 1911.[9] Freud was interested in establishing the basic factors that brought about paranoia in a patient and in determining the manifestations such a disorder exhibited. He observed in Schreber a psychosis characterized by persistent but logically reasoned delusions of persecution and grandeur. Freud attributed this psychological condition to the consequences of an Oedipus complex Schreber suffered in his youth.

Canetti's interest in Schreber's case is quite different from Freud's. Canetti does not try to establish the cause of paranoia but wants to illustrate the profound similarities between a paranoiac and a despotic ruler. Among the factors in Schreber's case that Canetti examines is the victim's belief that he is functioning in the entire universe and through an eternity of time – something like the manager of a planetary system.

Schreber developed a complex organizational structure for human souls in which he observed a plot whereby his psychiatrist and God were engaged in "soul murder" or "soul theft" (*CP*, 438), a conspiracy that would lead to "the destruction of Schreber's reason" (*CP*, 439). The process included a multitude of souls speaking as voices to him in his sleep, often living as "little men" for a short while in his head (*CP*, 440). "In soul-language I was called 'the seer of spirits,' " Schreber reports, and believes he has in this way come into contact "with the totality of all souls and with the very Omnipotence of God" (*CP*, 440). In his delusion, Schreber concludes that he is the only individual who can take the initiative to save the universe from catastrophe and dissolution.

Canetti maintains that Schreber's illusory concept of self is "a precise model of political power" (*CP*, 441), and he develops the way in which that concept of madness, or paranoic behavior, reveals the elements of the crowd, of power, and of how the seeker of ultimate power becomes the last man alive – the survivor. For Canetti the importance of the analysis of Schreber's paranoia is the demonstration that it is really "an illness of power" (*CP*, 448). Schreber could only attain that power in his dementia, but there have been others who achieved it in reality. Nevertheless, "A madman, helpless, outcast and despised, who drags out a twilight existence in some asylum, may, through the insights he procures us, prove more important than Hitler or Napoleon, illuminating for mankind its curse and its masters" (*CP*, 448).

Conclusion

In this examination of his book, many other examples of crowds and power could have been selected to illustrate Canetti's thesis. Indeed, over the years Canetti himself has mentioned in interviews that he had the materials for a second volume of *Crowds and Power*. But such a volume would probably alter only slightly the basic views he presents in the existing volume. Examples might come from manifestations of crowds and power in the years since 1960, when the book was first published, but Canetti has been quick to point out that his work should in no way be seen as a historical study. He uses materials from ancient cultures to make more understandable the almost incomprehensible phenomena of the present ("Gespräch," 114).

It may also be instructive to read this work from the perspective that Canetti suggests in the opening paragraph to the section on "African Kings." "It is not for a European of the twentieth century to regard himself as above savagery. His despots may use more effective means, but their ends often differ in nothing from those of the African Kings" (*CP*, 411). *Crowds and Power* does not present a unified theory or methodology for investigating this urgent contemporary problem, but it can serve as a rich source book for others to consult in examinations of these issues.

Chapter Five

Recordings

The Human Province, The Secret Heart of the Clock

In 1965 Canetti wrote the essay "Dialogue with the Cruel Partner."[1] It was included in a volume in which modern authors were asked to discuss the function and the importance that the keeping of a diary had had in their work. There he noted that he actually kept three different types of diaries: notes or jottings (*Aufzeichnungen*), memo books (*Merkbücher*), and diaries (*Tagebücher*).

The memo books serve as a private calendar in which Canetti registers names of people he encounters, sudden ideas that come to mind, titles of especially important books that have had a profound impact on him, and the names of places he has visited. The diaries are reserved for the occasions when the author speaks to himself, when the fictional "I" addresses the writer on the most urgent and difficult issues confronting him. Canetti insists that the memo books and diaries are of such a personal nature that he will not make them available to readers, perhaps even destroying them eventually.

The notes or jottings, although also personal adjuncts to his works, have been published in four volumes: *Aufzeichnungen 1942-1948* (Notes 1942-48)[2]; *Alle vergeudete Verehrung: Aufzeichnungen 1949-1960* (All squandered veneration: notes 1949-60)[3]; *Die Provinz des Menschen: Aufzeichnungen 1942-72*, which contains the first two volumes and materials from 1961 through 1972; and *Das Geheimherz der Uhr: Aufzeichnungen 1973-1985*. Consequently, these last two texts contain all of the *Aufzeichnungen* and have been translated as *The Human Province* and *The Secret Heart of the Clock*, respectively.

Canetti had been a note taker for many years. In the autobiography, he mentions in 1924-25 keeping "true notebooks," as opposed to the notebooks for lectures, where he "jotted down every exuberance, as well as my sorrows" (*TE*, 109). During that same time period, he relates going off to the mountains with two notebooks and Freud's study of mass psychology. One notebook was to contain his observations on Freud; the other was reserved for his personal life. "I talked to myself a lot, probably to articulate the chaos of hatred, resentment, and confinement . . . I wanted to put that chaos into words, organize it, and banish it" (*TE*, 150).

The most important collection of notes, however, not just for the young Canetti in 1929 and 1930 but for his entire life, was the preliminary work on his projected eight-part novel *The Human Comedy of Madmen*. Although the "book man" was the only character to be fully developed in *Auto-da-Fé*, the others remained as important personality types to be elaborated in detail and variations in the notes and jottings from 1942 until 1985.

The "Phantast," for example, that technological visionary who disliked everything around him, may have been the one to whom this 1942 observation should be attributed: "Oh, for a stethoscope, a fine stethoscope to identify the generals in their wombs!" (*HP*, 8). In 1957, when the first manmade satellite orbited the earth, that same character emerged briefly, suggesting that "the rivalry between the technologically active powers" can now be played out in outer space rather than leading to the annihilation of the earth (*HP*, 175). Of course, a dozen years thereafter, in 1969, when the first man walked on the moon, Canetti's "Phantast" was in his glory: "Lovers already feel spied upon from the moon. . . . Settlement of the moon by aircontinents. Wars over air" (*HP*, 250). The live television broadcasts of the moonlanding evoked the following: "The lack of any other creature there. Robinson Crusoe among minerals, as a robot, taking no step without an order from afar. Functioning remote orders, a dreadful vision of the future. Do this, do that; and in between, silly jokes for the audience on earth" (*HP*, 251). And two final observations on the subject: "Moon hermits as earth worshipers" and "Secrets deposited on the moon" (*HP*, 251). More than a decade later, in 1980, Canetti includes the following cryptic entry, which may also be attributable to a "Phantast" who has gone beyond the earth's limitation: "They have seen us. We will never learn about it" (*SH*, 65).

In much the same way, the other characters who were to have made up *The Human Comedy of Madmen* can be found in the notes. Some, such as the "actor," the "collector," and the "spendthrift," appear in every imaginable disguise. The "religious fanatic" and the "enemy of death" represent topics of such great importance for Canetti that they become major issues that transcend these volumes; consequently, they are a part of every work.

Closely associated with the eight "madmen" are countless character sketches, of which only 50 were included in the volume *Earwitness.*[4] Rather than writing an essay or a story in which he develops a particular type of human behavior, Canetti generates in a line or two, at most in one page, a snapshot of a specific personality. The "earwitness," for example, eavesdrops on everyone and indiscriminately uses the information thus gathered against the speaker. Another, called the "early worder," is a person who "says nothing he has thought over, he says it beforehand. It is not his heart that runneth over, but the tip of his tongue" (*EW*, 39). Others, such as the "long-changer," are perhaps not much more than examples of Canetti's delight in playing with words. This "long-changer" is the opposite of the person who normally short-changes others.

In *The Human Province* Canetti has included several hundred personality types. For example, he talks about "twosome and threesome people" who can only experience important events in their lives in groups of two or three (*HP*, 149). Another type is a "flatterer": "A man flatters until one finally replies amicably in order to get rid of him. He builds his reputation on these replies" (*HP*, 192). A third example: "The most lamentable man I ever knew was a storekeeper who was cast away under words; he put them in his mouth grain by grain and, ruminating, indited a poem" (*HP*, 126). A final example from this volume is the "well-read man," described in a longer entry that serves to illustrate not only Canetti's power of observation of human behavior but also to demonstrate his fine talent for satire. This "well-read man" is really a lazy or slothful fop whose preference is to pass himself off as a reader, even though he reads only two or three simply written books a year. He actually doesn't even read these books but rather opens each at random, skipping back and forth, searching for passages that appeal to him so he can astound strangers with his counterfeit erudition. He selects only popular books and relies on reputable critics to establish the distinction of the book before he even begins to leaf through. He purchases the book from a distinguished book seller and displays it prominently on his coffee table. If the "well-read man" "is the topic and if he can grasp at first sight the very first page he opens to, then he need not read on. He has discovered a masterpiece, his masterpiece, and from now on he tells it to everyone" (*HP*, 180).

In the final volume of notes, *The Secret Heart of the Clock*, the character sketches tend to be terse and pithy: "A terrible man searching for terrible ancestors" (*SH*, 73); "The story of the unjust man: He sides with the one who would have been the winner" (*SH*, 90); "The slanderer who follows after the eulogist, to liven up the action" (*SH*, 120). In 1982, Canetti reflected on his intentions in developing the characters that illustrate the multitude of behaviors he had observed over the four decades during which he wrote these notes: "There is more than one reason for working with characters. One of them, the important and right one, is directed against destruction. The other, the worthless one, has to do with a self-love that wants to see itself variously reflected. There is an interplay between both these reasons; their relationship determines whether one's characters are universally valid or vain" (*SH*, 108).

To fully understand the origin and function of these notes and how they became a part of his published work, it is necessary to turn to Canetti's autobiography, in which he reveals that he became preoccupied with the phenomenon of the masses as early as 1925. Although he interrupted his systematic study for a relatively short period in the early 1930s to write his novel and two plays, he returned to this topic and pursued it with intense determination until he completed the manuscript of *Crowds and Power* in the last days of 1959. In March 1938, when Hitler marched into Vienna and annexed Austria to the German empire, Canetti resolved not to write any purely literary work and to devote himself instead exclusively to the study of crowds and power. Admitting that his knowledge was still inadequate and that he might require many more years of study, he began in 1942 – as a type of "safety valve" – to devote one or two hours each day "to write down whatever thoughts come to my mind" (*Aufzeichnungen*, 8). Many entries from the 1942-48 period are directly related to his work; the extensive reading of documents in such fields as mythology, religion, history, anthropology, and biography provide the basis for his book. At the same time, however,

Canetti also reacts in his notes to the news reports of the times – the progress of the war, the massacre and holocaust, and the terrible consequences of the dropping of the atomic bombs.

The second volume, recording the years 1949-60, continues in much the same way and covers the period when Canetti wrote *Crowds and Power*. No longer subject to his self-imposed wartime prohibition of not writing purely literary works, Canetti during this time allowed himself to write his drama *Life-Terms* and the report of his visit to Marrakesh, *The Voices of Marrakesh*.[5] And after 35 years, including 7 of intensive study and 12 of writing, he finally completed what he regarded as his life's work. The daily activity of writing for one or two hours continued, however, and the last two volumes of the notes are the result of this personal and intellectual exercise. Canetti instructs the reader already in the introduction to the first volume that he has included only a selection of the notes he wrote and that he has neither revised nor edited them for publication. Nevertheless, the four volumes from over 44 years make up an estimated 3,000 entries.

It is not possible to easily categorize the wealth found in all those notes. Even though they reflect Canetti's most wide-ranging thinking, there are virtually no entries of a personal nature. On perhaps no more than a dozen occasions does he refer to a specific person, and then he hides the name behind a single mysterious letter, making identification impossible. In the fourth volume, for example, there are numerous entries that could refer to his daughter, Johanna, and yet they could just as easily be about the relationship that any youth might have with an older person. And it is only during the last few years that Canetti includes any entries in which he actually refers to himself: first-person or "I" entries. Likewise, although there are various observations and reactions to specific world and personal events, with the exception of the note entitled "August 1945," none of the statements are explicitly associated with any date.

Canetti has used the word "*Aufzeichnungen*" (notes, jottings) as title and description of these four volumes. Although such a nonspecific word encompasses all entries adequately, many can be more precisely identified as aphorisms. The aphorisms are concise statements – ranging from one or two lines to no more than a page – articulating with terseness and effectiveness specific thoughts or principles. Aphorisms normally present a certain thesis, but without a conclusion, forcing the readers or listeners to continue thinking and thus to formulate answers or conclusions of their own.

The aphorism has not been a popular form of prose, yet there have been distinguished German and European writers who have used this genre with great success. Some forerunners to the German aphorists – and included in Canetti's reading – were the Elizabethan essayist Sir Francis Bacon, the Spanish Jesuit philosopher and writer Baltasar Gracian, and the French moralists of the seventeenth century Pascal and LaRochefoucauld. Among the German aphorists, Canetti mentions that Veza, his future wife, introduced him in the mid-1920s to Georg Christoph Lichtenberg, the first and most important writer of aphorisms. Later, in 1968, Canetti says of Lichtenberg that he "wrote the richest book in world literature" (*HP*, 240). Other German authors whose aphoristic writings Canetti found stimulating were Goethe, Schopenhauer, and Nietzsche, as well as Nestroy, Karl Kraus, and Robert Musil.

Perhaps Canetti already saw himself as a part of this literary tradition in 1943 when he wrote: "The great writers of aphorisms read as if they had all known each other very well" (*HP*, 34). Just over a decade later, in 1954, Canetti writes again about collections of aphorisms and asks which sentences should be written down. He begins by suggesting that "the sentences that confirm one" might be included since they could illustrate the "pure joy in meeting a truly congenial mind" (*HP*, 145), yet he warns that such association must be undertaken with the greatest caution. Other sentences, not of a personal nature, that should be included are those which are funny and those which arouse an image. Funny sentences, which appear with great regularity in Canetti's collection, are those that "amuse one with an unexpected turn of phrase or with terseness; as sentences they are new and have the freshness of new words" (*HP*, 145). Sentences that arouse images are of considerable interest to Canetti because they allow him to explicate long-considered but as yet unarticulated thoughts. Another sentence type that Canetti insists on including is one that puts the writer to shame by confronting him with a "sentence from the outside" that reveals a foible or shortcoming he has been unwilling to perceive in himself (*HP*, 146). Finally, he mentions "untouchable or sacred sentences" (*HP*, 146), which should not be included because they are of such magnitude that they should be reserved for a page or book all by themselves.

A first glance at the *Aufzeichnungen* offers a reading list of the scores of authors Canetti read and studied during the decades since he started keeping these notes. Any attempt to just list names and titles (there is no index) would be foolish because there is no evidence that Canetti commented on everything he read; quite the contrary should be assumed. Furthermore, even when Canetti makes a specific reference to a particular title or offers a quotation from an author, he gives no bibliographical information. Readers can pursue the task of coming to terms with this aspect of the *Aufzeichnungen* in two ways: they can answer the question of what Canetti is saying in all those entries, or they can search for the answer to why he has come to a particular conclusion as a result of his reading a specific author. Both ways offer a rich intellectual experience, but the latter might take a lifetime to complete. An entry from 1943 illustrates not only Canetti's intentions but also the enormity of the task for the reader. "My whole life is nothing but a desperate attempt to overcome the division of labor and think about everything myself, so that it comes together in a head and thus becomes one again" (*HP*, 34).

Canetti, however, is in no way arrogant enough to believe that it is possible for him to actually know everything. On the contrary, he is engaged in a constant battle with philosophers who establish elaborate systems that allege complete answers or solutions to specific issues. Three who have written extensively on the question of power – Thomas Hobbes, Joseph de Maistre, and Friedrich Nietzsche – become lifelong enemies to whom Canetti returned frequently throughout all those years, challenging their systems and confirming his own views rejecting the notion that there exists one or another desirable system to rule people.

The seventeenth-century political philosophy of Thomas Hobbes argues that people in their urge toward self-preservation create societies in which they contract with a temporal sovereign to provide for their protection and peace. The royalistic and ultramontane philosopher of the early nineteenth century Joseph de Maistre, on the other hand, developed the idea that the world should be one, ruled absolutely by the pope as spiritual ruler, with no temporal ruler having independent authority. And the German philosopher Friedrich Nietzsche condemned traditional morality as the code of the slavish masses and preached the superiority of the aristocrat, the morality of masters, in which a life by the might of its own superiority will survive. In none of his readings, whether philosophy, world history and religions, or mythology and anthropology, did Canetti find any evidence that these views offered any solution to the problem of establishing an agreeable and worthy – as well as humane – way for people to live in a society.

Two topics that evoke Canetti's ire over the years are psychology and history. Already in the mid-1920s he has a major confrontation with Freud's *Mass Psychology and Ego Analysis*, a book that he says in his autobiography "repelled me from the very first word and still repels me no less fifty-five years later" (*TE*, 147). In the mid-1940s he observes people who dwell on instincts and other people's drives, who cultivate and admire such characteristics: "it all reminds me of the loyalty in a club of criminals" (*HP*, 84). And the venom has not abated when Canetti, at age 80, notes: "The elimination of concepts becomes a necessity when one has heard them too often: expectorations of the mind. – That's how you feel these days about fetish, Oedipus, and other abominations" (*SH*, 132-33).

There is equal wrath and outrage when Canetti writes about historians and historiography. On almost the first page of *The Human Province* he says of history that it "strikes one as a fixated vendetta of the masses . . . and that is exactly what condemns history" (*HP*, 5). And not much later he writes: "I hate the respect of historians for Anything merely because it happened, their falsified, retrospective standards, their impotence, their kowtowing to any form of power" (*HP*, 24). He continues to accuse history of being a report on what happened to the stronger groups and of "consisting mainly of diabolical cruelty" (*HP*, 135). At a moment of great pessimism, Canetti observes the most ominous aspect of history when it records models: he is reminded that Caesar's Persian campaign was modeled on Alexander, just as Hitler's Russian battle plans were developed to surpass those of Napoleon. Canetti concludes these observations with the questions: "Who will imitate Hitler, who will emulate our other leaders? Whose children's children will die for this or that epigone?" (*HP*, 167).

It is Canetti's contention that history, like psychology, is essentially based on faulty premises that consequently propose and perpetuate unacceptable systems of thought. The only solution he offers to this dilemma are aphorisms that stimulate thought and consideration of the problem. Two examples are typical. In 1957 he wrote:

"There is no historian who does not praise Caesar for at least one thing: the fact that the French now speak French. As though they would be mute if Caesar had not killed a million of them!" (*HP*, 167). A quarter-century later, with his highly developed acerbic wit, he proposes "a historiography according to which the losers would have always been right" (*SH*, 90).

Despite the treatment of philosophers, psychologists, and historians, most of Canetti's notes and comments about writers are quite positive. During the first period, from 1942 to 1948, the number of authors mentioned is relatively small, but it increases enormously thereafter, and with each year the breadth of the reading expands. In the case of some writers whom Canetti admires greatly, entries abound, while the one or two notes devoted to other writers can undoubtedly be attributed to concurrent reading. It must be recalled that these *Aufzeichnungen* served not only as a "safety valve" while Canetti was writing *Crowds and Power*, but also are an adjunct to his essays and autobiographical writings. Consequently, to appreciate the full importance to Canetti that specific writers have had, one must bear in mind what he said about them elsewhere. For example, he acknowledges his debt to Kraus, Kafka, Musil, and Broch in his Nobel Prize acceptance speech and recognizes in his essays the importance that they and other writers had for him.

There are a few writers who appear to have been enormously important to Canetti throughout his life, and one almost wonders why he has not given them greater prominence. Three names provide examples: Stendhal, Dostoyevski, and Goethe. The French novelist Stendhal (1783-1842) first served as a model of masterful writing style when Canetti was writing his own novel. At a later date Canetti used Stendhal as an example of literary immortality in the brief, one-page chapter "Immortality" in *Crowds and Power*. Reflecting on Stendhal's autobiography *Henri Brulard*, Canetti is intrigued by Stendhal's ability to create models and antimodels and by his successful representation of "experiences of death, so true and powerful as to haunt the reader" (*HP*, 270). And in this same note from 1971 Canetti writes: "I owe Stendhal the conviction that every person – were he to succeed in getting himself fully down on paper – would be exciting and amazing and also irreplaceable" (*HP*, 271). This observation undoubtedly enhanced Canetti's courage to make out of every character sketch and every person in his autobiography a fine literary miniature. After numerous other entries, Canetti in 1985 writes a very personal note: "Stendhal is to be envied for many things. Most of all for his complete exposure after his death" (*SH*, 141). Canetti is clearly longing for a similar literary immortality.

The role the great Russian novelist Fyodor Dostoyevski (1821-81) plays in Canetti's life is interesting. Although *The Idiot* and *The Brothers Karamazov* are included in a list of books important to Canetti in the mid-1920s, the first entry in the notes comes as late as 1971, and it is not of any consequence. Then, in late 1980, it seems as if Canetti is making amends for his years of silence as he writes on Dostoyevski: "Minds that become the program of a life. Their impact is so tremendous that even after decades one doesn't dare to know them completely" (*SH*, 86). A year later, writing about the *Notes from the Underground*, Canetti asserts that this critical work about the solitary hero, the embittered clerk who as a nihilist discovers the dark and destructive attributes of man's rational and social pretenses, is "the root of how many things, down to the literature of our day!" (*SH*, 93). He calls Dostoyevski a "prophet of the underground. . . the first and most urgent one" (*SH*, 93). He observes that "self-degradation and self-vilification" are a hallmark of Dostoyevski's character and writing (*SH*, 93) and, on a later occasion, calls him "the poet whose art resides in his lack of detachment" (*SH*, 115). In the final pages of the notes, Canetti asserts that it is only through Dostoyevski that the works of Franz Kafka can continue to live – and it is well-known that Canetti considers Kafka to be one of the most significant writers of the twentieth century.

The Nobel Prize laudation began: "The exiled and cosmopolitan author Canetti has one native land and that is the German language. He has never abandoned it and he has often avowed his love of the highest manifestations of the classical German culture" ("Nobelpreis," 43). Consequently, it is not at all surprising that Canetti holds the greatest German writer, Johann Wolfgang von Goethe (1749-1832), in the highest esteem. Without reference to specific works Canetti read in his youth, his list of important books in the mid-1920s merely gives the name "Goethe," without elaboration. Throughout the autobiography the reader can find more than ample evidence, both direct and indirect, of the immense influence that Goethe had on Canetti. In the first volume of the *Aufzeichnungen*, Goethe is the first German author mentioned, and the last name given in the fourth volume is that of Goethe.

Canetti pays homage to Goethe as he does to almost no other writer. In 1943 he writes: "If, despite everything, I should survive, then I owe it to Goethe, such as one owes it only to a god. It is not one work, it is the mood and care of a full existence that suddenly overwhelmed me" (*HP*, 34). It should be remembered that this entry was written at the height of World War II, that Canetti had not written any major work in a decade, and that he had already devoted many years to his study of crowds and power with no clear understanding of when and how that work would be completed. But reading Goethe and observing the vastness and multiplicity of Goethe's life and works gave Canetti the courage to pursue his work. It freed him from any doubts he might have had, or that others may have suggested, that his research of "more and more areas of knowledge and thought" was of questionable value (*HP*, 35). Goethe freed him, as he writes, to proceed even with his interest in animals and his preference for reading myths. "Since I've been reading Goethe, everything I undertake strikes me as legitimate and natural . . . he gives me the right: Do what you have to, he says, even if it is nothing tumultuous; breathe, observe, reflect!" (*HP*, 35). And almost a quarter-century later Canetti once more meditates on Goethe and again concludes that his greatness "gives one the strength not of boldness but of persistence" to work and to live (*HP*, 236).

There are many other writers and books that Canetti considers in these *Aufzeichnungen*. Along with frequent references to the Bible and holy books from other religions, he surveys many cultures of the world and the myths of countless societies. Virtually all the names of classical literature appear along with the major philosophers of the Western world, yet he shows great interest in writings from the Eastern and Oriental world as well. The names range from the well-known (Shakespeare, Dante, Homer) to the obscure, such as a seventeenth-century English antiquary, John Aubrey, or a quotation from the "Essays on Idleness" written about 1340 by the Japanese poet and court official Yoshida Kenko.

Animals are mentioned in almost the same number as authors. Many of these entries are aphorisms, reminiscent of the medieval bestiaries. For example, "I would be relieved if just one bull would send those heroes, the toreadors, into a lamentable flight – a whole bloodthirsty arena, too. But I would prefer an uprising by the lesser, gentle victims, the sheep and cows. I won't admit that it can never happen; that we will never tremble before them, before them of all creatures" (*HP*, 115). On the distribution of power: "My greatest wish is to see a mouse devour a cat alive. But first she has to play with it long enough" (*HP*, 3). An apparent truth, slightly skewed: "When camels are sold to a stranger they get sick, out of disgust at the price" (*HP*, 151). In an animal utopia: "People stood humbly before the thrones of the animals, awaiting their judgment" (*HP*, 205). Or another view of utopia: "There everyone is ruled by an innate worm and takes care of him and is obedient" (*HP*, 205). Canetti also shows great concern for animals and humankind's absurd cruelty when he observes that a special 12-volume edition of 998 copies of the *Codex Atlanticus* is to be published: "For the leather cover, the skins of about twelve thousand cows are required, since each one is sufficient for only one volume" (*SH*, 9). And an indisputable truism: "When the parasite has sucked himself full of your blood, you let him go. You wouldn't lay hands on your own blood" (*SH*, 145). Finally, just two examples from a host of delightfully funny images that Canetti creates with his animals: "Fraternal kiss between octopuses" (*SH*, 64) and "A whale full of believers" (*SH*, 70). These brief stories and quips serve Canetti, and the reader, with momentary relief from the overwhelming seriousness of most notes and aphorisms. Canetti may have had the reader in mind when he wrote: "That is an aphorism, he says, and quickly shuts his mouth again" (*SH*, 10).

"I read *The Plowman of Bohemia* in school, and I have to read it again today" (*HP*, 244). This 1968 reference to the most important German book from the fifteenth century, written by Johann von Tepl (c. 1350-1414), illustrates Canetti's lifelong preoccupation with the subject of death. Already in the early pages of the autobiography he talks about death, and following the sudden death of his father in 1912 nothing seems to engage him so much as his father's death and the topic of death in general. Canetti's novel and dramas deal with death in one form or another; his study of crowds and power considers the question of death from a great variety of perspectives. And death is a central issue in the *Aufzeichnungen*, a topic of discussion coming up over and over again.

The Plowman of Bohemia is written in the form of a dialogue between a peasant, whose wife has just died, and Death. The sad and embittered peasant curses Death, but Death calmly explains (in 32 chapters) how God has ordained that it is each human being's destiny to die. When the peasant finally understands, he submits to the divine will and, in the last two chapters, God sets the seal of his approval on the final relationship between the two litigants, the peasant and Death. At the conclusion of the book, the peasant prays in submission for the salvation of his wife's soul.

Like the peasant, Canetti has engaged in a lifelong disputation with Death, but he has never accepted the notion of predestination or preordination. Canetti has consulted all the gods and religions of the world without finding an acceptable reason for Death to be triumphant over Man. He has examined all the systems but has discovered none that offers Death as a rational conclusion to life.

In one of the last entries of 1985, Canetti writes defiantly: "Here he stands, looking at Death. Death approaches him, he repels it. He will not do Death the honor of taking it into account. If he finally does break down in bewilderment – he didn't bow before Death. He called it by its name, he hated it, he cast it out. He has accomplished so little, it is more than nothing" (*SH*, 150).

This part of Canetti's oeuvre – the notes and aphorisms – is aptly described by the titles of the two final volumes: it is an examination of the condition of humankind – The Human Province – from a very personal point of view over a very long life – The Secret Heart of the Clock.

Chapter Six

In Search of Ancestors and Self

The Conscience of Words

In his reply to the encomium and bestowal of the Nobel Prize for Literature, Canetti acknowledges his indebtedness to four European writers: Karl Kraus, Franz Kafka, Robert Musil, and Hermann Broch. These four are not the only writers who influenced Elias Canetti, but they do represent major aspects of Canetti as writer and thinker. All were his senior by many years and all were intimately associated with Canetti's formative period – from age 19 to age 33 in Vienna (1924-38). The second and third volumes of his autobiography report extensively on this period, with the greatest detail devoted to his turbulent encounter with Kraus (1874-1936), which started just a few months after Canetti's arrival in Vienna. Canetti knew Kafka (1883-1924) only from his writings; records show that he met with Musil (1880-1942) only in 1933 and that their acquaintance was by no means personal; Broch (1886-1951), however, whom he met in 1932, seems to have served as a mentor for the young Canetti.

Kraus, whom Canetti calls "the greatest German satirist" is cited for teaching Canetti "to listen . . . to the sounds of Vienna," an endowment that would influence his lifelong style of writing – both literary and nonliterary ("Nobelpreis," 49). A second and more important gift from Kraus was that "he inoculated me against war, an inoculation which was at that time still necessary for many people." Canetti suggests that such instruction is no longer required in contemporary times because "since Hiroshima everyone knows what war is, and the fact that everyone knows it is our only hope." Kraus was Canetti's idol – both positive and negative – from whom he learned the power of the "acoustic mask," which not only plays such a dominant role in the early plays and the novel, but which also can be easily detected in the later autobiographical and essayistic writings. And Canetti's pacifism and preoccupation with crowds and

power were undoubtedly influenced and furthered by his reading
and attending Karl Kraus's lectures.

Franz Kafka "had the talent to transform himself into a small
being and thus withdraw from power" ("Nobelpreis," 49). Canetti's
first experience with Kafka's writings came while he was working on
Auto-da-Fé. He had finished only the first eight chapters when he
read *The Metamorphosis*. In the essay "The First Book," written
more than 40 years later, Canetti pays homage to his teacher:
"Nothing more fortunate could have happened to me at this point.
There, in utmost perfection, I found the antipode to literary non-
commitment, which I hated so much; there was the rigor that I
yearned for. There, something was achieved that I wanted to find for
myself. I bowed to this purest of all models, knowing full well that it
was unattainable, but it did give me strength" (*CW*, 211). Kafka was
to serve Canetti as a most important model in the effort to articulate
with great precision his struggle against power. "Kafka's Other Trial,
The Letters to Felice" is Canetti's longest and perhaps most poetic
essay, showing Kafka as the keenest observer of the conditions of
power in society. This essay alone could rank Canetti as one of the
great essayists of his time.

From Musil, whom "I had known during my Vienna years,"
Canetti learned "that one can undertake a task for decades without
knowing whether it can be completed, a recklessness made up primarily of a patience that presupposes an almost inhuman obstinacy"
("Nobelpreis," 49). Here Canetti is referring not only to Musil's
writing of the monumental novel *The Man without Qualities* but
also to his own lifelong attempt to understand this literary masterpiece. It is perhaps curious that Canetti has written no essay on
Musil, although he did devote one chapter of his autobiography to
this novelist.

"I was a friend of Hermann Broch," says Canetti ("Nobelpreis,"
49). He suggests that it was not Broch's work that influenced him,
but that he has been intrigued his whole life by one of Broch's special aptitudes: his "*Atem-Gedächtnis*" or "breath-memory." Canetti
first mentions this cryptic concept in the essay "Hermann Broch,
Speech for His Fiftieth Birthday, Vienna, November 1936" (*CW*, 1-
13). On that occasion, Canetti referred specifically to Broch's novella
"The Homecoming," a story that has only the briefest plot: a man ar-
rives in a small town, leaves the square in front of the train station,

and rents a room in the home of a widowed baroness and her daughter. The uniqueness of the novella is the way in which Broch had created a rare aura – or breath of air – in which each character and place has enclosed itself, not to isolate itself but to preserve its singularity. No person or place is subordinated to another; there is no power-play at work; there is only a true and productive equality. At the conclusion of the essay, Canetti submits that Broch's writings, although advocating pacifism, are nevertheless the work of a sober-minded and realistic thinker.

From a survey of the bibliography, it might be tempting to say that all of Canetti's essays are included in the volume *The Conscience of Words*, but that would actually be untrue. There are essays embedded in virtually all of his writings. One need only recall some of the sinological studies in *Auto-da-Fé* or the scores of portraits of people and societies that form the core of *Crowds and Power*. The three volumes of Canetti's autobiography are filled with remarkable essays on artists who had a major impact on his life and work. And the notes and aphorisms, published in *The Human Province* and *The Secret Heart of the Clock* and written over a period of more than four decades, include hundreds of sketches or short essays on persons, cultures, and countries. But in *The Conscience of Words*, Canetti's essays can be divided into three broad categories: (1) on the lives and works of writers who are important to him; (2) on issues of power; and (3) on himself as a writer and thinker – *Dichter und Denker*. Yet, if we were to attempt to classify these essays from the author's perspective, there would be but one common characteristic theme: Elias Canetti, a responsible writer and thinker on power, searching for his place. This study examines and discusses three representative essays.

"The Writer's Profession"

In 1976 the University of Munich conferred an honorary doctoral degree on Canetti. On that occasion he gave as a speech the essay "The Writer's Profession" (*CW*, 236-46), which serves well as a statement not only of Canetti's views on the responsibility of writers but also of personal disclosure and self-definition.

Canetti begins his essay by expressing irritation with those who claimed that the German word *Dichter* (author, writer, or poet) had

fallen into disrepute and that literature was dead. Indeed, he believes that there are people who call themselves "someone who
writes" (avoiding the label *Dichter*) who are in fact doing what a
Dichter has always done, namely writing serious and important
books for a world that is very much in need of such writing. Yet
Canetti immediately imposes his personal trademark on the *Dichter*
by insisting on two criteria: on the one hand, the *Dichter* must
"seriously doubt his right to be one" (*CW*, 237), while on the other,
he must be fully convinced of the necessity and the importance of
what he writes. "The man who does not see the state of the world
we are living in has scarcely anything to say about it" (*CW*, 237).
Canetti categorically rejects the idea that literature is dead but asks
what contribution writers can make to today's world.

As an example, Canetti cites the lamentation of an anonymous
writer, who, on 23 August 1939, one week prior to the start of World
War II, exclaimed, "But everything is over. If I were really a writer, I
would have to be able to prevent the war" (*CW*, 237). At first, Canetti
was inclined to see that statement as arrogance and vainglorious
bombast. On closer inspection, however, he noted that the statement carried the precise opposite meaning: this writer admits to
"complete failure" in preventing the war from commencing and, furthermore, assumes "responsibility" for the outcome of the war
before it has begun. "In his despair at what has to happen now, he
accuses himself" because he knows "the true bearers of the responsibility" (*CW*, 238). Canetti concludes that the anonymous writer
knew precisely what a *Dichter* "ought to be and the fact that he considered himself one until the moment, when, with the outbreak of
war, everything collapsed for him" (*CW*, 238). Indeed, this may seem
like an "irrational claim to responsibility" (*CW*, 238), but not for the
Dichter who is committed to use the power of words. Canetti proposes the dilemma: "If words can do so much" to bring about war,
" – why cannot words hinder it?" (*CW*, 238-39).

The *Dichter*, Canetti continues, is someone who must have great
trust in words, using them with candor and skill, with passion and
reverence. Occasionally the *Dichter* may not even be fully cognizant
of what he is saying with his words, while at other times his words
have a power that can destroy him. Nevertheless, the *Dichter* must
defend everything that his words have said and be responsible for
the failure of each word used. If the writer seeks credence he must

take the initiative for "fictive responsibility" (*CW*, 239), rather than wait until others request his leadership, because, as Canetti has stated numerous times, it is a responsibility that the *Dichter* cannot abdicate even when he anticipates total failure. In the final analysis, Canetti demands that the significant writers, "the authors of the essential works of mankind" (*CW*, 240), are truly only those who have provided "an awareness of what constitutes mankind" (*CW*, 240). From them we receive "our daily bread; we are nourished and carried by them" (*CW*, 240).

Canetti introduces the most important attribute of the *Dichter* with a term he has used frequently in his writings on the role and function of the writer: the word *metamorphosis*. In this essay, he maintains that the writer's most important task is to be "the keeper of metamorphosis" (*CW*, 240). He understands this in a twofold sense: one, "he will make mankind's literary heritage . . . his own" (*CW*, 240), and two, he will "keep practicing the gift of metamorphosis" (*CW*, 242).

The first notion of metamorphosis – the making of all literatures his own – truly reflects Canetti's lifelong passion for reading not only all the major works of world literature but also the myths told by large and small tribes from around the world. Here he limits himself in his examples of metamorphoses from world literature to three: (1) from Roman literature, Ovid's *Metamorphoses* (c. A.D. 2-8), (2) from Greek literature, Homer's *Odyssey* (c. eighth century B.C.), and (3) from Assyro-Babylonian literature, the *Gilgamesh* epic (perhaps composed during the third millennium B.C.).

Ovid, in his poem of the *Metamorphoses*, attempts to provide a chronological account of the metamorphoses of human beings and inanimate objects from the beginning of creation through the deification of Julius Caesar in the fourth decade B.C. Each of the 246 stories, most of which are myths, ends with a metamorphosis; "an almost systematic collection of all the known, mythical, 'higher' metamorphoses" (*CW*, 240). Canetti identifies Homer's *Odyssey* as an "adventurous metamorphoses." In this epic, the protagonist, who had suggested building the huge wooden horse that led to the defeat of the Trojans and the freeing of Helen, must wander for 10 years before he comes home to Ithaca. When eventually he returns to his kingdom, he must perform a final metamorphosis in which he has to kill his wife's suitors before he can reveal his identity to Penelope.

Canetti notes that these two works have had a legendary impact on European literature and culture since long before the Renaissance.

Canetti acknowledges that the Mesopotamian *Gilgamesh* epic has played a most significant role in his life as a reader and writer. It was as a 17-year-old in Frankfurt that he heard Carl Ebert read from the *Gilgamesh*. "No work of literature, literally none, has so decisively determined my life as this epic, which is four thousand years old and, until one hundred years ago, was unknown" (*CW*, 241). He continues and admits that not only has he read this work with great regularity since then but the fact that such a significant literary work had been discovered after millennia filled him "with expectation for things still unknown to us" (*CW*, 241). Such a confession certainly reveals Canetti's endeavor to make all literature his own, including any work still to be discovered.

The *Gilgamesh* epic demonstrates two issues of major importance to Canetti: a metamorphosis and a confrontation with death. In the long and complex narrative, the character of Gilgamesh may retain the same outward features throughout the story, but as he tries to establish a name for himself he must undergo a process of individuation that demands physical, emotional, and spiritual preparation for an initiating encounter with Humbaba, the demonic guardian of the cedar forest. Gilgamesh endures even greater metamorphoses in the second half of the epic when, having lost his friend and brother Enkidu, he must pass through stages of melancholia and self-dissolution, emerging a profound and mature human being. Enkidu, on the other hand, represents continual metamorphosis. This is the story of Enkidu's birth, his initial development in the wilderness, his gradual reception into the life of civilization, his courageous acts, and his death. In what is certainly the most stirring death scene in all of ancient literature, Gilgamesh eulogizes Enkidu and in deep grief sets off on a long search, insisting that there must be some ultimate meaning in the death of his friend. The unknown author of the *Gilgamesh* epic has met the most basic and important requirement Canetti has established for the writer by providing "an awareness of what constitutes mankind" (*CW*, 240).

During the long years Canetti worked on *Crowds and Power* he discovered another form of metamorphosis in the hundreds of myths he examined from tribes around the world. He chides those who have brought about the demise of cultures that had such rich oral traditions perpetuating myths, "an inexhaustible spiritual legacy" (*CW*, 241). Nonetheless, Canetti is grateful that scholarship has recorded and preserved so many examples of "mythical experiences" (*CW*, 241). Yet, in the final analysis "its true preservation, its resurrection to our life" is the task of the *Dichter* (*CW*, 241).

The second notion of metamorphosis describes the relationship that the *Dichter* must have with the world. "He should be able to become anybody and everybody, even the smallest, the most naive, the most powerless person" (*CW*, 242). The way in which that process of metamorphosis is accomplished is by "experiencing others from the inside" (*CW*, 242), by understanding precisely the full meaning of the discourse of others. Canetti suggests that although some people have used the word "empathy" to describe this process, he prefers the word *metamorphosis* to define the mysterious way in which the *Dichter* will approach another human being (*CW*, 242). Unlike those in our society whose goal orientation requires ever greater specialization for success, Canetti sees the *Dichter* as someone who seeks to understand not only all manner of people but also the "inner structure of every branch of knowledge" for no predetermined purpose whatsoever (*CW*, 243). The acquisition of everything will, of course, create a state of chaos in the mind of the writer similar to the chaos the writer perceives in the world; from this follows the responsibility to conquer it for others as well as for him- or herself, because the writer abhors chaos.

The two metamorphoses – the one acquired from literature, the other from keen observations of people – now combine in the *Dichter*, who can create characters and myths. Working within such a strictly delimited framework, Canetti concludes that it will provide the writer with "the feeling of certainty and incontestability, that was what it was, that was the only thing it could be" (*CW*, 244).

Canetti concludes the essay – and articulates his lifelong aspiration to be a writer – by recalling that the *Dichter* is a person who feels compassionately responsible for life. Through metamorphosis, the writer brings into being new myths that reflect the writer's own times and give him or her "the strength to oppose death" (*CW*, 245), in this way creating a work with universal validity. Canetti formulates all this into a law for the *Dichter*. "One shall repulse nobody into nothingness who would like to be there. One shall seek nothingness only to find a way out of it and one shall mark the road for everyone.

Whether in grief or in despair, one shall endure in order to learn how to save others from it, but not out of scorn for the happiness that the creatures deserve, even though they deface one another and tear one another to pieces" (CW, 246).

"Dr. Hachiya's Diary of Hiroshima"

In 1971 Canetti wrote two essays that related directly to World War II: "Hitler, According to Speer" and "Dr. Hachiya's Diary of Hiroshima" (CW, 184-91). The former had been prompted by the publication of Albert Speer's Memoirs.[1] Speer had served for many years as Hitler's personal architect and, for the last three years of the war, as minister for armaments and munitions. His Memoirs were published after he had served a 20-year sentence for major war crimes. Canetti's essay, however, concentrates primarily on Speer's effort as an architect to realize Hitler's paranoic visions through the building of monumental structures. In this essay, Canetti directly applies to Hitler his views on crowds and power; indeed, the essay could easily have served as another chapter in the section on "Rulers and Paranoiacs" of Crowds and Power.

"Dr. Hachiya's Diary of Hiroshima" is a very different essay. If Karl Kraus inoculated Canetti against war, as he said in his Nobel Prize speech, this essay may be Canetti's endeavor to do the same for his readers. Canetti may have thought that "since Hiroshima everyone knows what war is, and the fact that everyone knows it is our only hope," but this essay assures that everyone will know what Hiroshima really is.

The essay is based on Canetti's reading of the diary of Michihiko Hachiya, the director of a hospital in Hiroshima, a medical doctor, and a patient.[2] Hachiya's diary begins on 6 August 1945 (the day the atomic bomb was dropped on the city) and continues to 30 September of that year. Canetti says "it is written like a work of Japanese literature: precision, tenderness, and responsibility are its essential features" (CW, 184). Exactly the same qualities hold for Canetti's writing style in this essay. From his autobiography, it is known that Canetti has been reading the classics of Japanese literature since his student days in Vienna, but it is only now, a half-century later and after reading Dr. Hachiya's diary, that Canetti feels he really knows the Japanese.

Without introduction or indication of whether the author of the diary is being quoted, Canetti offers, in a typically Japanese style reminiscent of haiku, a series of short but poetic phrases describing Hiroshima during the first few hours and days after the atomic bomb fell.

"The melted faces of Hiroshima, the thirst of the blind."
    "A cadaver on a bicycle."
    "At night, the only illumination: the fires of the city, blazing corpses."
    "The stillness, the figures moving soundlessly, it is like a silent film."
    "The visits to the patients in the hospital: the first reports on the events, the annihilation of Hiroshima." (*CW*, 184)

Canetti establishes the entire timbre of his essay with these finely honed and sharply focused phrases. But he includes a perplexing question at the end of this opening: "The city of the forty-seven ronins; was that why it was picked?" (*CW*, 184). Canetti's typically Western readers must seek their own clarification, for he neither explains who the forty-seven ronins are nor describes the role they play in Japanese history and literature. Knowledge of this story is essential to understanding the personality of Dr. Hachiya, as well as the Japanese and their traditional relationship to their Emperor, an important aspect of Canetti's essay.

In Japanese feudal times, the ronins were masterless samurai who assumed the role of knight errant or soldier of fortune during periods of war. The story of the 47 ronins was greatly popularized by Chikamatsu (1653-1724), sometimes referred to as the Shakespeare of Japan. The play tells of a feudal lord who had fallen into disgrace and was compelled to commit suicide and to forfeit his property. Forty-seven followers, now ronins, were obligated to avenge him and assassinated the man responsible for his downfall. Although their loyalty was greatly admired, their code demanded that they all commit suicide.[3]

Canetti introduces Dr. Hachiya as a "modern doctor," a description of a profession easily understood. He is, however, also described as a person "so Japanese that he believes steadfastly in the Emperor, even when the latter announces the capitulation" (*CW*, 184) (an event that occurred 10 days after the bombing). The Emperor's surrender speech is broadcast to the Japanese people in an incomprehensible "archaic language of the court" (*CW*, 188) that must be translated and certified as the Emperor's by the few who recognize his voice and understand the proclamation.

In Japanese tradition, everyone at Dr. Hachiya's hospital bows "at the mention of the imperial name" (*CW*, 188). It is clear to these listeners that the militants had started the war, not their Emperor, whom they still celebrate as the imperial divinity. Because of their reverence for the Emperor and given his repudiation of the war, the people accept their defeat. Yet, Canetti observes in Dr. Hachiya's diary, there are nevertheless two groups of people who emerge in this time of hopelessness and uncertainty: those who favor continuing the war and those who oppose it.

In this double crowd of the defeated, those who favored continuance of the war faced great opposition because they were seen as contradicting the Emperor's orders. The officers of the militaristic government who had ruled as totalitarians for years not only had brought defeat but – much more importantly – they had humiliated the Emperor. As believers and subjects of the imperial divinity, the people, too, were humiliated. They now had to accept the idea that their enemy was not a hostile foreigner, but some in their own midst. Had the story of the 47 ronins come true? Was the Emperor so disgraced that he would have to forfeit his life, his lands, and his loyal servants? Such a fate for the Emperor is totally unacceptable to Dr. Hachiya and the people because their "continuity of life depends on his continuity" (*CW*, 189). For Canetti, this surely serves as another example of a people perpetuating one of their most basic and powerful myths.

Canetti also observes in this diary the dominant topic of life and death. Other accounts and records of Hiroshima reveal that half the population perished within the first few weeks of the attack. Canetti, however, cites only one example of mass destruction: Dr. Hachiya attempts to compare Hiroshima to the ancient city of Pompeii, buried by a volcanic eruption, a terrible act of nature. But for Canetti, the bombing of Hiroshima was "the most concentrated disaster that ever broke in on human beings" because it was "a catastrophe that was carefully calculated by human beings and perpetrated by them" (*CW*, 185). Of all the massive abuses of power cited in *Crowds and Power*, none receives Canetti's wrath and outrage as does this one.

The great power of the essay, however, is in its treatment of the life and death of unnamed individuals immediately following the bombing. At the very outset of the diary, Dr. Hachiya writes of the peoples' initial encounters – "You're alive? You're alive?" (*CW*, 184) – and wonders how often he has to hear those cries. Dr. Hachiya plays a dual role as a "physician with forty wounds" (*CW*, 184), often comparing his own condition to that of his dying patients. Although trained as physician and scientist, he knows of no way to treat them; a week passes after the catastrophe before he even learns – from a visitor to the city – that an atomic bomb had fallen. No one knew what had happened. They spoke only of the "*pikadon*," a word that described what they had experienced: *pika* refers to the intensely shining light and *don* to the terrible sound heard from a distance. Only later did the word *pikadon* assume the meaning of atomic bomb. Dr. Hachiya even records the reaction of a man who observed the cloud from a greater distance; he was "overwhelmed by its beauty: the colorful glow, the sharp edges, the straight lines spreading out into the sky" (*CW*, 186).

Of all the cases of life and death, one is especially poignant. A hospital patient had escaped his burning home but was unable to rescue his wife. Well enough to return, he finds bones on the spot where he last saw her, and he takes them to the hospital altar. When he has recovered sufficiently to travel a greater distance, he takes the bones to the country where his wife's family lives. Upon arrival, he finds his wife alive and well, living with her family; she had managed to escape the burning home. Canetti, without adding further information, is overwhelmed by this account, which he calls "more than survival, it is a return from the dead, the most powerful and most wonderful experience that human beings can possibly have" (*CW*, 187).

The closing section of the essay fully demonstrates Canetti's concept of the *Dichter:* a person who feels responsible for life and does so with compassion. He has portrayed Dr. Hachiya as a man of science, but also as a man who upholds the traditions of his country. Although thoroughly accustomed to experiencing death in his professional life, he still venerates each new death. On a memorial day, seven weeks after the calamity, Dr. Hachiya sought out "every place that is hallowed by the dead, his own and also those whom he has learned about" (*CW*, 190), and he prayed for these dead. Canetti wonders whether there were equally generous people praying for the dead in the European cities ravaged by the war. With this essay

Canetti has satisfied his requirements for the *Dichter* to attain a universal reality. He has created a new myth through the metamorphosis of the compassionate Japanese doctor. More important, however, by asking his European and Western readers to pray for their dead, Canetti wants them to experience the same compassion and a similar metamorphosis.

"Kafka's Other Trial: The Letters to Felice"

The writings of Franz Kafka have nourished Canetti and served him as lifelong companions. He first encountered Kafka's writings while he was still in the early stages of writing *Auto-da-Fé*. Throughout the years, Canetti has reflected on Kafka and his writings; there are scores of references and entries in the autobiographical and aphoristic writings. A 1947 entry from Canetti's collected aphorisms can serve as an introduction and fitting eulogy to Kafka: "Kafka truly lacks any writer's vanity, he never boasts, he cannot boast. He sees himself as small and proceeds in small paces. Wherever he sets his foot, he senses the uncertainty of the ground. . . . One has to walk the small paces with him and one becomes modest. There is nothing in modern literature that makes one this modest. He reduces the swelled head of every life. One turns good when reading him, but without being proud of it" (*HP*, 98).

Canetti's affinity for Kafka found its most forceful and passionate expression in the major 1968 essay, "Kafka's Other Trial: The Letters to Felice" (*CW*, 60-139). The stimulus for the essay was the publication in 1967 of the letters Kafka had written to Felice Bauer between 1912 and 1917,[4] perhaps the most creative but also the most tormenting and turbulent period in Kafka's life.[5]

Records for 1912-17 show what Kafka wrote: "The Judgement," "The Metamorphosis," "In the Penal Colony," the 14 stories collected in *A Country Doctor*, "The Hunter Gracchus," "The Great Wall of China," the story of "The Stoker" (which later became the first chapter of *Amerika*), and, most important, a substantial part of one of Kafka's major novels, *The Trial*. What the records did not show prior to the publication of the letters to Felice Bauer was the agony Kafka experienced during those five years. The source of much of his distress, Felice previously had been identified only by the letter *F* in Kafka's writings, as well as in the secondary literature.

Canetti's essay is divided into two parts, the first concentrating more on Kafka's life and his writings between the fall of 1912 and the summer of 1914, and the second dealing with the period from then until Kafka breaks his second engagement to Felice in late December 1917. Since there are fewer letters from the second period – they make up less than 20 percent of the correspondence – Canetti draws on other documents to fill in his portrayal of Kafka's life. Additionally, the second part of the essay offers more of an interpretation of Kafka's writings, presenting him as "the greatest expert on power" (*CW*, 111).

Kafka met Felice on 13 August 1912 at a dinner party in the home of Max Brod's father in Prague. At that time, Felice worked as an executive secretary in a Berlin firm and was now en route to Budapest. Five weeks after that first meeting, on 20 September, Kafka began corresponding with her. Unfortunately, her letters to him seem to have been lost, but there are ample references to Felice's writing in Kafka's letters, so it is possible to infer the views she expressed. Included in the volume of letters are some letters from Kafka to Grete Bloch, Felice's friend, and a few other letters directly associated with Kafka's relationship to Felice. To appreciate the enormity of time and energy Kafka expended on these letters (the volume is some 750 pages), one must note that there were times, sometimes months, when Kafka did not write to Felice at all, while at other times he would write two and even three 20- to 30-page letters on a single day.

The outward facts of Kafka's relationship with Felice Bauer are easily summarized. In late summer 1912 they meet and begin to correspond shortly thereafter. In March 1913 Kafka goes to Berlin for a first meeting with Felice since their introduction and returns for a two-day visit in early May. They discuss marriage, about which Kafka has great doubts, but by mid-June, Kafka has proposed to Felice by letter. For the remainder of the year, Felice rarely responds when Kafka writes and he even suspends corresponding with her for about a month. Then, on 1 November, Kafka meets Grete Bloch, who has come to Prague to speak to him on behalf of her friend Felice. Ten days later the correspondence with Grete begins; it will continue for several years.

In early January 1914, Kafka writes to renew his request for Felice's hand in marriage, and she responds evasively. They meet in

Berlin in March, where Felice offers various arguments against their marriage. Kafka returns at Easter time, in mid-April, and they unofficially announce their engagement, with plans to marry in September. The engagement is announced officially at a reception at the Bauers' home in Berlin on 1 June. In the next few weeks, Kafka suffers from a profound existential crisis, agonizing particularly about his obligations to his writing and the impact that Felice might have on his work. He writes to Grete Bloch, outlining his qualms about Felice and the impending marriage. Grete shares this information with Felice. Six weeks after the official announcement, when Kafka returns to Berlin on 12 July, the two women confront him with his statements and the engagement is broken.

For the next three years, from summer 1914 to summer 1917, the records show that Kafka and Felice met once or twice a year at various spas and vacation resorts. Following a meeting in July 1916 in Marienbad, Kafka drew up a list of reasons for and against marriage. One year later, however, Felice visits him in Marienbad and they announce their engagement for a second time. This engagement, too, was to be short-lived. After a period of hemorrhaging in 1917, Kafka is diagnosed with tuberculosis, the cause of his death not quite seven years later. When Felice comes to Prague in late December 1917, the second engagement is broken. There is no evidence that Kafka and Felice saw or corresponded with each other again.[6]

Having lived with Kafka's writings for so many years, Canetti was now motivated to write this essay after reading the letters, and it is clear that he followed the guidelines he articulated in "The Writer's Profession." His understanding of Kafka is based on almost four decades of intensive reading, not only of everything that Kafka wrote but also a great deal of what friends and critics had written about him. Canetti, however, does not prepare the traditional scholarly essay; rather, he attempts to understand the letters as "testimonies of existence" (*CW*, 61) that will allow him to understand Kafka in a new and more profound way. He recalls that Kafka found sustenance in the letters of his literary forefathers, Kleist, Flaubert, Hebbel, and Grillparzer, and he looks upon Kafka as one of his own important and powerful predecessors. Canetti acknowledges that "most people, luckily, are aware of the horror of life only sometimes; a mere few, however, appointed as witnesses by internal forces, are always aware of it. And there is only one comfort for that horror of life: aligning it with the horror of preceding witnesses" (*CW*, 60-61).

In this essay, Canetti's style is quite similar to that which he used in other essays dealing with literary documents; indeed, it is similar even to *Crowds and Power*. He begins his portrait of Kafka with an examination of the letters to Felice as well as the literary works, diaries, and other notes that relate to that time. To all this Canetti adds his understanding of the complete works of Kafka, establishing the significance of the specific to the whole. Finally, he includes a study of the time period under consideration to show that he is examining both the afflictions of the individual and the disorder of a time. As an example of this style and synthesis, Canetti observes that there is a direct relationship between Kafka and Felice's dissolution of their first engagement in July 1914, the beginning of Kafka's work on *The Trial*, and the outbreak of World War I only a few weeks thereafter. The successful integration of all these elements is, according to Canetti, the hallmark of a great writer.

> The man who believes that it is given to him to separate his inner world from the outer world has absolutely no inner world from which anything could be separated. But with Kafka, the weakness he suffered from, the intermittent halting of his vital energy, permitted him to focus on and objectivize his "private" events only very sporadically. To achieve the continuity that he regarded as crucial, two things were necessary. One was a very powerful but yet somehow false shock like that "trial," which would mobilize his torments of precision for a defence against the outside world. The other was a linking of the external hell of the world with his inner one." (*CW*, 99-100)

And now Canetti sets out to establish and describe that link between Kafka's inner and outer world with rigor and magnanimity.

The first half of the essay portrays the personality of Franz Kafka from the day he met Felice Bauer until their first engagement was broken off. Without citing specific sources, Canetti draws a picture of the evening they met. The meeting was rather fortuitous. Kafka was at the Brod family home to discuss some final details of the manuscript of short prose pieces that were to make up *Betrachtungen* (Meditations), his first published volume. Felice had stopped in Prague for the evening to visit the family. In addition to talking about the manuscript, they looked at some photographs of a trip that Max

Brod and Kafka had taken a month earlier, and they talked about a
trip to Palestine that Kafka planned for the next year. At the conclusion of the evening, Brod's father and Kafka walked Felice to her
hotel. All in all, for the average person, an average evening. But not
for Franz Kafka.

The callous or cynical reader of the first few pages of Canetti's
essay – or for that matter, of Kafka's letters and diary entries from
the period – might be inclined to see Kafka as merely a smitten and
immature young man in love to the point of distraction. And in a
way, that is true. Canetti even reminds the reader that "any life that
one knows well enough is ludicrous" (*CW*, 128). But he continues
and maintains that "when one knows it [this life] even better, it becomes serious and dreadful" (*CW*, 128). Indeed, in the early days of
the relationship with Felice, Kafka lost his heart as many others have
in youthful romances. Yet, he simultaneously analyzes every aspect
and possible consequence of his relationship with Felice Bauer. And
it is this "serious and dreadful" dimension of Kafka's life that Canetti
delineates in this essay.

The episode of the photographs exemplifies Canetti's story-
telling technique. The photographs handed around the dinner table
that evening are the basis of a rather convoluted account that foretells much of the conflict that Kafka and Felice will experience. These
pictures were taken while Kafka and Max Brod were in Weimar in
July 1912, a trip they referred to as their "Thalian journey" in honor
of Goethe and Schiller (*CW*, 62). It seems that Kafka had befriended
"a beautiful girl," the daughter of the custodian of the Goethe
house. He had also become acquainted with her parents and was
able to visit the house frequently and not only during normal visiting
hours. He had taken several photos of her in the gardens of the
house, and he often saw her in the small town, usually in the company of young students. On one occasion, Kafka made an appoint-
ment to see her, but she did not show up, leaving him to conclude
that she preferred the company of students. After he left Weimar they
exchanged a few postcards, and Kafka even included the content of
one of her cards in a letter he wrote to Brod. In that same letter
Kafka posed the following prophetic question: "For if I am not disagreeable to her, I am still as unimportant to her as a pot. But then
why does she write just as I want her to? Could it be that one can
bind a girl by writing?" (*CW*, 62).

Canetti has recreated this episode from a variety of sources. The first hint of the event is a portion of only one sentence in the first letter Kafka wrote to Felice: he identifies himself as "the one who handed you across the table, one by one, photographs of a Thalia trip" (*Felice*, 43). From this short reference, Canetti goes on to find further discussions of the trip in the Kafka-Brod correspondence and in various diary entries and notes Kafka made at the time. All these sources come together to make up a vignette that not only describes the event but also contains the core of the entire story.

There is considerable importance for Canetti in the facts that Kafka's trip took him to the city of Weimar and that it was called the "Thalian journey." Kafka had journeyed to the great center of German literature and paid tribute to the titans of German classicism. Furthermore, by assigning to the journey the name of one of the muses, there is the implication that this was a voyage where Kafka was to receive creative inspiration from the goddess. Consequently, the photographs serve as evidence that the aspiring young writer had completed the journeyman's tour and was now ready to establish himself as a master. Evidence of this accomplishment is, of course, the manuscript that Kafka had brought with him that evening.

The "beautiful girl" in the photographs becomes Felice. Canetti will gradually transform the daughter of the custodian in the home of the great writer into the woman Kafka wants as a wife. This is an example of Canetti's portrayal of metamorphosis, which he sees as the essential core of the development of literary characters. And just as the young girl in Weimar is an unreliable friend who prefers the company of students, so Felice will be as she favors writers whom Kafka considers greatly inferior. The exchange of postcards following Kafka's departure from Weimar parallels his correspondence with Felice.

The inclusion of the quotation from another source, here the Kafka-Brod correspondence, is a device Canetti uses with frequency throughout his essays. The purpose is twofold: on the one hand, it offers information and plot to tell the story, but on the other, it serves to anticipate the major issues and themes to be developed. By quoting just these few seemingly unimportant lines about the girl in Weimar, Canetti introduces the entire dilemma of Kafka's relationship with Felice. The statement begins with the double negative – "not disagreeable" – that Kafka seems to use whenever he refers to himself. It is followed by an even stronger deprecatory remark – "as unimportant . . . as a pot." Canetti will show in the essay that this manner of negative self-description, of humiliating himself and taking on the image of a lowly thing or animal, is actually a device that makes Kafka an expert on power. He reserves unto himself the freedom to identify himself, rather than giving others the power to humiliate him. Kafka's meeting the girl in Weimar is just as coincidental as his meeting Felice. Likewise, he will pursue Felice even when she shows little passion in return, and, indeed, even when she exhibits real antipathy toward him. The comment about writing is, of course, the major aspect of the stormy five-year relationship. Felice will learn to be and to write as Kafka wishes, but the essay shows that all will be tormentingly and catastrophically unsuccessful.

At first glance, the first letter that Kafka wrote to Felice is innocuous, especially if read only from Felice's perspective and without reference to all the documents that Canetti uses to posit the letter as a central event in Kafka's life. But Canetti finds evidence in the first two paragraphs forecasting Kafka's passion for Felice. Kafka reminds Felice that they had shaken hands in a promise to travel together to Palestine the following year. Canetti interprets the promise in the following way: the handshake is understood "as a *Gelöbnis*" (pledge) (*CW*, 62), a word that is semantically and etymologically closely related to "the word *Verlobung*" (betrothal) (*CW*, 62). He then associates the word *Verlobung* with Kafka's strong desire to travel to Palestine, which he perceives to be "the promised (*gelobte*) land" (*CW*, 62). Thus, concentrating on only three words, Canetti highlights Kafka's initial amativeness – a personal and emotional response – and his intellectual curiosity – a practical matter that could easily be accomplished with Felice's help.

Canetti does not mention every diary entry or each letter Kafka wrote to Felice, but he examines all the material with such care that there emerges a double portrait of Franz Kafka: one, the individual trying to come to terms with his personal life and his relationship to Felice Bauer, and two, the writer demonstrating in his works of fiction the agony of that personal life. Of course, the more the reader of Canetti's essay knows about Kafka's life and work, especially about the novel *The Trial*, the more informative and enjoyable the essay is. But Canetti's style of writing – one is tempted to say his style of story-telling – is so instructive and inclusive that even the reader who knows little about the topic will easily understand the essay.

There is, however, another aspect of the essay on Kafka that is most intriguing: the uncanny parallel between the portrayal of Kafka and the character of the book man Peter Kien in *Auto-da-Fé*. A review of the chronology discloses immediately that Canetti's novel was written at least a half dozen years before any biographical information on Kafka might have been available. Furthermore, the letters to Felice only became available in 1967, a good 35 years after Canetti wrote his novel. Consequently, it is impossible to suggest that Kafka's life served as a model for the character of Peter Kien. Another conclusion is equally impossible. Canetti in no way manipulated the materials on Kafka's life and works when he wrote his essay in 1968. Indeed, both Kafka and Kien were recluses who had dedicated their lives to writing: Kafka sought refuge in work at night and in total seclusion. In the often-quoted letter of 14-15 January 1913, he describes his ideal to Felice:

> Once you said that you wanted to sit near me while I write; you must realize I couldn't write in that case. . . . Writing means opening oneself to an excessive degree. . . . That is why one cannot be too alone when one is writing, that is why it cannot be quiet enough when one is writing, the night is insufficiently night. That is why one doesn't have enough time, for the roads are long, and one easily goes astray. . . . I have often thought that the best life for me would be with paper and pen and a lamp inside the innermost room of a vast, locked cellar. Food would be brought and placed far from my own room behind the outermost door of the cellar. The walk to the food, in my housecoat, through all the cellar vaults, would be my sole promenade. I would return to my table, eat slowly and deliberately, and then resume writing immediately. What things I would then write! From what depths would I tear it out! (*CW*, 83-84)

But Kien is just like Kafka. Kien's ideal is to be locked in his study on the top floor of his apartment house, where all the walls are lined with books and light comes only through skylights he installed when he had the windows bricked over, and where the housekeeper brings the meals that he eats alone while continuing his work. The only real difference between the two is that Kafka did write, while there is no evidence that Kien ever produced anything.

Another example of the similarities between Kien and Kafka is their interest in Chinese writings. Kien is the world's expert in sino-

logical studies and owner of the largest library on that topic in the
entire city. Canetti found the first example of Kafka's predilection for
Chinese poetry and nocturnal work in a letter dated 24 November
1912, written while Kafka was in the midst of work on *The Metamorphosis*. Felice apparently had told him that she had written him a letter while in bed one night. He replied that "she should leave the
nocturnal writing to him" (*CW*, 83) and continued with the poem "In
the Dead of Night" by the popular eighteenth-century Chinese writer
Yüan Tzu-tsai. This poem, one of Kafka's favorites, tells how a
"scholar, pouring over his book, forgets to go to bed. His mistress,
making a great effort to control her anger, finally grabs away his lamp
and asks: 'Do you know what time it is?' " (*CW*, 83). And Kafka also
reports to Felice "that night work belongs to men everywhere, even
in China" (*CW*, 83), implying quite directly that she, or for that matter any woman, is not suited for nocturnal creative work.

The similarities between *Auto-da-Fé* and the essay can even be
seen in the character of Therese and Felice Bauer. Both are uncom-
plicated persons with little interest in literature, except perhaps for
its commercial value. Therese is initially charged to dust the books;
eventually she pawns them. Felice's function in Kafka's letters, as he
sees it, is merely to be someone with whom he can conduct a
"dialogue with himself" (*CW*, 68). Felice is also known as Kafka's
"dearest businesswoman" (*CW*, 60), who eventually sells his letters.

There are other similarities between Kafka and Canetti's novel. A
careful scrutiny of the sources available to Canetti at the time he
wrote the essay demonstrates without a doubt that he was scrupu-
lously fair in his representation of Franz Kafka. The only explanation
for the similarities between the two works is that Canetti was particularly attracted to this period in Kafka's life because it was analogous
to his fictional character.

In the first part of his essay, Canetti describes in the greatest
detail how Kafka's relationship with Felice Bauer developed from the
time of their first meeting until they broke their engagement some
two years later. He tells the story primarily from Kafka's perspective
because, on the one hand, only Kafka's letters have been preserved,
and, on the other hand, he is interested in showing how the personal experiences – the "other trial" – become the direct and
immediate source for the novel *The Trial*.

Canetti demonstrates how Kafka's experiences during the engagement were transformed into the episode of the arrest of Josef K. in the first chapter of *The Trial* while the subsequent meeting with Felice and Grete became the basis of the execution in the last chapter. The records show that Kafka wrote these two chapters starting in August 1914, a few months after these events. Canetti adds a third trial to Kafka's personal and novelistic trials when he observes that at precisely the same time Europe was experiencing the tormenting events that led to the commencement of World War I. Here is the merger of Kafka's inner and outer world, "linking . . . the external hell of the world with his inner one" (*CW*, 100).

The purpose of Canetti's work, in the final analysis, is not just to present a traditional biography or an interpretation of the novel – although these are important – but to articulate the manner in which Kafka the writer and the protagonist of his novel, Josef K., serve as models of power. Canetti will demonstrate that in spite of the misfortunes the writer and his character experience, their particular behavior will bring about a unique form of survival. This will be perhaps the only possible way of sustaining life that Canetti can perceive for the modern world.

To introduce his study of *The Trial*, Canetti extracts several salient issues from each of the three parts that make up the first chapter of the novel. The bizarre "Arrest" to which Josef K. is subjected on that "one fine morning" contains numerous important elements. Even though the initial encounter with the strangers who have come for Josef K. takes place in his bedroom, they finalize the arrest in the adjacent room belonging to Fräulein Bürstner. The uniqueness of the arrest is that neither the Inspector nor his assistants can tell Josef K. the reasons for it. The implication is that the charge is very serious, yet he remains free to pursue his work and can move about without any restrictions.

Kafka experienced his engagement in a similar way, and the passage Canetti quotes from the diary describes what should have been a happy event: "I was as bound up as a criminal. If they had dumped me in a corner with real chains and put gendarmes around me and let me watch from there, it wouldn't have been worse. And that was my engagement" (*CW*, 101). What made the occasion as horrifying as it was – for both Josef K. and Kafka – was the public nature of the event. Josef K.'s arrest took place in the lodgings of a virtual stranger and in the presence of people basically unknown to him. Kafka's engagement to Felice in Berlin was similarly celebrated in the company of strangers from her family and even his own.

Two elements warrant special attention: one, the nature of the arrest and the engagement, and two, the public place where each occurs. In the case of Kafka's engagement, Canetti has offered ample evidence that Kafka's perception of marriage was unique. It is quite understandable that Kafka would react with horror and confusion when he then had to experience a traditional, bourgeois engagement. He was being forced into something he had never even imagined. Likewise, the public place and nature of the engagement were troublesome. Up to that moment, Kafka had only written his most intimate thoughts, both pro and con, regarding marriage, but now this very private man with very private thoughts was exposed to a public with whom he was unable to interact on even the most superficial level. Like the true *Dichter* – as Canetti has identified him – Kafka takes full responsibility for his words, even when they have the power to destroy him. Yet, in this episode, it is not Kafka the writer but Kafka the man who confronts an incomprehensible world. When he creates the character of Josef K., Kafka transforms his personal disbelief into that guilty charge that remains unspoken throughout the novel.

The second part of the first chapter, "Conversation with Frau Grubach," Josef K.'s landlady, serves as an interlude between the arrest of the morning and an encounter with Fräulein Bürstner later that night. Canetti identifies the fictional character of Fräulein Bürstner with Grete Bloch. Kafka's relationship to Grete at the time of his engagement to Felice had taken an unusual turn. Canetti's analysis of the letters that Kafka wrote to Grete and to Felice in the months prior to the engagement reveals that Kafka perceived his marriage to Felice to be "complete only if he thought of her [Grete] as a part of it" (*CW*, 96). "He was also moved by the vaster notion that a marriage which he viewed as a kind of duty, as a moral achievement, could not succeed without love, and it was the presence of Grete Bloch, for whom he felt love, that would bring love into the marriage" (*CW*, 97). Neither Felice nor Grete shared with Kafka these curious views on marriage.

The final section of the first chapter of *The Trial*, "Fräulein Bürstner," tells of Josef K.'s effort to have a few words with her about that morning's events. When she finally came home, he attempted to tell her that the "Court of Inquiry" had used and disturbed her room in the morning and that he wished to be pardoned for causing the upheaval. The only evidence of the incident, however, were some photographs on the wall not in the order in which she had left them. Josef K. becomes quite agitated as he relates this story and raises his voice to a point where a neighbor knocks on the door to quiet the shouting. "Fräulein Bürstner feels compromised and is unhappy," and Josef K. "kisses her on the forehead as though to comfort her" (*CW*, 102). Her efforts to have him return to his room and leave her alone are countered with further kisses "on the mouth and then all over her face, the way a thirsty animal laps greedily at the spring water it has finally found. At last, he kissed her on the neck, right on the throat, and there he let his lips rest for a long time" (*CW*, 102). Finally Josef K. returns to his room, and prior to falling asleep, "he thought a little about his behavior, he was satisfied with it, but surprised that he wasn't even more satisfied" (*CW*, 102).

Like Kafka pursuing Grete Bloch, Josef K., continues his pursuit of Fräulein Bürstner in the most aggressive manner. Canetti's description of Josef K.'s physical attack on Fräulein Bürstner is a direct quotation from Kafka's novel. It could, however, have come straight from the chapter "Seizing and Incorporation" in *Crowds and Power*, in the discussion of which it was pointed out that the most basic manifestation of power and survival exhibited by humans was seizing and incorporating – overpowering and devouring the other. Josef K. was stalking and lying in wait, he found a way of tricking, he chases and seizes, overpowers and eventually devours Fräulein Bürstner just like "a thirsty animal" (*CW*, 102). Having accomplished that, he returns to his room and celebrates his victory with satisfaction. Neither Kafka nor the protagonist in his novel can understand their aberrant behavior and, consequently, find it impossible to comprehend the nature of their guilt.

Canetti examines only the parallels between Kafka's life and the first and last chapters of his novel because these two chapters relate specifically to the question of power. One could easily read the intervening chapters and see that they are also based on real experiences from Kafka's life: apartments he had visited, lawyers he had known, large group meetings he had attended, various members of his family, as well as characters and events from his extensive reading of classical and modern literature. In this way, Kafka is the *Dichter*, "the keeper of metamorphosis" (*CW*, 240), making not only his personal experiences but also "mankind's literary heritage . . . his own" (*CW*, 240).

The concluding chapter of the novel begins one year after the events described at its beginning. The parallel experiences in Kafka's life, however, are separated by only six weeks. Following the engagement where he "was bound up as a criminal," Kafka resumed his correspondence with Grete Bloch. In these letters he was quite candid about his feelings and fears regarding his marriage to Felice. His relationship to Grete, however, is rather ambiguous. Canetti discovered one surviving letter from Grete to Kafka in which she admits that she has ceased to serve as intermediator and now feels like a jilted lover. To atone for her guilt in deceiving Felice – and perhaps even to seek revenge and break up the engagement – Grete shows Felice Kafka's letters to her, underlining every passage expressing reservations about his marriage and criticisms of Felice. These are, in summary, the events leading to the "tribunal" in Berlin on 12 July 1914.

Kafka is confronted by the evidence that Grete has supplied. Felice quoted passage upon passage from the letters, requesting explanations. Kafka, however, remained silent throughout the entire proceeding. The result of the trial was the dissolution of the betrothal. It was clear that Kafka had no defense to offer, but it is equally clear that – again – he was incapable of verbalizing his views on the spur of the moment. Only a few weeks later, however, he started writing *The Trial*, and, working in his own medium, he became both the most articulate defense attorney and the severest judge.

Canetti now turns to the novel and examines the parallel experiences in the life and execution of Josef K. The protagonist is visited by two men who summon him for his execution. Unlike the previous encounters with the law, Josef K. does not resist. He admits his guilt even though he still does not know the charge against him. He is led to a stone quarry where he is executed. Canetti uses Kafka's words to describe the execution, where one of the men was holding Josef K. while "the other thrust the knife into his heart and turned it twice" (*CW*, 106). In the final moment, Josef K. observes how the two men are witnessing this final act. "'Like a dog!' he said; it was as if the shame must outlive him" (*CW*, 106).

Canetti's interpretation of Kafka's experiences and the last chapter of the novel is based on the documents relating to the "tribunal" in Berlin and the concurrent "execution" with the breaking off of the engagement. He cites a few lines from the first letter Kafka wrote in reply to one Grete Bloch had sent in mid-October 1914, three months after the Berlin meeting. In it Kafka tells Grete: "You did sit in judgement over me . . . but it only looked that way; in reality, I was sitting in your place and I still have not left it" (*CW*, 104). Canetti understands these lines to indicate that Kafka rejected Grete as his judge and that there is "no external tribunal that he recognizes, he is in his own court" (*CW*, 104). In this context, however, it is absolutely crucial to acknowledge that Kafka's "court will always be in session" (*CW*, 104). When Kafka resumed his correspondence with Felice a fortnight later, he was of the same opinion. The only aspect of "the trial" that troubled him greatly was the way in which Felice had humiliated him again in public: "there were things that ought to have been almost impossible to say in private" (*CW*, 105). Two issues are important to Canetti here: one, that of being one's own judge, and two, the avoidance of humiliation.

It became clear to Kafka that he was "destined to remain alone" (*CW*, 106), because he recognized that Felice would always be an interference and danger to his work. He realized his duty as a *Dichter*, an obligation from which he could never withdraw. Recall that in the "cellar dweller" letter Kafka stated his need for total solitude in order to be creative. Canetti also quotes from a later entry in Kafka's journal where he complains about Felice's attempt to impose her way of life on him: "my watch had been one and a half hours fast for three months now and she sets it at the real time" (*CW*, 110). This imposition of her wishes on his watch is totally unacceptable to Kafka, and Canetti determines that "the fact that his watch runs differently from others is a tiny piece of freedom for him" (*CW*, 110). However trivial this may appear, Canetti sees it as a significant example of an "obstinate attempt of a powerless man to escape power in any form" (*CW*, 111). Regardless of the circumstances or persons involved, power can only be retained by never allowing others to sit in judgment.

The issue of the avoidance of humiliation is closely related to the question of power, a problem Canetti has also examined extensively in *Crowds and Power*. Only a superior being has the ability to humiliate an inferior person. Canetti maintains that the ideal way to escape humiliation is to grow so small and insignificant that one disappears from the sight and touch of the powerful; this in turn makes one even more powerful against the superior being. In this essay on Kafka, Canetti quotes numerous passages where Kafka complains about his poor health, his skinny body, his headaches and inability to sleep – all examples of inferiority. Yet he overcomes all these deficiencies when he functions as a writer.

Canetti examines the theme of power or powerlessness in Kafka's other works. Indeed, it becomes clear that virtually every work – from "The Judgement" or "The Metamorphosis" to *The Trial* and *The Castle* – has as its core the conflict between those who exert power over others and those who are attempting to escape this power. In "The Judgement" Canetti observes that Georg Bendemann rejects his father's humiliation and verdict, even though that act costs him his life. The character of Gregor Samsa in "The Metamorphosis" humiliates his family and is then destroyed by that family, whom he had previously nourished and supported. In *The Trial*, Josef K.'s guilt is brought about by his implacable search for the court, while his counterpart in *The Castle* is unsuccessful in gaining entrance to the castle to speak to the very authority that had summoned him. And, of course, there were Kafka's great confrontations with his family, eloquently portrayed in the famous "Letter to his Father." This serves as yet another example of an encounter with superior powers who are powerless in the face of someone who refuses to accept their power. In each of these examples, the protagonists escape power and humiliation only when they withdraw to the point where they become invulnerable. Canetti ends this investigation of the power to judge and the avoidance of humiliation with a quotation in which "Kafka himself summed up what 'smallness' means for him: 'Two possibilities: to make oneself infinitely small or to be infinitely small. The latter is perfection, that is, inactivity; the former is beginning, that is, action'" (*CW*, 121-22).

The essay concludes with a study of the letters from the other half of Kafka's relationship to Felice Bauer: from early 1915 when they meet again after the "court of law" until the second and final breakup of their engagement in December 1917. Canetti notes that the character of the letters has changed to reflect the different nature of Kafka's personality. Whereas Kafka had courted Felice during the first period, Felice now takes the initiative to gain Kafka's affections. To achieve some insight into this period, Canetti is obliged to use a variety of other sources, making this account far less personal and the parallel between Kafka's life and work less compelling.

Because of poor health Kafka frequents numerous spas during these years, and the records show that he and Felice met on various occasions in Bodenbach, Karlsbad, Marienbad, and elsewhere. In early July 1917 they spend 10 days in Marienbad and then decide to marry, even though both had articulated good and compelling reasons why they should not. Elsewhere Canetti found a letter that Kafka wrote to Max Brod in which the strange euphoria of the moment is described: "Our contract is in brief: To marry soon after the war's end, rent two or three rooms in a Berlin suburb, each person taking care of his or her own domestic needs. F. will work again as before, and I, well I – I can't say as yet. . . . Nevertheless – there is peace in it now, and hence a possibility of life" (*CW*, 125). That moment of bliss is shattered only a few weeks later when Kafka begins coughing blood and receives the diagnosis that he has tuberculosis. But Canetti has discovered in an obscure source that Kafka had already quarreled with Felice shortly after the engagement and may well have been looking for a way to escape this second betrothal.[7] Consequently, Canetti concludes that the diagnosis of the illness "launch[ed] a new period in his life. The pronouncement by this authority, whom he forced himself to recognize, rescued him from Felice, his fear of the marriage, and his hated job. But it tied him for all time to the disease of which he ultimately died" (*CW*, 135).

The first engagement was dissolved when Grete Bloch intervened, and Kafka was liberated to write some of his greatest works. When he needed rescuing again, he was released for a short time by a fatal disease. Canetti ends the essay with Kafka's statement: "The work to be done is enormous" (*CW*, 139).

Chapter Seven

Recognition and Honors

The day after the Swedish Academy announced that the 1981 recipient of the Nobel Prize for Literature was Elias Canetti, the *New York Times* page 1 article detailing the event was headlined "Writer of Central Europe Wins Nobel Prize" and identified him as "the first native of Bulgaria to win the prize."[1] Two days later the *Sunday Times* of London reminded its readers that Canetti was "the first British citizen to win the Literature prize since Winston Churchill" and called him "as exotic a successor to Kipling, Galsworthy and Churchill as one could wish for."[2] News magazines reported "laurels for an obscure wanderer, widely praised but little known"[3] and, recalling that the prizes for literature the previous two years had been awarded to unknown Greek and Polish poets, labeled Canetti "the dark horse" for 1981.[4] The press in the Federal Republic of Germany virtually ignored the announcement, but the Austrians delighted in calling Canetti their Nobel laureate; the literary journal *Literatur und Kritik* wrote that "Canetti is not an Austrian citizen, but in recognition of his acknowledgment we may include him in our literature. He is the first author of truly Austrian spirit who has received the Nobel Prize."[5] The Spanish press took note of the fact that Canetti's forefathers had lived in that country until expelled by the Inquisition 500 years earlier; despite the intervening centuries, Canetti became a Spanish laureate.

Canetti could easily have clarified matters for the press by announcing the facts in an interview. Basically shy and apparently angry that he had been long ignored by the media, however, he let his London agent, John Wolfers, give notice that he was not available for comment. Indeed, shortly after accepting the most distinguished prize ever conferred upon him, Canetti vented his wrath by imposing an extraordinary ban on British publishers. The *Times* of London reported that Canetti had taken this action "as a protest at the way he had been neglected here until the Nobel prize made him world-famous. Only four of his seven books had been published in Britain and they have been allowed frequently to go out of print."[6]

Canetti's English publishers blamed the reading public for the British neglect, but the records reveal that some of Canetti's writings were not reviewed even when they were published in Britain. And even when they were reviewed, the commentary was slapdash and superficial: *Auto-da-Fé*, for example, had been described by the *Times* in 1946 as "ponderous and trivial." *The Voices of Marrakesh* was considered "so idiosyncratic that it failed to attract a single newspaper review."[7] In 1985, with considerable reluctance, Canetti lifted the ban that had prevented the publication of more than half of his books in Britain.

Unlike other Nobel laureates, Canetti's rise to fame has been slow and often unfairly influenced by events that had nothing to do with his writing. To understand his current status, it is interesting to trace the path towards recognition in the English-speaking and German-speaking worlds. Since sources from the early critical reception are not widely available, they are inspected in greater detail here than those from more recent years.

Early Reception in the English-Speaking World

An examination of critiques in distinguished literary journals and scholarly writings in prestigious academic periodicals reveals a curious paradox. Prior to 1970 in the English-speaking world, the readership of Canetti's works remained quite small, but the limited number of critics and scholars who did write on his works viewed them very favorably.

When *Auto-da-Fé* was first published in England in 1946, it was reviewed for the *Spectator* by Kate O'Brien.[8] With considerable perspicacity, she demonstrates how the novel must be read as a "gigantic fable" in which Canetti "shows us, in agonisingly slow detail, the destruction of the mad, pure mind of one man, a kind of genius, by one or two mindless, sub-brutal fellow creatures." In the closing lines of her critique, O'Brien foretells the predicament that Canetti will experience in attracting readers to this novel: "The author asks too much of us; we are too tired for this. Swift and Joyce had more mercy, and each also had the weakness, if you like, of spiritual reference which they could not evade. There is none of that here. There is no God, from any theology; there is no light. Only vileness enthroned, and reason nobly flying to its own obliteration. A mad, magnificent work which we are not able to endure, which perhaps we are right not to accept, but of which we dare not deny the genius or the justification."

Readers of the third volume of Canetti's autobiography, *The Play of the Eyes*, can find many examples where Canetti himself records similar observations about *Auto-da-Fé*. Already upon completing the manuscript Canetti expresses his fear of having portrayed a reality too horrible even to contemplate. Friends who read the manuscript or who heard Canetti read selections were terrified by the catastrophe of unimaginable proportions predicted by the novel; they not infrequently warned Canetti, as Dr. Sonne said, that "the book would have a hard life" and that Canetti should be forewarned of "the attacks that were to be expected" (*PE*, 209).

Yet despite these predictions, major critics continued to praise the novel. In 1950, Jacob Isaacs, distinguished professor of literature at the University of London, presented a series of lectures broadcast on the BBC and published the next year as *An Assessment of Twentieth-Century Literature*.[9] Examining literature created during the first half of the twentieth century, Isaacs names *Auto-da-Fé* "the finest book . . . I have ever read. . . . an allegory of man's resistance against the power of evil and the evil of power." He observes of the novel that "it has the crystal clarity and directness of all great allegory," and he places Canetti's work in the company of the fiction of Dante, Bunyan, and Kafka. Even if one were to attribute a degree of hyperbole to these assertions, Isaacs clearly announces Canetti's novel as a very significant work of contemporary fiction.

With the publication of *Crowds and Power* in 1960 as *Masse und Macht* in Germany and then in translation in 1962, two English scholars examined Canetti's novel and his socioanthropological study and confirmed that Canetti's work was, indeed, worthy of a greater and more positive reception. At the time the English translation was published, Iris Murdoch evaluated *Crowds and Power* for the *Spectator*.[10] She notes the breadth and depth of Canetti's erudition, which resulted in this "extremely imaginative, original and massively documented theory of the psychology of crowds." Murdoch believes that Canetti expanded our understanding of crowds and power in areas where both Marx and Freud had been deficient.

Canetti offers the reader "a satisfactory theoretical explanation of Hitler," and, unlike other investigators, he provides a unique insight into the question "of the political power of a church over its adherents." It is pointed out that Canetti has developed a new concept that articulates "the interaction of 'the mythical' with the ordinary stuff of human life. The mythical is not something 'extra': we live in myth and symbol all the time." The review of this "great original work on a vitally important subject" ends with a laudation that says of Canetti: "We need and we shall always need the visions of great imaginers and solitary men of genius."

In 1969 Ian Watson published an engaging essay, "Elias Canetti: The One and the Many," in which he offers valuable insights into similarities between *Auto-da-Fé* and *Crowds and Power*.[11] With wit and keen perception, Watson starts his essay with the suggestion that the "scientific study in social psychology . . . might have been written by Dr. Peter Kien himself, midway . . . between his scholarly theses on Chinese Philosophy and his later demented Swiftian project for a Psychology of Trousers." The essay illustrates how the two works constantly "impinge upon one another: the madness of the one provides the method of the other." The novel is a study of the isolation and alienation of the individual, and the nonfiction study is an investigation of the psychology of the crowd: "The One and the Many are not separate phenomena but rather polar opposites, which . . . depend upon one another for their existence." This essay is one of the earliest attempts to focus on Canetti's lifelong pursuit of the understanding and the expression in various genres of the make-up and the power of crowds.

The reception in England by the serious press and the academic community prior to 1970 was, for the most part, very promising. The popular reception of Canetti's two major works, however, was disappointing. In 1960, for example, the first English publisher of *Auto-da-Fé*, Jonathan Cape, acknowledged that the novel had been out of print for some years and a second printing was ordered. Sales were very slow; only 2,500 copies were sold in the following 10 years (Lebracht 1982, 8a).

In the United States, Canetti's novel was first published in 1947 under the title *The Tower of Babel*; it was republished as *Auto-da-Fé* shortly after the English version of *Crowds and Power* became available in the early 1960s. With the exception of a few newspaper re-

views in 1947 and slightly more interest in the 1960s, Canetti seems
to have had a limited American readership before 1970. The most interesting commentary – entitled "The World as Inferno" – appeared
in the *Partisan Review*[12]; it was written by the peripatetic American
scholar Leslie Fiedler. Fiedler suggests that the different titles portray
metaphorically three contemporary visions of evil: the German title,
Die Blendung, "as hallucinatory displacement"; the English "as im-
molation by fire"; and the American edition, *The Tower of Babel*, "as
failure of communication" (316). Fiedler categorizes the work as a
city-novel, exhibiting all the elements of the modern urban world:
"the terrible seediness of the pawnshop, the dive, the police court,
the hotel corridor, the streets where ennui waits to become terror"
(316). Peter Kien, who has lived his entire life in a private world, is
thrust into an incomprehensible inferno the moment he makes his
first "gesture at human engagement" and can never recover from this
mistake (316). Every encounter with society, even the assistance of
his brother, leads to his holocaust. The failure of communication
forms the foundation of the human predicament. Fiedler speculates
on the symbolism of the Oriental philosophers Mencius and Confucius that pervades the novel. He poses the question of whether the
reader is "to accept an implied Mencian analysis, that where the Intellectual refuses the leadership of the people . . . disorder and evil
results" or is to perceive Canetti's intention to be "a larger irony,"
which suggests that "behind the phantasmagoria of actual evil the
noble falsehoods of the Chinese sages" exists (318).

Early Reception in the German-Speaking World

Canetti has written extensively about the genesis of his novel in *The
Play of the Eyes* and in the 1973 essay "The First Book – *Auto-da-
Fé*" (the essay was republished in *The Conscience of Words*). The
autobiographical record shows that he concluded work on the
manuscript in fall 1931 and that it was published under the German
title *Die Blendung* in late fall 1935. The lapse of four years between
completion and publication should not be considered especially
long; after all, Canetti was basically an unknown and unpublished
young writer at the time. Had he been more assertive and perhaps
more self-confident, he might sooner have found a willing publisher
ready to take the risk of bringing out the novel.

Numerous factors having no bearing on the quality of the novel must nevertheless be considered in understanding its fate during its first 10 to 15 years. Although the European cultural scene during the 1920s was open to the most diverse experimentation in all areas of the arts, by the beginning of the 1930s Hitler's national socialism and other conservative political views had attained considerable power and influence in Germany. This trend did not go unnoticed in neighboring Austria, where the publishing business was always dependent on a readership in Germany for financial success. In May 1933 the new Nazi government organized a book burning in Berlin, as well as in several other cities. Burned were an estimated 20,000 books written by some of the world's most distinguished authors, including a host of writers who also happened to be Jews. The event served notice to publishing houses that from then on the Propaganda Ministry directed by Goebbels would not allow the printing of books it considered experimental and in style (such as those by expressionist, surrealist, or impressionist artists), books whose authors were politically opposed to the new government, or those written by Jews and other ethnic or religious groups identified as enemies of the state. Although Canetti's novel is not highly experimental and does not specifically offer a political point of view, judged from today's perspective *Die Blendung* might well have fallen into the category of books the Nazis would have prohibited. As to the fact that Canetti was born into the Jewish faith – even though he has been a lifelong critic of that religion – the 1935 Nuremberg Laws could easily have been applied to him, prohibiting the publication and distribution of his work in Germany.

Despite this unfavorable climate, the publishing house of Herbert Reichner, with offices in Vienna, Leipzig, and Zurich, took the chance and published the avant-garde *Die Blendung* by the Jewish Elias Canetti. Only two and a half years later, in March 1938, Hitler completed the annexation of Austria, compelling Herbert Reichner to emigrate and shortly thereafter forcing the dissolution of his publishing house. Exact records are unavailable, but it is estimated that between 2,000 and 3,000 copies of the first edition were sold,[13] certainly not enough to make the novel known to a wide reading public. Given the massive destruction during World War II, there are surely only a few copies of that first printing still in existence.

Very little research has been undertaken evaluating the reception the press gave the first printing of the novel.[14] Although the response seems to have been positive by and large, the critics expressed bewilderment. One summarizes the general reaction: "It is a most curious and unusual book" (Dissinger, 91). Hermann Hesse's review in a Zurich newspaper in January 1936 was positive but with reservations, saying that the novel was "exciting but also agonizing" (Dissinger, 93). The only newspaper in Germany with a review of the book was the *Frankfurter Zeitung;* in its literary supplement of April 1936, Peter von Haselberg's essay "Experimenting with the Novel" attempts to place Canetti's work within the tradition of the European novel and concludes that it is "the first step beyond Joyce's *Ulysses*" because "the boundary between real happenings and fantasies is . . . experimentally shifted."[15] The Viennese critic Ernst Waldinger, who became acquainted with Canetti's work at various public readings, wrote in the June 1936 issue of *das silberboot* that *Die Blendung* belonged stylistically in the company of James Joyce's prose and that it is conceptually linked to Balzac's great cycle of novels of the *Human Comedy.*[16]

Of much greater importance to Canetti than the reviews – whether good, bad, or wrong – were the views of his acquaintances and fellow writers. In *The Play of the Eyes* he wrote at length how he valued the opinions expressed by Dr. Sonne. Canetti also records the positive reactions of Hermann Broch and Robert Musil after they heard him read selections of *Die Blendung*. Broch was very generous in an introduction to one of Canetti's public readings and encouraged and assisted him in publishing his novel. The composer Alban Berg, to whom Canetti sent a copy of the published work, wrote in a letter that he had read the novel with great interest and enthusiasm. The painters Georg Merkel and Fritz Wotruba were, likewise, impressed by Canetti's accomplishment.

The name of Thomas Mann appears twice in the early history of *Die Blendung*. Shortly after Canetti had completed the manuscript, he sent Mann a copy, believing that he was honoring the world-famous author and certain that if Mann opened the manuscript on any page he "would then be unable to put it down again" (*CW*, 212). Much to Canetti's chagrin, Mann returned the manuscript a few days after receipt saying that he did not have the strength to read such a long work. Canetti, however, was not discouraged. When the novel was printed he sent Mann an autographed copy and, this time, received a very gracious and insightful letter, dated 14 November 1935.[17] Mann made the usual apologies for his earlier behavior and said that of all the books he had read during that year, Canetti's novel and his brother's *Henri IV* had impressed him the most. Of Canetti's book, Mann wrote that he was "candidly captivated and pleasantly impressed by its intricate fullness, the abundance of its fantasy, the provocation of its conception"; he ended the letter with congratulations for "that which has been completed and in anticipation of that which is to come in the future."

Canetti was genuinely pleased with the support he received from friends and colleagues. This early joy, however, was followed by the disappointment of an almost 30-year hiatus. In the years following World War II, the Munich publisher Willi Weismann attempted to continue the German literary tradition that had existed before 1933, but without success. Readers and critics were enthusiastic about the writings of the Group 47 authors rather than honoring continuity from former times. Nevertheless, Weismann brought out a second edition of 5,000 copies of *Die Blendung* in 1948; these sold well enough to encourage another printing of the same number in 1949. In 1950 Weismann even printed 2,000 copies of the German edition of *Comedy of Vanity*. The entire project, however, fell victim to the currency reform of 1948 and Weismann went bankrupt, leaving most of the 1949 printing and the play to be remaindered.[18] The only more extensive article published at this time was Rudolf Hartung's "Fable and Character: Observations on a Novel by Elias Canetti," appearing in Weismann's in-house publication *Literarische Revue* with, most likely, limited circulation.[19]

There is no evidence that the publication of the English edition of *Auto-da-Fé* helped to attract a German readership. Nor was the successful 1949 French translation *La Tour de Babel* to have an impact on the German market, even though that year it won the first literary prize Canetti was to receive, the Grand Prix International du Club Française du Livre. During the 1950s, the dramas became available, the monograph "Fritz Wotruba" was published in Vienna, and some of the notes on Canetti's trip to Marrakesh became known. At the end of that decade, Canetti sent his manuscript for *Masse und Macht* to the publisher in Hamburg. At that time, now 55 years old, the author was virtually unknown in the German-speaking world.

Gradual Recognition

In 1960 *Masse und Macht* appeared in Germany, and slowly Canetti's work became known to a wider circle of readers and critics. Rudolf Hartung, who had by then become an editor at Carl Hanser publishers in Munich, contributed considerably to promoting Canetti's work. In 1963 Carl Hanser became Canetti's exclusive publisher (except for *Masse und Macht*, published by Claassen of Hamburg); they began a regular program of publishing and republishing his works. Starting with a new edition of *Die Blendung* in 1963, Canetti finally acquired a greater readership. In the first two years almost 10,000 hard-bound copies of the novel were printed, followed in 1965 by a paperback edition of 47,000 copies (Bischoff, 145-46). Other works were published in equally high numbers, some with special editions distributed by German book clubs. Also in 1965 the two plays, *Komödie der Eitelkeit* and *Hochzeit*, received their premiere performances in Braunschweig. Finally, in only five years, Canetti, at age 60, became known.

Almost annually for the next two decades, Canetti received along with popular success virtually every literary prize that the Federal Republic of Germany, Austria, and Switzerland bestow on their most distinguished authors. The honors and distinctions include the Writer's Prize of the City of Vienna 1966, the German Critics' Prize 1967, the Great Austrian State Prize 1968, the Literature Prize from the Bavarian Academy of Fine Arts 1969, the Literature Prize from the Cultural Division of the Union of German Industry 1971, the Georg Büchner Prize 1972, the Franz Nabl Prize and the Nelly Sachs Prize 1975, the Gottfried Keller Prize 1977, the distinction Pour le Mérite from the Federal Republic of Germany 1979, the Johann Peter Hebel Prize 1980, the Nobel Prize for Literature and the Franz Kafka Prize 1981, and the Great Service Cross of the Federal Republic of Germany 1983. In addition, Canetti received honorary doctoral degrees from the University of Manchester in 1975 and the University of Munich in 1976. The sales of his books were never so large that he could be considered a best-selling author, but the honors Canetti has received for his writings clearly demonstrate their extraordinary value.

Once his work became more readily available, critics also took note of Canetti.[20] In addition to Rudolf Hartung, Germanists such as

Dieter Dissinger and Manfred Durzak began to write extensively and critically in scholarly journals in the late 1960s. In 1972, the American Germanist Dagmar Barnouw published the first in a host of penetrating examinations of various aspects of Canetti's literary and essayistic works. She was joined by colleagues around the world, such as David Roberts in Melbourne, Claudio Magris in Trieste, Roberto Corcoll Calsat in Barcelona, and Gerald Stieg in Paris. Of course, there were numerous scholars in Austria, Switzerland, the former German Democratic Republic, and the Federal Republic of Germany who devoted considerable attention to Canetti's work.

Special volumes of essays have been published to celebrate important birthdays: in 1975, on the occasion of Canetti's seventieth birthday, his publisher Carl Hanser issued the volume of essays *Canetti lesen – Erfahrungen mit seinen Büchern*; in 1980, *Hommage à Elias Canetti à l'occasion de son 75ème anniversaire* was published in France; and, to celebrate the eightieth birthday in 1985, Carl Hanser again published a series of essays, the volume *Hüter der Verwandlung*. This last appeared in English translation as *Essays in Honor of Elias Canetti* and serves as a fine introduction to Canetti scholarship for those not able to read German.

In the period following Canetti's receipt of the Nobel Prize, there were numerous meetings and symposia where his works were discussed by scholars from universities in Europe and the United States. In 1983 the journal *Modern Austrian Literature* published a special Canetti issue presenting a cross-section of scholarship on *Auto-da-Fé*. It also touches on some of the other works (6 of the 13 articles are in English). Since the late 1980s almost yearly at various Austrian universities or literary centers there have been symposia reporting the results of penetrating and discerning scholarship. The number of dissertations on Canetti in American and European universities remains very small.

Canetti himself has paid tribute to many authors, both famous and unknown, in his essays. He acknowledged, for example, the important impact that Franz Kafka had on him and his writings, but second to Kafka was the little-known Swiss writer Robert Walser. In his autobiography Canetti wrote extensively on Hermann Broch and Robert Musil, but there is perhaps no commentary more sensitive and gracious than his brief homage to Ludwig Hohl in *The Secret Heart of the Clock* (pp. 76-78).

Many writers have likewise praised Canetti. Hermann Broch was the first to publicly express admiration, introducing his young colleague as Canetti was about to read from his important, but as yet unpublished, novel (which still had the title *Kant fängt Feuer*).[21] Another early but rather different form of recognition came when Iris Murdoch dedicated *The Flight from the Enchanter* to Canetti, perhaps using Canetti as a model for the character of the philosopher. In the mid-1960s, in Saul Bellow's novel *Herzog*, the following entry certainly refers to Canetti: "And then this Bulgarian, Banowitch, seeing all power struggles in terms of paranoid mentality. . ."[22] The character of Moses Herzog may not have flattered Canetti, but the author does take note of the importance of *Crowds and Power*.

In 1980 the American writer and essayist Susan Sontag published her major Canetti study, "Mind as Passion."[23] She reviewed and analyzed Canetti's life and work with a sensitive perspicaciousness, celebrating his originality, the keenness with which he understands his times, and his dogged opposition to death. What Sontag admires most in Canetti is the power of his mind and the strength of his words.

> Canetti is someone who has felt in a profound way the responsibility of words, and much of his work makes the effort to communicate something of what he has learned about how to pay attention to the world. There is no doctrine, but there is a great deal of scorn, urgency, grief, and euphoria. The message of the mind's passions is passion. "I try to imagine someone saying to Shakespeare, Relax!" says Canetti. His work eloquently defends tension, exertion, moral and amoral seriousness.

Any serious student of Canetti should carefully read and take to heart Susan Sontag's essay.

In his essay "Krieg zwischen Küche und Kopf" (war between kitchen and head), the German writer Siegfried Lenz, whose many works attempt to come to terms with Germany's past, tries to make amends for Canetti's oblivion.[24] Lenz suggests that *Die Blendung* lost some of its power and effectiveness when it became inaccessible to readers during "the time of the blinding" (he calls the Hitler period this, "*die Zeit der Verblendung*"). Postwar readers could read the novel only with a sense of guilt for allowing themselves to have been blinded. Nevertheless, Lenz believes that this story – "the neverending conflict between reality and fantasy" – is "an archetypal and permanent part of the human experience" and, as such, this metaphor for the antagonism between the intellect and reality will continue to find a new readership.

Salman Rushdie represents the younger generation of writers who look to Canetti as their teacher, as a writer's writer. In a delightfully humorous radio presentation, "The Worm of Learning Turns, Swallows Its Tail, and Bites Itself in Half," Rushdie laments that Canetti has become famous, because for years Canetti had been Rushdie's "secret pleasure," along with Grimmelshausen, Machado de Assis, and Borges. As a 19 year old, Rushdie read *Auto-da-Fé*, recognized that the older form of the novel was still very much alive, and learned from Canetti's work how he wanted to write. "I decided that all I had to do was – like Canetti – to combine vast erudition and awesome intricacies of structure with a sort of glittering, beady comic eye."[25] With greater maturity, however, Rushdie compares Canetti's writing with that of Musil, Döblin, Thomas Mann, and Kleist because he finds in their great novels "an irony that at first seems simply deadpan and ends up being utterly deadly" (83). Rushdie takes note of the deadliness in *Auto-da-Fé* that can become prophetic: "There are moments in every writer's life when he finds that what he created as fantasy is no less than the literal truth; and the nightmare of Elias Canetti ended up as the world's bad dream" (84). Speaking of present-day book burning in Indonesia, of Hitler's burning of books, of the way the American Moral Majority in essence "burned" books by banning them, Rushdie could not have then imagined that he would be the victim of an auto-da-fé only a few years later.

As a final example of tribute and research one should carefully consider B. W. Powe's idiosyncratic, postmodernist essay *The Solitary Outlaw*.[26] Powe's book-length study explores the "power, passion, and accountability of words" (13) and the "techniques of communication" (17) of the writer Wyndham Lewis, the media guru Marshall McLuhan, Pierre Elliot Trudeau when he was prime minister of Canada, the pianist Glenn Gould, and Elias Canetti, whom Powe identifies as the "author who tried to speak out to all" (13). In the final chapter, Powe brings Canetti and McLuhan together: Canetti's *Auto-da-Fé*, with its book man who lives a solitary life of abstraction without moral imagination, and McLuhan's *The Gutenberg Galaxy: The Making of Typographic Man* (1962), announcing the current era

of postliteracy and the end of the age of books. Although Kien's life
ends as he blindly sets fire to the books, Canetti emerges, in Powe's
view, as the prophet who has identified the individual, the "I,"
within the mass in *Crowds and Power*, and who celebrates the conscience of words and the human province. McLuhan, whom Powe
describes as the "chronicler of disintegration and reintegration"
(183), has discovered in his writings "the inner necessity of creating
a calm 'I' in the midst of terror and turbulence" (184). Powe believes
that Canetti and McLuhan are united in "their effort for the mainte-
nance of a humanism in the vortex of mass society" (185).

Further Studies

Elias Canetti is, without a doubt, one of the great creative artists and
seminal thinkers of the twentieth century. Much superb scholarship
has been devoted to his work in the years since his writings have increased in number and circulation, but much more remains to be
done.

Salman Rushdie reported that the doorbell at Canetti's house in
Hampstead has not worked since 1960; Canetti, this very private
man, has been quietly at work in his immense library, "books rising
in Himalayan splendor from floor to ceiling" (Rushdie, 83). In addition to publishing his writings on a regular basis for the past three
decades, Canetti has revealed, in his essay "Dialogue with the Cruel
Partner," that he has been keeping a diary, memo books, and notes
(*Aufzeichnungen*) for many years. A selection of the notes and aphorisms have been published, but the great majority of Canetti's private
writings are still unavailable and may remain so for some time to
come. We must hope that Canetti does not destroy them; if made
available to a knowledgeable scholar, they could offer still greater insight into the published work. Like Canetti's own essay on Kafka, a
sensitive artist studying Canetti's files might write an important essay.

Although Canetti has published three volumes of his autobiography, more than a half century of his life remains unknown to his
readers. And the entire life of this extraordinary man who lived in extraordinary times should be the topic of a critical biography. There
are many issues and questions that might be resolved in such a study
of Canetti's life and work.

Very little work has been devoted to the reception and impact that Canetti's novels and dramas have had on other artists. It is insufficient to suggest that Canetti is "a writer's writer" without investigating how his writings have influenced others. In conjunction with such a study, it would be interesting to know how the various works were received in translations in different countries, as, for example, the Chinese or Serbocroatian version of *Auto-da-Fé*, the Bulgarian or Japanese translations of the plays, or, closer to home, the Spanish or French rendering of the autobiography.

The short pieces of fiction that are embedded in the notes and aphorisms, that make up the Earwitnesses, and that constitute some of the voices Canetti found in Marrakesh could be investigated more extensively and placed within the oeuvre.

Only preliminary work has been done on understanding and formulating a basic philosophical view from the notes and aphorisms. They contain a wealth of information and thought, but since they, as well as *Crowds and Power*, are not written in the traditional discourse of scientific writing, scholars may wish to explicate and interpret Canetti's views. Such a study could enhance some of the existing philosophical and comparative anthropological investigations already published by various scholars and lead to an expanded understanding of Canetti's fundamental philosophical concepts. Other far-reaching and iconoclastic investigations could lead to new and very different insights into Canetti's thoughts.

Further studies would surely confirm the Nobel Prize tribute: In his versatile writings the cosmopolitan Canetti attacks the sicknesses of our age and serves the cause of humanity with intellectual passion and moral responsibility.

Abbreviations

The following abbreviations are used in the text and in the notes:

A   *Auto-da-Fé*. Translated by C. V. Wedgwood. New York: Far-
        rar, Straus & Giroux, 1984.

CP   *Crowds and Power*. Translated by Carol Stewart. New
        York: Farrar, Straus & Giroux, 1984.

CV   *Comedy of Vanity*. Translated by Gitta Honegger. New
        York: Performing Arts Journal Publications, 1983.

CW   *The Conscience of Words*. Translated by Joachim Neu-
        groschel. New York: Farrar, Straus & Giroux, 1984.

EW   *Earwitness*. Translated by Joachim Neugroschel. New York:
        Farrar, Straus & Giroux, 1986.

FW   *Fritz Wotruba*. Vienna: Rosenbaum, 1955.

HP   *The Human Province*. Translated by Joachim Neugroschel.
        New York: Farrar, Straus & Giroux, 1986.

LT   *Life-Terms*. Translated by Gitta Honegger. New York: Per-
        forming Arts Journal Publications, 1983.

PE   *The Play of the Eyes*. Translated by Ralph Manheim. New
        York: Farrar, Straus & Giroux, 1987.

SH   *The Secret Heart of the Clock*. Translated by Joel Agee. New
        York: Farrar, Straus & Giroux, 1989.

TE   *The Torch in My Ear*. Translated by Joachim Neugroschel.
        New York: Farrar, Straus & Giroux, 1982.

TF   *The Tongue Set Free*. Translated by Joachim Neugroschel.
        New York: Farrar, Straus & Giroux, 1983.

VM   *The Voices of Marrakesh*. Translated by J. A. Underwood.
        New York: Farrar, Straus & Giroux, 1984.

W   *The Wedding*. Translated by Gitta Honegger. New York:
        Performing Arts Journal Publications, 1986.

names that include in their names the German word *Bad* (spa) are localities in which mineral springs exist.)

The better-known spas tend to offer not only a medicinal service but also a cultural environment that promotes mental health. Spas generally have a staff of health care providers, including physicians, dietitians, physical therapists, and those who oversee such activities as the drinking of mineral waters or the taking of therapeutic baths. At some spas, residents can attend concerts, lectures, or other cultural events. European doctors have long believed in the curative benefits of visits to spas.

Two spas that Canetti's mother visited are examples of such places. Bad Reichenhall is located in the foothills of the Bavarian Alps in Germany. It is known for its brine baths, where patients spend long hours each day in water that is strongly impregnated with salt. The Waldsanatorium in Arosa, Switzerland, is a famous sanatorium for consumptives; nearby are spas in the towns of St. Moritz and Davos, places also noted for their fine winter sports facilities. It is believed that exposure to the fine air in mountainous regions can inhibit tuberculosis and other progressive wasting diseases of the body.

13. August Strindberg (1849-1912), Swedish writer, known today primarily for his naturalistic and expressionistic dramas that reflect a brooding pessimism and a profound divulgement of sinister forces in nature. He had gained widespread popularity with fin-de-siecle audiences who were interested in uncovering the dark powers of the unconscious mind. The dramas present characters that are dominated by emotions, instinct, and passions; he most powerful exhibit his particular views on women and sexuality. For trindberg, love was a cruel and vicious encounter in which men and omen attempt to dominate and overwhelm each other. From his own unfortunate and disquieted life he concluded that women represented a onysian power in nature whose main aspiration it is to suppress the paic intellectualism and spirituality of men, who exemplify the Apollonian wer of nature. The great misogynist philosopher Friedrich Nietzsche was moved by Strindberg's play *The Father* that he wrote to the playwright: —read your tragedy twice over with deep emotion; it has astonished me nd all measure to come to know a work in which my own conception ve – with war as its means and the deathly hate of the sexes as its fundamental law – is expressed in such a splendid fashion" (quoted by Eric ley, "On Strindberg," in *Six Plays of Strindberg*, trans. E. Sprigge [New : Doubleday, 1956], vi).

4. *Coriolanus*, a tragedy by Shakespeare, tells the story of a legendary n general whose tragic fall came about as a result of the haughty arce and deliberate pride this great and noble man exhibited toward mmon people.

Elias Canetti, *Die Blendung* (Vienna: Herbert Reichner, 1935); *Auto-trans.* C. V. Wedgwood (London: Jonathan Cape, 1946); republished

Notes

Chapter One

1. Elias Canetti, *Die gerettete Zunge: Geschichte einer Jugend* (Muni Carl Hanser, 1977); *The Tongue Set Free: Remembrance of a Europ Childhood*, trans. Joachim Neugroschel (New York: Continuum, 19 hereafter cited in text as *TF*.

2. Elias Canetti, *Die Fackel im Ohr: Lebensgeschichte 1921* (Munich: Carl Hanser, 1980); *The Torch in My Ear*, trans. Joachim groschel (New York: Farrar, Straus & Giroux, 1982); hereafter cited as *TE*.

3. Elias Canetti, *Das Augenspiel: Lebensgeschichte 1931-1937* (Carl Hanser, 1985); *The Play of the Eyes*, trans. Ralph Manheim (N Farrar, Straus & Giroux, 1986); hereafter cited in text as *PE*.

4. Friederike Eigler, *Das Autobiographische Werk von Elia* (Tübingen: Stauffenburg, 1988) offers a good summary study of points of view proposed by different scholars.

5. In Elias Canetti, *Das Gewissen der Worte* (Munich: C 1975; 2d ed., 1976); *The Conscience of Words*, trans. Joachim (New York: Continuum, 1979); hereafter cited in text as *CW*.

6. Quoted in Bernd Witte, "Der Erzähler als Tod-Feind," 28 (1982): 65; trans. mine.

7. Elias Canetti, *Die Provinz des Menschen: Aufzeichnun* (Munich: Carl Hanser, 1973); *The Human Province*, trans. groschel (New York: Seabury, 1978), 45; hereafter cited in t

8. Elias Canetti, *Masse und Macht* (Hamburg: Claasser *and Power*, trans. Carol Stewart (London: Victor Golla York: Viking, 1962); hereafter cited in text as *CP*.

9. See Friedrich Schlegel, *Philosophische Vorlesunge*

10. See Novalis, *Heinrich von Ofterdingen*, 1800.

11. In *The Tongue Set Free* see "Father's Death; The *The Play of the Eyes* see "The Final Version."

12. The European tradition of spending time at spa early times, "taking the waters" or "taking the cure" activity for the past several centuries, not only for the more prosperous members of the middle class. Mai areas that have mineral springs, have good climatic c restful retreat from the life of major urban centers.

as *The Tower of Babel* (New York: Alfred A. Knopf, 1947); hereafter cited in text as *A*.

16. "Rede zur Verleihung des Nobelpreises 1981 (Nobel address), *Moderne Språk* 76, no. 1 (1982): 49; hereafter cited in text as Nobelpreis, all trans. mine.

17. Two works provide fine studies of Kraus and his times: Harry Zohn, *Karl Kraus* (New York: Twayne, 1971); Edward Timms, *Karl Kraus: Apocalyptic Satirist. Culture and Catastrophe in Habsburg Vienna* (New Haven: Yale University Press, 1986).

18. Allan Janik and Stephen Toulmin, *Wittgenstein's Vienna* (New York: Simon and Schuster, 1973), 69-70.

19. See *TE*, the chapter "The Fifteenth of July," pp. 244-52 and numerous references throughout the autobiography and Canetti's essays. The same day and event also became the core of Heimito von Doderer's monumental novel *Die Dämonen*. After describing the experiences of more than two dozen characters in the chapter "The Fire," Doderer concludes: "Thus ended for us the day which quite incidentally signified the Cannae of Austrian freedom" (Heimito von Doderer, *Die Dämonen* (Munich: Biederstein, 1956); *The Demons* (New York: Alfred A. Knopf, 1961), 1311).

20. Karl Kraus, *The Last Days of Mankind*, ab. and ed. Frederick Ungar (New York: Ungar, 1974), act 1, scenes 27 and 28, pp. 58-60; hereafter cited in text.

21. Walter Benjamin, "Karl Kraus," in *Reflections*, ed. and intro. Peter Demetz (New York: Harcourt Brace Jovanovich, 1978), 263; hereafter cited in text.

22. Elias Canetti, *Hochzeit* (Munich: Carl Hanser, 1964); *The Wedding*, trans. Gitta Honegger (New York: Performing Arts Journal Publications, 1986); hereafter cited in text as *W*.

23. Elias Canetti, *Kömodie der Eitelkeit* (Munich: Weismann, 1959); *Comedy of Vanity*, trans. Gitta Honegger (New York: Performing Arts Journal Publications, 1983); hereafter cited in text as *CV*.

24. An excellent overview of Wotruba's life and work is *Fritz Wotruba: Figur als Widerstand. Bilder und Schriften zu Leben und Werk*, ed. Otto Breicha (Salzburg: Verlag der Galerie Welz, 1977).

25. Elias Canetti, *Fritz Wotruba* (Vienna: Brüder Rosenbaum, 1955); hereafter cited in text as *FW*.

26. Elias Canetti, *Das Geheimherz der Uhr: Aufzeichnungen 1973-1985* (Munich: Carl Hanser, 1987); *The Secret Heart of the Clock: Notes, Aphorisms, Fragments 1973-1985* (New York: Farrar, Straus & Giroux, 1989), 22; hereafter cited in text as *SH*.

27. Martin Buber, *Briefwechsel aus sieben Jahrzehnten*, vol. 1, 1897-1918 (Heidelberg: Schneider, 1972), 506; trans. mine.

Chapter Two

1. *Die Blendung* has been translated into many languages, including two English versions entitled *Auto-da-Fé* and *The Tower of Babel*. Since each title suggests a slightly different meaning, it is interesting to examine their implications.

Die Blendung is the German equivalent of the English phrase "the blinding." The title refers directly to the state in which the major characters function, that is, they are totally blind to what is happening in their external worlds. It does not, however, refer in any way to Peter Kien's death by fire at the end of the novel.

Auto-da-Fé alludes to the ritual of the Spanish Inquisition during the late fifteenth century that led to the burning on a public pyre of a person condemned as a heretic. Although Kien dies as a result of the fire he sets to his library, he was never found guilty of heresy in any court. The French expression *faire un autodafé des ses manuscrits* (to commit one's manuscripts to flames) describes the events more correctly, but it also omits the idea of self-immolation.

The Tower of Babel recalls the Biblical story in the book of Genesis where the building of the tower that was to reach heaven was interrupted by the confusion of everyone speaking a different language. This title calls to mind the fact that all the major characters of the novel are unable to comprehend the real meaning of the language they use with one another.

2. There are many good books that describe life in Berlin during the early years of the twentieth century. Particularly valuable is Henry M. Pachter, *The Fall and Rise of Europe: A Political, Social, and Cultural History of the Twentieth Century* (New York: Praeger, 1975).

3. Aristotle, *Poetics*, trans. Benjamin Jowett, in *The Pocket Aristotle*, ed. Justin D. Kaplan (New York: Pocket Library, 1958), 351.

4. Robert Humphrey, *Stream of Consciousness in the Modern Novel* (Berkeley: University of California Press, 1968), 3.

5. The word *krummholz* means dwarf or scrub pine.

6. This episode undoubtedly relies on the "Historical Record" written by the "Father of History," the Han historian Ssu-ma Chin (also known as the Herodotus of China).

7. The topic of the masses and their place in and impact on society was to become the core of Canetti's later study *Crowds and Power*.

8. This concept is similar to the attitude expressed in Goethe's *Faust*: "Whoever strives in ceaseless toil, / Him we may grant redemption" (lines 11936-37).

9. It should be noted that Canetti wrote this book several years prior to the 1933 book burning ordered by the Nazi minister of propaganda, Josef Goebbels.

10. There actually was a person by this name. José Raoul Capablanca (1888-1942), world chess champion from 1921 until 1927, was known for his flawless playing techniques. This serves as another example of Canetti's inclusion of materials from the real world in his fictitious world of headless or worldless characters.

11. For further information see Detlef Krumme, *Lesemodelle: Canetti, Grass, Höllerer* (Munich: Carl Hanser, 1983), 73-75.

12. A *landsknecht*, or lansquenet, was a mercenary foot soldier, frequently armed with a pike or lance, who had been used by German (and other) armies since the fifteenth century. Of course, the mercenary Pfaff has turned against his masters.

Chapter Three

1. Interview with Elias Canetti and Friedrich Witz, 23 August 1968, Radio DRS, II. Programm, Studio Zurich. Quoted in A. M. Bischoff, *Elias Canetti – Stationen zum Werk* (Bern: Herbert Lang, 1973), 70; trans. mine.

2. Karl Kraus, "Nestroy und die Nachwelt," *Die Fackel*, nos. 349-50 (1912): 23; trans. mine.

3. Elias Canetti, *Welt im Kopf*, intro. and sel. Erich Fried (Graz: Stiasny, 1962); hereafter cited in text, all trans. mine.

4. The number "500 words" must be understood figuratively rather than literally because it would be impossible to limit anyone's speech to such a low number if one were to count each word the individual utters. Canetti undoubtedly was suggesting that the "word-poor" person's vocabulary is restricted by the small number of concepts he might discuss in such a setting. Linguists have examined this issue extensively and have concluded that "the claim that . . . some individual people . . . manage with a vocabulary of only a few hundred words . . . is mere fantasy" (Robbins Burling, *Patterns of Language* [San Diego: Academic Press, 1992], 64).

5. Elias Canetti, *Die Befristeten* (Munich: Carl Hanser, 1964); *Life-Terms*, trans. Gitta Honegger (New York: Performing Arts Journal Publications, 1983); *The Numbered*, trans. Carol Stewart (London: Calder & Boyars, 1984); hereafter cited in text as *LT*.

6. Paul Kruntorad, "Kompromißlose Texttreue," *Frankfurter Rundschau*, 1 October 1985; trans. mine.

7. Günther Rühle, "Ein Skandal in Braunschweig," *Frankfurter Allgemeine Zeitung*, 9 February 1965; trans. mine.

8. Peter Iden, "Vom Ich zum Wir und wieder zurück," *Die Zeit*, 17 February 1978; trans. mine.

9. Hans Hollmann, "Working on Canetti's Plays," in *Essays in Honor of Elias Canetti*, 240-45.

10. "Playhouse Theatre, Oxford – The Numbered," *Times* (London), 6 November 1956.

11. "The Playhouse – The Numbered by Elias Canetti," *Oxford Magazine*, n.d., p. 1.

12. egw., "Warten auf Canetti," *Die Welt*, 21 November 1967; trans. mine.

13. Siegfried Kienzle, "Der verordnete Tod," *Darmstädter Echo*, 7 February 1983; trans. mine.

14. Gitta Honegger in a letter to me dated 3 October 1989.

15. Susan Sontag, *Under the Sign of Saturn* (New York: Farrar, Straus & Giroux, 1980), 190.

Chapter Four

1. Sigmund Freud, *Massenpsychologie und Ich-Analyse* (1920); authorized translation James Strachey, *Group Psychology and the Analysis of the Ego* (New York: Liveright, 1949).

2. For a complete examination, see Michael D. Biddiss, *The Age of the Masses: Ideas and Society in Europe since 1870* (New York: Harper & Row, 1977); Serge Moscovici, *The Age of the Crowd: A Historical Treatise on Mass Psychology*, trans. J. C. Whitehouse (Cambridge: Cambridge University Press, 1985).

3. See Sigrid Schmid-Bortenschlage, "Der Einzelne und seine Masse – Massentheorie und Literaturkonzeption bei Elias Canetti und Hermann Broch," in *Experte der Macht: Elias Canetti*, ed. Kurt Bartsch and Gerhard Melzer (Graz: Droschl, 1985), 116-32.

4. For more information on this extraordinary group, see Martin Jay, *The Dialectical Imagination: A History of the Frankfurt School and the Institute of Social Research, 1923-1950* (Boston: Little, Brown, 1973).

5. Virtually all examples used in this study refer to the roles men have played in the myths and stories under consideration; the absence of references to women is most conspicuous. The fault may be a lack of materials available to Canetti in the years he was preparing this study. The bibliography consists of many investigations that were conducted during the nineteenth and early twentieth centuries by men who pursued research in the spirit of romanticism or who were members of the foreign service in remote locations of the world; they may have been biased.

6. "Gespräch mit Joachim Schickel," in Elias Canetti, *Die gespaltene Zukunft: Aufsätze und Gespräche* (Munich: Carl Hanser, 1972), 129-30; hereafter cited in text as "Gespräch."

7. *Senatspräsident* is Schreber's title. It cannot be accurately translated because it refers to a legal office that has no equivalent in systems of jurisprudence outside of Germany.

8. Daniel Paul Schreber, *Denkwürdigkeiten eines Nervenkranken* (Leipzig: Oswald Mutze, 1903); *Memoirs of My Nervous Illness*, trans. Ida MacAlpine and Richard A. Hunter (London: Wm. Dawson & Sons, 1955).

9. Sigmund Freud, "Psychoanalytic Notes upon an Autobiographical Account of a Case of Paranoia (Dementia Paranoides)," *Collected Papers*, trans. Alix and James Strachey (New York: Basic Books, 1959), 3:387-470. Canetti shows his long-felt antipathy toward Freud in that he does not even include this work in the bibliography of *Crowds and Power*.

Chapter Five

1. Originally published in *Das Tagebuch und der moderne Autor* (Munich: Carl Hanser, 1965). Republished in *The Conscience of Words*, 40-54.

2. Elias Canetti, *Aufzeichnungen 1942-1948* (Notes 1942-1948) (Munich: Carl Hanser, 1965); hereafter cited in text, all trans. mine.

3. Elias Canetti, *Alle vergeudete Verehrung: Aufzeichnungen 1949-1960* (All squandered veneration: notes 1949-1960) (Munich: Carl Hanser, 1970).

4. Elias Canetti, *Der Ohrenzeuge: Fünfzig Charaktere* (Munich: Carl Hanser, 1974); *Earwitness: Fifty Characters*, trans. Joachim Neugroschel (New York: Farrar, Straus & Giroux, 1979); hereafter cited in text as *EW*.

5. Elias Canetti, *Die Stimmen von Marrakesch: Aufzeichnungen nach einer Reise* (Munich: Carl Hanser, 1967); *The Voices of Marrakesh: A Record of a Visit*, trans. J. A. Underwood (New York: Farrar, Straus & Giroux, 1978); hereafter cited in text as *VM*.

Chapter Six

1. Albert Speer, *Erinnerungen* (Berlin: Propylaen, 1969), translated as *Inside the Third Reich: Memoirs* by R. and C. Winston (New York: Macmillan, 1970).

2. For those interested in reading the entire diary in English, there is an excellent edition available: Michihiko Hachiya, *Hiroshima Diary: The Journal of a Japanese Physician, August 6-September 30, 1945*, translated and edited by Warner Wells (Chapel Hill: The University of North Carolina Press, 1955). In addition to identifying the prominent places and people and including a glossary of words whose meanings were not easily translated, the editor provides copious footnotes explaining virtually everything not known to a Westerner whose understanding of Japan, medicine, and the power of an atomic bomb may be limited.

3. For further information, see W. G. Aston, *A History of Japanese Literature* (Rutland, Vt., and Tokyo: Charles E. Tuttle, 1972).

4. Franz Kafka, *Briefe an Felice*, ed. Erich Heller and Jürgen Born, intro. Erich Heller (Frankfurt am Main: S. Fischer, 1967); hereafter cited in text as *Felice*, all trans. mine.

5. For further information, see the excellent biography by Peter Mailloux, *A Hesitation before Birth – The Life of Franz Kafka* (Newark: University of Delaware Press, 1989).

6. The history of the letters themselves, however, continued for many years. Felice, who married a wealthy banker in 1919, kept Kafka's letters even during her years in exile in Switzerland and the United States. Although she had vowed to destroy them rather than make them public, she sold them to Schocken Books in 1955 after several extensive hospital stays had put her in desperate need of money. Felice died in New York in 1960. The letters were published in Germany in 1967, 43 years after Kafka's death, and in translation in the United States in 1973.

7. Rudolf Fuchs, "Reminiscences of Franz Kafka," Appendix 3 to Max Brod, *Franz Kafka. A Biography* (New York: Schocken Books, 1960), 257.

Chapter Seven

1. John Vinocur, "Writer of Central Europe Wins Nobel Prize," *New York Times*, 16 October 1981, 1.

2. Salman Rushdie, "The Invisible Master," *Sunday Times* (London), 18 October 1981, 39.

3. J. D. Reed, "Laurels for an Obscure Wanderer," *Time*, 26 October 1981, 86.

4. Jean Strouse, "Man of Parts," *Newsweek*, 26 October 1981, 94.

5. Anon. ed., *Literatur und Kritik*, November 1981, 576; trans. mine.

6. Norman Lebrecht, "Don't Publish Me, says Nobel Man," *Times* (London), 31 March 1982, 8a; hereafter cited in text.

7. Norman Lebrecht, "Nobel Author Ends Ban on Britain," *Times* (London), 12 May 1985, 4a.

8. Kate O'Brien, "Fiction: 'Auto-Da-Fé'," *Spectator*, 24 May 1946, 540.

9. Jacob Isaacs, *An Assessment of Twentieth-Century Literature* (London: Secker & Warburg, 1951), 60; reprinted in *Essays in Honor of Elias Canetti* (New York: Farrar, Straus and Giroux, 1987), 304-5.

10. Iris Murdoch, "Mass, Might, and Myth," *Spectator*, 7 September 1962, 337-38.

11. Ian Watson, "Elias Canetti: The One and the Many," *Chicago Review* 20-21, nos. 4 and 1 (May 1969): 184-200.

12. Leslie Fiedler, "The World as Inferno," *Partisan Review*, June 1947, 316-20.

13. Alfons-M. Bischoff, *Elias Canetti, Stationen zum Werk* (Bern: Herbert Lang, 1973), 143.

14. See Dieter Dissinger, "Erster Versuch einer Rezeptionsgeschichte Canettis am Beispiel seiner Werke 'Die Blendung' und 'Masse und Macht' " and "Bibliographie" in *Canetti lesen − Erfahrungen mit seinen Büchern*, ed. Herbert G. Göpfert (Munich: Carl Hanser, 1975), 90-105 and 136-66; hereafter cited in text, all trans. mine.

15. Included in translation in *Essays in Honor of Elias Canetti*, 297-99; unfortunately, only half of the review is reprinted there.

16. Waldinger's entire review appears in *Essays in Honor of Elias Canetti*, 299-302.

17. Reprinted in *Canetti lesen*, 122-23; trans. mine.

18. Alfons-M. Bischoff, *Elias Canetti: Stationen zum Werk* (Bern: Herbert Lang, 1973), 143-44; hereafter cited in text.

19. Reprinted in *Essays in Honor of Elias Canetti*, 310-14.

20. Specific works are listed in the Selected Bibliography, Secondary Sources, of this volume.

21. Hermann Broch, "Einleitung zu einer Lesung von Elias Canetti in der Volkshochschule Leopoldstadt am 23.Januar 1933" in Göpfert, *Canetti lesen*, 119-21.

22. Saul Bellow, *Herzog* (New York: Fawcett, 1965), 99.

23. Reprinted in Susan Sontag, *Under the Sign of Saturn* (New York: Farrar, Straus & Giroux, 1980), 181-204; the passage quoted is on 203. Reprinted in *Essays in Honor of Elias Canetti*, 88-107.

24. Siegfried Lenz, "Krieg zwischen Küche und Kopf: Zu Elias Canettis *Die Blendung*," *Elfenbeinturm und Barrikade: Erfahrungen am Schreibtisch* (Hamburg: Hoffmann & Campe, 1983), 146-51; trans. mine.

25. Salman Rushdie, "The Worm of Learning Turns, Swallows Its Tail, and Bites Itself in Half," in *Essays in Honor of Elias Canetti*, 82; hereafter cited in text.

26. B. W. Powe, *The Solitary Outlaw* (Toronto: Lester & Orpen Dennys, 1987); hereafter cited in text.

Selected Bibliography

PRIMARY WORKS

Canetti's major works published in the original German are listed in chronological order; English translations are listed in alphabetical order.

Original German Editions

Hochzeit (*The Wedding*). Berlin: S. Fischer, 1932 (printed as manuscript); Munich: Carl Hanser, 1964. (Drama.)

Die Blendung (*Auto-da-Fé*). Vienna, Leipzig, Zurich: Herbert Reichner, 1935/36; Munich: Willi Weismann, 1948; Munich: Carl Hanser, 1963. (Novel.)

Komödie der Eitelkeit (*Comedy of Vanity*). Munich: Willi Weismann, 1950; Munich: Carl Hanser, 1964. (Drama.)

Fritz Wotruba. Preface by Klaus Demus. Vienna: Brüder Rosenbaum, 1955. (Essay.)

Masse und Macht (*Crowds and Power*). Hamburg: Claassen, 1960. (Anthropological/sociological study.)

Welt im Kopf (World in his head). Edited by Erich Fried. Graz, Vienna: Stiasny, 1962. (Anthology.)

Die Befristeten (*Life-Terms*). Munich: Carl Hanser, 1964. (Drama.)

Dramen. Includes *Hochzeit* (The Wedding), *Komödie der Eitelkeit* (Comedy of Vanity), *Die Befristeten* (Life-Terms). Munich: Carl Hanser, 1964.

Aufzeichnungen 1942-1948 (Notes 1942-1948). Munich: Carl Hanser, 1965. (Aphorisms.)

Die Stimmen von Marrakesch: Aufzeichnungen nach einer Reise (*The Voices of Marrakesh: A Record of a Visit*). Munich: Carl Hanser, 1967. (Travel report.)

Der andere Prozess: Kafkas Briefe an Felice (*Kafka's Other Trial: The Letters to Felice*). Munich: Carl Hanser, 1969. (Essay.)

Alle vergeudete Verehrung: Aufzeichnungen 1949-1960 (All squandered veneration: notes 1949-1960). Munich: Carl Hanser, 1970. (Aphorisms.)

Die gespaltene Zukunft: Aufsätze und Gespräche (The fractured future: essays and conversations). Munich: Carl Hanser, 1972. (Essays.)

Macht und Überleben: Drei Essays (Power and survival: three essays). Berlin: Literarisches Colloquium, 1972. (Essays.)

Die Provinz des Menschen: Aufzeichnungen 1942-1972 (*The Human Province*). Munich: Carl Hanser, 1973. (Aphorisms.)

Der Ohrenzeuge: Fünfzig Charaktere (*Earwitness: Fifty Characters*). Munich: Carl Hanser, 1974. (Prose fiction.)

Das Gewissen der Worte (*The Conscience of Words*). Munich: Carl Hanser, 1975; enl. ed, 1976. (Essays.)

Der Überlebende (The survivor). Frankfurt, Main: Suhrkamp, 1975. (Selections from *Masse und Macht*.)

Der Beruf des Dichters (The writer's profession). Munich: Carl Hanser, 1976. (Essay.)

Die gerettete Zunge: Geschichte einer Jugend (*The Tongue Set Free: Remembrance of a European Childhood*). Munich: Carl Hanser, 1977. (Autobiography.)

Die Fackel im Ohr: Lebensgeschichte 1921-1931 (*The Torch in My Ear*). Munich: Carl Hanser, 1980. (Autobiography.)

Das Augenspiel: Lebensgeschichte 1931-1937 (*The Play of the Eyes*). Munich: Carl Hanser, 1985. (Autobiography.)

Das Geheimherz der Uhr: Aufzeichnungen 1973-1985 (*The Secret Heart of the Clock: Notes, Aphorisms, Fragments 1973-1985*). Munich: Carl Hanser, 1987. (Aphorisms.)

English Translations

Auto-da-Fé. Translated by C. V. Wedgwood. London: Jonathon Cape, 1946. Republished as *The Tower of Babel*. New York: Alfred Knopf, 1947.

Comedy of Vanity. Translated by Gitta Honegger. New York: Performing Arts Journal Publications, 1983.

The Conscience of Words. Translated by Joachim Neugroschel. New York: Seabury Press, 1979.

Crowds and Power. Translated by Carol Stewart. London: Victor Gollanz, 1962; New York: Viking, 1962.

Earwitness: Fifty Characters. Translated by Joachim Neugroschel. New York: Seabury Press, 1979.

Fritz Wotruba. Preface by James S. Plaut. Vienna: Brüder Rosenbaum, 1955.

The Human Province. Translated by Joachim Neugroschel. New York: Seabury Press, 1978.

Kafka's Other Trial: The Letters to Felice. Translated by Christopher Middleton. London: Calder & Boyars, 1974; New York: Schocken, 1974.

Life-Terms. Translated by Gitta Honegger. New York: Performing Arts Journal Publications, 1983. Translated by Carol Stewart as *The Numbered*. London: Calder & Boyars, 1984.

The Play of the Eyes. Translated by Ralph Manheim. New York: Farrar, Straus & Giroux, 1986.

The Secret Heart of the Clock: Notes, Aphorisms, Fragments 1973-1985. Translated by Joel Agee. New York: Farrar, Straus & Giroux, 1989.

The Tongue Set Free: Remembrance of a European Childhood. Translated by Joachim Neugroschel. New York: Seabury Press, 1979.

The Torch in My Ear. Translated by Joachim Neugroschel. New York: Farrar, Straus & Giroux, 1982.

The Voices of Marrakesh: A Record of a Visit. Translated by J. A. Underwood. London: Calder & Boyars, 1978; New York: Seabury Press, 1978.

The Wedding. Translated by Gitta Honegger. New York: Performing Arts Journal Publications, 1986.

Miscellaneous Works

Canetti, Veza. *Der Oger* (The ogre). Postscript by Elias Canetti. Munich: Carl Hanser, 1991.

_____. *Die Gelbe Strasse.* Foreword by Elias Canetti. Munich: Carl Hanser, 1990. Translated by Ian Mitchell as *Yellow Street.* London: Peter Halban, 1990; New York: New Directions, 1991.

_____. *Gedult brigt Rosen* (Patience brings roses). Munich: Carl Hanser, 1992.

Sinclair, Upton. *Alkobol.* Berlin: Malik, 1932. Canetti's translation of *The Wet Parade*, 1931.

_____. *Leidweg der Liebe.* Berlin: Malik, 1930. Canetti's translation of *Love's Pilgrimage*, 1911.

_____. *Das Geld schreibt. Eine Studie über die amerikanische Literatur.* Berlin: Malik, 1930. Canetti's translation of *Money Writes!*, 1927.

Uber die Darstellung des Tertiärbutylcarbinols (on the presentation of tertiary butyl methylalchol). Dissertation, University of Vienna, 1929.

SECONDARY WORKS

Bibliographies

Bensel, Walter, ed. *Elias Canetti. Eine Personalbibliographie.* Giessen: DUX Verlag, 1989. Lists all editions of primary works, speeches, interviews, translations, and over 1,000 entries for secondary literature.

Bischoff, Alfons-M. *Elias Canetti: Stationen zum Werk.* Bern: Herbert Lang, 1973. 141-49. An accurate listing of the earlier secondary literature, especially for the period 1936-69.

Dissinger, Dieter. "Bibliographie zu Elias Canetti." In *Canetti lesen. Erfahrungen mit seinen Büchern,* edited by Herbert G. Göpfert, 139-66. Munich: Carl Hanser, 1975. A precise listing of the earlier work, including German and foreign reviews of Canetti's works.

Stieg, Gerald. "Kommentierte Auswahlbibliographie." *Zu Elias Canetti*, edited by Manfred Durzak, 171-80. Stuttgart: Ernst Klett, 1983. An annotated bibliography of the major studies.

Books

Arnold, Heinz Ludwig, ed. "Elias Canetti." *Text + Kritik* 28. Stuttgart: Boorberg, 1970, 1973, 1982. All three editions have fine introductory articles on the major works.

Aspetsberger, Friedbert, and Gerald Stieg, eds. *Elias Canetti. Blendung als Lebensform.* Königstein/Ts: Athenäum, 1985. A collection of 10 articles, 4 on *Auto-da-Fé*, the remaining on other major works.

Barnouw, Dagmar. *Elias Canetti.* Stuttgart: Metzler, 1979. The first study to concentrate on Canetti's earlier works; includes a penetrating study of *Crowds and Power.*

Bartsch, Kurt, and Gerhard Melzer, eds. *Experte der Macht. Elias Canetti.* Graz: Droschl, 1985. A series of articles on basic questions regarding Canetti's work by distinguished scholars.

Bischoff, Alfons-M. *Elias Canetti: Stationen zum Werk.* Bern: Herbert Lang, 1973. An examination of Canetti's early works; especially complete bibliography for materials prior to 1969.

Curtius, Mechthild. *Kritik der Verdinglichung in Canettis Roman "Die Blendung": Eine Sozialpsychologische Literaturanalyse.* Bonn: Bouvier, 1973. A detailed examination of *Auto-da-Fé* from a Marxist and Freudian perspective.

Daviau, Donald, ed. "Special Elias Canetti Issue" of *Modern Austrian Literature* 16, nos. 3/4 (1983). A series of essays, half in English, primarily on *Auto-da-Fé* and *Crowds and Power.*

Dissinger, Dieter. *Vereinzelung und Massenwahn: Elias Canettis "Die Blendung."* Bonn: Bouvier, 1971. A meticulous analysis of various aspects of the structure of *Auto-da-Fé* and its relationship to *Crowds and Power.*

Durzak, Manfred, ed. *Zu Elias Canetti.* Stuttgart: Ernst Klett, 1983. A series of fine articles on basic Canetti research written primarily for those well-acquainted with Canetti's work.

Eigler, Friederike. *Das autobiographische Werk von Elias Canetti.* Tübingen: Stauffenburg, 1988. Examines autobiographical elements in the three volumes of the autobiography and in other works, as well as the concept of transformation.

Feth, Hans. *Elias Canettis Dramen.* Frankfurt, Main: R. G. Fischer, 1980. A detailed examination of the three plays and Canetti's theory of drama.

Göpfert, Herbert G., ed. *Canetti lesen: Erfahrungen mit seinen Büchern.* Munich: Carl Hanser, 1975. A series of essays published on the occasion of Canetti's seventieth birthday.

Hommage a Elias Canetti a l'occasion de son 75eme anniversaire. Rouen: Université de Haute-Normandie, 1980. A collection of articles written by distinguished friends and scholars on the occasion of Canetti's seventy-fifth birthday.

Hüter der Verwandlung. Beiträge zum Werk von Elias Canetti. Munich: Carl Hanser, 1985. Translated by Michael Hulse as *Essays in Honor of Elias Canetti*. (New York: Farrar, Straus & Giroux, 1987). To celebrate Canetti's eightieth birthday a group of internationally renowned scholars wrote essays on all aspects of Canetti's work, including a reception history of *Auto-da-Fé*. This is the only major collection of essays available in English.

Kaszynski, Stefan H., ed. *Elias Canettis Anthropologie und Poetik*. Munich: Carl Hanser, 1984. An interesting collection of articles, most of them written by scholars from Poland.

Krumme, Detlef. *Lesemodelle: Elias Canetti, Günter Grass, Walter Höllerer*. Munich: Carl Hanser, 1983. A major study that compares Canetti novel with Grass's *Tin Drum* and Höllerer's *Elephantenuhr*.

Lawson, Richard A. *Understanding Elias Canetti*. Columbia: University of South Carolina Press, 1991. A fine, but brief, introductory study for undergraduates.

Meeuwen, Piet van. *Elias Canetti und die bildende Kunst: von Bruegel bis Goya*. Frankfurt, Main: Peter Lang, 1988. The only study that examines how Canetti integrates references to major art works in his writings.

Meili, Barbara. *Erinnerung und Vision: Der lebensgeschichtliche Hintergrund von Elias Canettis Roman "Die Blendung."* Bonn: Bouvier, 1985. An examination of the autobiographical elements in *Auto-da-Fé*.

Pattillo-Hess, John, ed. *Canettis Masse und Macht oder Die Aufgabe des gegenwärtigen Denkens*. Vienna: Bundesverlag, 1988. A series of articles that examine *Crowds and Power*.

Piel, Edgar. *Elias Canetti*. Munich: C. H. Beck, edition text + kritik, 1984. An introductory study to Canetti's work up to the early 1980s.

Powe, B. W. *The Solitary Outlaw*. Toronto: Lester & Orpen Dennys, 1987. A fascinating postmodern study on the status of language and writing at the end of the twentieth century.

Roberts, David. *Kopf und Welt: Elias Canettis Roman "Die Blendung."* Munich: Carl Hanser, 1975. A meticulous reading and interpretation of *Auto-da-Fé*.

Parts of Books and Articles in English

Barnouw, Dagmar. "Elias Canetti – Poet and Intellectual." In *Major Figures of Contemporary Austrian Literature*, edited by D. Daviau, 117-41. New York: Peter Lang, 1987. A comprehensive study of Canetti's oeuvre, with emphasis on *Crowds and Power*.

Beller, Manfred. "The Fire of Prometheus and the Theme of Progress in Goethe, Nietzsche, Kafka, and Canetti." *Colloquia Germanica* 17, nos. 1/2 (1984): 1-13. Examines the various ways in which a common metaphor has been used to express different perceptions of progress.

Berman, Russell A. "The Charismatic Novel: Robert Musil, Hermann Hesse, and Elias Canetti." In *The Rise of the Modern German Novel. Crisis and Charisma*, edited by Russell A. Berman, 179-204. Cambridge: Harvard University Press, 1986. A comparative study of contemporaneous novels.

Cohen, Yaier. "Elias Canetti: Exile and the German Language." *German Life and Letters* 42, no. 1 (1988): 32-45. Traces Canetti's single-minded loyalty to the German language during his extended exile in England.

Darby, David. "A Fiction of Detection: The Police Enquiry in Elias Canetti's *Auto-da-Fé*." In *Semiotics*, edited by Terry Prewitt, John Deely, Karen Haworth, 343-49. Lanham, Md.: University Press of America, 1989. Examines a critical episode in *Auto-da-Fé* that illustrates the chaos experienced by the protagonist rather than revealing the truth and reality of his existence.

Durzak, Manfred. "From Dialect-Play to Philosophical Parable: Elias Canetti in Exile." *Protest-Form-Tradition: Essays on German Exile Literature*, edited by Joseph Strelka, Robert Bell, Eugene Dobson, 35-56. Birmingham: University of Alabama Press, 1979. Examines the manner in which Canetti changed from writing fiction to essays and philosophical writings when he was forced to flee from Vienna.

Düssel, Reinhard. "Aspects of Confucianism in Elias Canetti's Notes and Essays." *Tamkang Review* (Taiwan) 18, nos. 1/4 (1987-88): 333-41. An introduction to an essential issue in all of Canetti's writings.

Gould, Robert. "*Die gerettete Zunge* and *Dichtung und Wahrheit*: Hypertextuality in Autobiography and Its Implications." *Seminar* 21, no. 2 (1985): 79-107. An in-depth examination of selected passages of the first volume of Canetti's autobiography discloses similarities to Goethe's work in the same genre.

Honegger, Gitta. "Acoustic Masks: Strategies of Language in the Theater of Canetti, Bernhard, and Handke." *Modern Austrian Literature* 18, no. 2 (1985): 57-66. An analysis of the unique "Austrianness" in the use of language of three contemporary playwrights.

McFarlane, J. W. "The Tiresian Vision." *Durham University Journal* 49, no. 3 (1957): 109-15. Assesses the manner in which "blindness" is used as a way of seeing reality in Canetti's *Auto-da-Fé* and in the work of other poets.

Parry, Idris. "Attitudes to Power." In her *Hand to Mouth and Other Essays*, 151-73. Manchester, England: Carcanet New Press, 1981. A detailed examination of the concept of power in *Auto-da-Fé*.

_____. "Elias Canetti's Novel *Die Blendung*." In *Essays in German Literature I*, edited by F. Norman, 145-66. London: London University, 1965. One of the first in-depth studies of *Auto-da-Fé*.

Russell, Peter. "The Vision of Man in Elias Canetti's *Die Blendung*." *German Life and Letters* 28 (1974-75): 24-35. An excellent review of the scholarly criticism of *Auto-da-Fé*.

Sacharoff, Mark. "Grotesque Comedy in Canetti's *Auto-da-Fé*." *Critique: Studies in Modern Fiction* 14, no. 1 (1972): 99-112. An analysis of the monomaniacal nature of the major characters of the novel.

Seidler, Ingo. "Who is Elias Canetti?" *Cross Currents: A Yearbook of Central European Culture* 20 (1982): 107-23. An introductory article that includes a lengthy translation of a representative selection of aphorisms from *The Human Province*.

Sokel, Walter H. "The Ambiguity of Madness: Elias Canetti's Novel *Die Blendung*." In *Views and Reviews of Modern German Literature: Festschrift for Adolf D. Klarmann*, edited by Karl S. Weimar, 181-87. Munich: Delp, 1974. Postulates that Kien's madness is the result of the dichotomy of his existence between two poles: the individual and the masses.

Sontag, Susan. "Mind as Passion." In her *Under the Sign of Saturn*, 181-204. New York: Farrar, Straus & Giroux, 1980. An important, penetrating examination of Canetti's major works.

Stenberg, Peter. "Remembering Times Past: Canetti, Sperber, and 'A World That Is No More.'" *Seminar* 17, no. 4 (1981): 296-311. Compares the impact that the culture of Vienna had on Canetti and Manès Sperber in their youth as revealed in their autobiographies.

Thomson, Edward A. "Elias Canetti's *Die Blendung* and the Changing Image of Madness." *German Life and Letters* 26 (1972): 38-47. Traces the literary metaphor of madness through the past two centuries, concluding with an examination of Kien as an example of the pure schizophrenic.

Thorpe, Kathleen. "Notes on *Die Blendung* by Elias Canetti." *Theoria* (South Africa) 67 (1986): 61-77. A close reading of the introductory chapters, illustrating the way in which they predetermine the conclusion of *Auto-da-Fé*.

Turner, David. "Elias Canetti: The Intellectual as King Canute." In *Modern Austrian Writing – Literature and Society after 1945*, edited by A. Best and H. Wolfschütz, 79-96. London: O. Wolff, 1980. A penetrating introduction to *Auto-da-Fé* and Canetti's three dramas.

Wiley, Marion E. "Elias Canetti's Refective Prose." *Modern Austrian Literature* 12, no. 2 (1979): 129-39. A close analysis of the essays, aphorisms, and shorter prose works.

Index

The Author

Thomas H. Falk was born in Germany but received most of his education in the United States, including a Ph.D. in German literature from the University of Southern California. For many years he taught German literature and language at Michigan State University, and he has conducted research and published on contemporary German and Austrian literature.

The Editor

David O'Connell is professor of foreign languages and chair of the Department of Foreign Languages at Georgia State University. He received his Ph.D. from Princeton University in 1966, where he was a National Woodrow Wilson Fellow, the Bergen Fellow in Romance Languages, and a National Woodrow Wilson Dissertation Fellow. He is the author of *The Teachings of Saint Louis: A Critical Text* (1972), *Les Propos de Saint Louis* (1974), *Louis-Ferdinand Céline* (1976), *The Instructions of Saint Louis: A Critical Text* (1979), and *Michel de Saint Pierre: A Catholic Novelist at the Crossroads* (1990). He is the editor of *Catholic Writers in France since 1945* (1983) and has served as review editor (1977-79) and managing editor (1987-90) of the *French Review*.